Pistis Sophia

The Mystical Teachings of Light and Redemption

A Modern Translation

Adapted for the Contemporary Reader

Anonymous
(Gnostic Tradition)

Translated by Tim Zengerink

Table of Contents

Preface - Message to the Reader

What If You Could Help Rebuild the Greatest Library in Human History?

Thousands of years ago, the Library of Alexandria stood as the crown jewel of human achievement — a sanctuary where the collected wisdom of every known civilization was gathered, preserved, and shared freely.

And then, it was lost.

Through fire, conquest, and the slow erosion of time, humanity lost not just books — but ideas, dreams, discoveries, and stories that could have changed the world forever.

Today, the Library of Alexandria lives again — and you are invited to be a part of its restoration.

Our mission is simple yet profound:

To rebuild the greatest library the world has ever known, and to translate all timeless works into every language and dialect, so that no seeker of knowledge is ever left behind again.

By joining our movement to rebuild the modern Library of Alexandria, you become part of an unprecedented mission:

- **Unlimited Access to the Greatest Audiobooks & eBooks Ever Written:**

  Instantly explore thousands of legendary works—Plato, Shakespeare, Jane Austen, Leo Tolstoy, and countless more. All instantly available to read or listen, placing a complete literary universe at your fingertips.

- **Beautiful Paperback & Deluxe Editions at Printing Cost**

  Own any title as an elegant paperback, deluxe hardcover, or stunning collectible boxset—offered to you at true printing cost, delivered straight to your door. Build your personal Library of Alexandria, crafted for beauty, built for durability, and worthy of proud display.

- **Fresh Translations for Modern Readers—in Every Language & Dialect**

  Enjoy timeless masterpieces reimagined in clear, contemporary language—no more outdated phrases or obscure references. Alongside the original versions, we're tirelessly translating these classics into every language and dialect imaginable, ensuring accessibility and understanding across cultures and generations.

- **Join a Global Renaissance of Literature & Knowledge**

  You directly support expanding our library, publishing deluxe editions at true cost, translating works into all global languages, and bringing humanity's greatest stories to people everywhere. By joining today, you're not just preserving a legacy of masterpieces; you set in motion a powerful wave of literary accessibility.

Become a Torchbearer of Knowledge.

Join us for free now at **LibraryofAlexandria.com**

Together, we will ensure that the light of human wisdom never fades again.

With gratitude and a shared love of knowledge,

The Modern Library of Alexandria Team

Visit:

www.libraryofalexandria.com

Or scan the code below:

Introduction

The Voice of Wisdom in the
Gnostic Cosmos

Pistis Sophia is one of the most profound and mysterious works in the corpus of early Christian Gnostic literature. Composed in Coptic and preserved in a single surviving manuscript, this text offers a window into the deeply mystical worldview of the Gnostic tradition. It is a book of cosmic vision, intricate theology, and spiritual yearning. Attributed to the early Christian Gnostics and written between the 3rd and 4th centuries CE, Pistis Sophia presents an extended series of teachings given by Jesus to his disciples after his resurrection, during a period of forty days in which he speaks not only to their outer ears but to the deeper listening of the soul. This is not a book of casual doctrine—it is a carefully layered spiritual revelation, crafted to guide the soul through its exile in the material world and back into the Light of the divine source.

At the heart of the narrative is the figure of Pistis Sophia, whose name means "Faith-Wisdom." She is not merely symbolic; she is a being of light who dwells in the higher realms but falls into the lower aeons through a misguided longing for the true Light. Trapped in the world of chaos and darkness, she laments, repents, and prays for redemption. Her journey forms a central allegory for the human condition—the soul's descent into matter, its confusion and suffering, and its eventual restoration through divine grace and inner awakening. Her cry is every soul's cry; her hope, every seeker's hope. Through her voice, we hear the struggle of spirit within the constraints of flesh, the longing to return to truth, and the trust that divine wisdom can and will lift the soul from darkness.

The text unfolds through dialogues between Jesus and his disciples—Mary Magdalene, John, Philip, Andrew, and others—who question him on the mysteries of the cosmos, the fate of souls, and the path to redemption. Jesus responds with layered teachings, revealing the structure of the heavenly realms, the names and roles of celestial powers, and the ways in which divine Light is concealed and revealed across the spiritual universe. These teachings are not abstract; they are addressed to the soul in exile, intended to awaken memory, ignite spiritual hunger, and guide the initiate toward the fullness of understanding.

One of the most powerful elements of Pistis Sophia is its insistence that knowledge—gnosis—is not merely intellectual but experiential and transformative. To know is to be changed, and to ascend is to shed the illusions and entrapments of the lower world. The Gnostic path is one of awakening, purification, remembrance, and ascent. The teachings of Jesus in this text are esoteric not because they are secret in the worldly sense, but because they require spiritual maturity and inner readiness. They speak to the soul that has already begun to feel that the world is not all there is—that something higher calls from beyond the veil of the visible.

In the Gnostic cosmos described here, the material world is not inherently evil but is governed by lesser powers, the archons, who do not comprehend the fullness of the divine plan. These rulers distort the Light and keep souls in bondage through ignorance, fear, and desire. But the spark of divine Light remains hidden within every human being, and through the guidance of Christ and the mysteries of wisdom, it can be awakened. Redemption is not a one-time event, but a continual unveiling—a peeling away of layers of darkness until the soul stands once more in the radiance of its original home.

Translated by Tim Zengerink

The Ascent of the Soul and the Role of Divine Knowledge

Central to Pistis Sophia is the idea that every soul has fallen from a higher state of being and is seeking its way back. This descent is not merely a punishment or a tragedy—it is part of a grand cosmic drama in which divine Light enters the depths of darkness in order to transform it. Just as Sophia descends into the lower aeons and lifts her voice in sorrow and supplication, so too does every soul, dimly remembering its origin, cry out for liberation. This is the spiritual plight of humanity—not ignorance alone, but forgetfulness. And the antidote is not merely faith in the outer sense, but inner illumination through truth, which Jesus in this text seeks to impart.

The journey of the soul is described as a passage through multiple realms, each guarded by powers and governed by laws that must be understood and transcended. These include the twelve aeons, the archons of the zodiac, and the spheres of punishment and purification. The soul must face and overcome the forces that have bound it—false rulers, distorted passions, deceptive lights. It must answer for its deeds, confess its ignorance, and cling to the Light that Christ brings into the world. The soul that has been prepared through the mysteries—baptism, renunciation, invocation, and prayer—can ascend safely, shielded by divine names and accompanied by the wisdom it has reclaimed.

Mary Magdalene emerges in this text as a chief disciple, not only asking the deepest questions but also interpreting the hidden meanings of Jesus' words. She is portrayed as the embodiment of spiritual insight—courageous, discerning, and devoted. Her prominence in Pistis Sophia reflects the Gnostic reverence for the feminine aspect of the divine, as well as the belief that wisdom (Sophia) is not distant from humanity, but intimately near and accessible. Through her voice and

6

through Sophia herself, we are reminded that the path of redemption is not governed by gender or hierarchy, but by spiritual receptivity and the purity of longing for the Light.

The teachings Jesus delivers are intricate, but always purposeful. They reveal that salvation is not an arbitrary act but a process of reorientation—of learning to recognize the false lights that bind us and attune ourselves to the true Light from above. The soul's path is gradual and demanding, but it is also filled with grace. Divine mercy is always present, responding to the cries of the fallen, lifting them from error and despair, and leading them into understanding. The knowledge imparted in Pistis Sophia is not cold or distant; it is born of compassion. It is the knowledge of a loving redeemer who has descended into the realms of chaos not to condemn, but to heal.

This modern translation has been created with the goal of preserving the mystical beauty and philosophical depth of the original while making its teachings approachable for today's readers. Each sentence has been carefully rendered with clarity, reverence, and faithfulness to the spiritual intent of the text. Archaic language has been refined, obscure terms clarified, and the dialogical structure preserved so that the reader can experience the unfolding of truth as the disciples themselves did—in questioning, listening, reflecting, and responding. The result is not merely a translation but a renewed invitation into a sacred dialogue.

Engaging the Mysteries of Sophia Today

Reading Pistis Sophia is not like reading any ordinary religious text. It requires attention, patience, and a willingness to encounter mystery. It speaks in the language of vision and symbol, of parable and paradox. Its meanings unfold slowly, like light rising through layers of shadow.

To read it well is not only to follow a story, but to enter a spiritual initiation. It is to listen as Sophia weeps, as Jesus teaches, and as the soul itself begins to awaken from slumber. The questions the disciples ask are the same questions we ask: Why do we suffer? What is the purpose of this world? How can we return to the divine? And the answers are given not as final formulas, but as paths of wisdom to walk.

The world in which we live is still filled with confusion and noise, with false lights and misleading voices. But the message of Pistis Sophia is that divine Light is never lost, only hidden. It shines within us, waiting to be uncovered. Through faith, wisdom, and perseverance, the soul can rise. The boundaries that seem impassable are not fixed. The voices of condemnation can be silenced by the Word of truth. The soul is not a prisoner forever. It is a wanderer, called home.

This text remains as relevant today as ever—not because of its cosmological diagrams or ancient names, but because it reveals a map of the human spirit's journey. It teaches that spiritual knowledge must be sought, cherished, and lived. That divine mercy is always near. And that the Light, no matter how far we have fallen from it, still calls us back.

Let this book be your guide through the complexity of the world and the complexity within yourself. Let Sophia's cry remind you of your own longing. Let Christ's voice, in its mystical depth and gentleness, lead you beyond the illusions of this age. And may the wisdom you gain from this journey not remain abstract, but become a force of love, clarity, and redemption in your life.

Enter Pistis Sophia not as a spectator, but as a seeker. Let its vision awaken your own. Let its mysteries open your heart. And let its Light, ever ancient and ever new, shine in you.

The Title

By carefully studying the clues and content of the manuscript, it becomes clear that while the story of Pistis Sophia—her struggles, repentance, songs, and their explanations—takes up a large part of the text, it is not the main focus. Instead, it is just one section of a bigger narrative. The mistaken title, The Second Book of Pistis Sophia, was added later by a different scribe in the middle of this part, which has caused confusion among scholars. This mistake led people to call the entire manuscript Pistis Sophia, even though that name is not accurate. By now, the title has been used for so long that it is unlikely to change. However, if a title were to be chosen based on the manuscript itself, a better option might be A Portion of the Books of the Savior. It is unclear whether this title would apply to the entire document, but the text we have appears to be parts of a larger collection of writings, possibly with at least two different layers.

The Askew Codex is more of a collection or anthology rather than a single, unified work. This makes it difficult to name each section in a consistent way. The common approach is to call the whole manuscript Pistis Sophia and to treat the first two sections as separate "Books," even though that does not match the content. The later sections seem to be parts taken from two different "Books," which may have been smaller sections of even larger writings.

It is very likely that the scribes who copied this manuscript did not create these sections themselves. Instead, they were working from an earlier version that had already been edited and put together before they copied it.

The Date of the Manuscript

It's hard to know exactly when this manuscript was written because dating Coptic handwriting is tricky. Most experts, following Schmidt, believe it comes from the 400s. However, not everyone agrees. Woide and Crum think it might be from the 300s, while Hyvernat suggests the 500s and Wright the 600s. Amélineau takes an even more extreme view, saying it could be from the 800s or 900s, but many have criticized his idea.

Translated from the Greek

The manuscript is written in the Sahidic dialect of Coptic, which was used in Upper Egypt and still shows many older features of the language. However, it was not originally written in Coptic. Like other Gnostic texts found in Coptic, it was first written in Greek. This is clear because many Greek words—including nouns, adjectives, verbs, and even connecting words—were left untranslated on almost every page. This is true for both Bible quotes and the rest of the text. In Schwartze and Petermann's Latin translation, all Greek words remain unchanged, while Schmidt's German version puts them in brackets.

The manuscript also contains complex terms like "Unapproachables" and "Uncontainables" that don't fit naturally in Coptic. The translator sometimes had trouble with Greek sentence structure, copying it word for word and then offering alternative translations.

Almost all scholars agree that this text was translated from Greek, and there is strong evidence to support it. For example, a document in the Berlin Codex, which has similar language patterns, was originally quoted in Greek by Irenaeus. While a few researchers, like Granger and Scott-Moncrieff, have questioned whether it was really translated, and Rendel Harris later suggested looking into the matter again, none of them have provided strong proof to challenge the Greek origin.

Anyone who has studied the text closely can see that its style doesn't match natural Coptic writing. Amélineau points out in his French translation that Coptic tends to be clear and direct, using short sentences. This manuscript, however, has long, complex sentences with multiple clauses—something common in Greek but unusual in Coptic. Because of this, the Coptic translator sometimes lost track of the structure, treating secondary clauses as main sentences. This strongly suggests that the original text was written in Greek, a language often used for scholarly writing.

Amélineau also highlights how complex the subject matter is, but while some parts feel mystical or abstract, the overall writing style is more straightforward, focusing on storytelling and descriptions. The text does not try to present deep philosophical arguments or logical reasoning. This further supports the idea that the original works behind the Askew Codex were in Greek, and all attempts to figure out where and when they were written are based on this assumption.

Originals Composed in Egypt

Even though many details are unclear, most experts agree that these texts were written or put together somewhere in Egypt. However, the exact place is unknown. While the writings do include some clear Egyptian influences, these are not the main focus. Instead, they seem to have been added to ideas that likely came from outside Egypt.

Figuring out when the texts were written is even more difficult. The answer depends on identifying the group or community that created the Pistis Sophia texts, but this is still uncertain. Scholars can only make educated guesses rather than give a definite answer.

The 2nd-Century Theory

Earlier scholars thought that Pistis Sophia was linked to Valentinus, an important thinker who died around the middle of the second century, or to one of his followers. This idea, known as the 2nd-century theory, was supported by researchers like Woide, Jablonski, La Croze, Dulaurier, Schwartze, Renan, Révillout, Usener, and Amélineau.

Amélineau, a French expert in Coptic and Egyptology, was the strongest supporter of this theory. In 1895, he translated Pistis Sophia, and in an earlier essay, he argued that Gnosticism began in Egypt. However, more recent studies have challenged many of his claims about Egyptian Gnosticism. In his essay, Amélineau compared Valentinus's ideas to those in Pistis Sophia to support his argument, but later scholars have not found his reasoning convincing.

The 3rd-Century Theory

In Germany, a new theory developed after Schwartze published his Latin version of Pistis Sophia in 1851. In 1854, Köstlin analyzed the text in detail and challenged the idea that it came from the Valentinian tradition. Instead, he suggested that it was influenced by Ophite teachings, a branch of early Gnosticism. He believed the text was written in the early 200s, a view later supported by Lipsius and Jacobi.

In 1891, Harnack built on Köstlin's work but looked at the text from a different angle. He focused on how it used scripture, its references to both the Old and New Testaments, and its descriptions of Christian beliefs and rituals. He also pointed out indirect clues, like mentions of persecution, suggesting it was written during a time when Christians faced legal troubles. Based on this, Harnack concluded that Pistis Sophia was most likely written in the late 200s.

Schmidt mostly agreed with Harnack but suggested that some parts of the text, especially the last sections, were older and belonged to the early 200s. This idea has gained widespread support and is now considered the most likely explanation. In Germany, scholars like Bousset, Preuschen, and Liechtenhan have backed this theory, while in France, De Faye has supported it. In England, researchers such as E. F. Scott, Scott-Moncrieff, and Moffat have also accepted this view.

In 1915, Legge tried to bring back the older idea that Pistis Sophia was written in the 100s and was directly connected to Valentinus. To support this, he argued that Harnack's comparisons between Pistis Sophia and the fourth gospel weren't convincing and that the text could just as easily be linked to the synoptic gospels. However, his argument isn't very strong, especially since the fourth gospel was first used in Valentinian circles. At first, I also supported the Valentinian theory, but I have since changed my mind. Now, the 3rd-century theory seems more likely, though it's still possible that Pistis Sophia was written in the early rather than late 200s, even if Harnack's reasoning is correct.

The "Ophitic" Background

Figuring out which group created Pistis Sophia is even harder. Calling it "Ophitic" isn't very accurate because the term is vague and often misused. In Gnostic history, Ophitism is not well-defined and can be confusing. Early Christian writers used the word to describe different sects, but none of these groups actually called themselves Ophites. Ideally, the term should refer to groups that either worshipped the serpent or made it an important symbol in their beliefs. However, most writings connected to this label don't actually focus on the serpent, which makes it difficult to say that Pistis Sophia has an Ophitic origin.

What we do know is that studying the early growth of Gnosticism within Christian communities means looking at these complicated traditions. This movement likely started in Syria, where different cultural and religious ideas mixed, including Babylonian, Persian, and Semitic influences. The Ophitic ideas in Pistis Sophia probably came from Syria but were further shaped in Egypt. While the text has some Greek (Hellenistic) influence, it is not deeply philosophical.

Three Vague Indicators

Are there any hints in Pistis Sophia that might help us figure out which group it came from within the different sects linked to Ophitism? There are three possible clues. First, Philip is named as the main person recording Jesus's actions and teachings, with Thomas and Matthew also mentioned. Second, Mary Magdalene plays a major role in one section, asking most of the questions. Third, another part of the text strongly condemns a certain act of sorcery, calling it the worst of all sins.

In the late 4th century, Epiphanius grouped several sects together, including the Nicolaitans, Gnostics, Ophites, Cainites, Sethians, and Archontics. These groups were known for their apocalyptic writings, including books called The Gospel of Philip and Questions of Mary. Epiphanius quotes parts of these texts, but the passages he includes are offensive and have nothing in common with Pistis Sophia. Some scholars, like Harnack, have suggested that The Little Questions of Mary might have been different from The Great Questions and could have focused more on strict religious practices, but Epiphanius treats them as the same. Even if part of Pistis Sophia could be called Questions of Mary, its content would fit better under the title The Great Questions rather than The Little Questions. Also, the texts Epiphanius refers to are from a completely different setting—while Pistis Sophia describes Mary asking Jesus questions in front of the other disciples, the texts Epiphanius mentions describe Mary speaking to Jesus alone.

Epiphanius often focused on shocking and immoral acts, claiming that many of these sects practiced them widely. Pistis Sophia also strongly condemns a similar offensive act, calling it the worst of all sins.

The text makes this point in a serious and intense way, with Jesus angrily telling Thomas, "Amen, I say unto you: This sin is worse than all others." However, Pistis Sophia does not suggest that such acts were common. Instead, it treats them as extremely rare and horrifying. If Epiphanius's claims were true, it would be hard to connect the Gnostics of Pistis Sophia to such an environment.

Epiphanius is not considered a reliable historian. His claims about widespread immoral behavior are difficult to believe, especially since his writings came much later. Liechtenhan suggested that the same collection of writings may have been rewritten in two different ways— one to support a looser, more permissive lifestyle, and the other to promote strict self-discipline. Scholars like Harnack have accepted this theory, but it oversimplifies things and does not fully explain the issue. Epiphanius's experiences as a young man with a radical religious group in Egypt may have strongly influenced his views. The shock of what he saw seems to have shaped his judgment, making him overly eager to report any rumors of scandal. Instead of carefully examining each claim, he gathered every disturbing story he could find and presented them as widespread truth.

Schmidt links the Severians, a strict religious group, to the sects Epiphanius described. According to Epiphanius, the Severians barely survived in the upper Thebaid region during his time. Schmidt suggests that Pistis Sophia might be connected to this group. However, even with close analysis, the limited information Epiphanius gives about the Severians does not match the beliefs and practices found in Pistis Sophia, making it very difficult to prove this connection.

The Bruce Codex offers a helpful comparison. Without relying only on the writings of early Church leaders, it is difficult to determine exactly which group created Pistis Sophia. However, Pistis Sophia is not the only Christian Gnostic text that has been preserved directly from Gnostic traditions, even if it came to us through translation. The

Bruce Codex, kept at the Bodleian Library in Oxford, contains two important manuscripts that help in this regard.

One of these, The Book of the Great Logos According to the Mystery, is closely related to the same literary tradition as Pistis Sophia, especially its fourth section. It is very likely that both texts come from the same background, though it is unclear whether this one is older or newer. Unfortunately, this manuscript does not give any more clues about when Pistis Sophia was written or which sect it belonged to. The second manuscript in the Bruce Codex is an unnamed apocalyptic text that seems to come from a different tradition. Schmidt, in his introduction to the translation, suggested that it likely belonged to the Sethian-Archontic group. At first, he thought it was written in the late 100s, but he later changed his view and placed it in the early 200s.

Schmidt's revised opinion is based on observations connected to a third set of Gnostic texts, which are still unpublished. These texts help provide context for understanding the religious and literary world in which books like Pistis Sophia and the Bruce Codex were written and shared.

Another important Gnostic manuscript, the Berlin Codex, was introduced to scholars on July 16, 1896, at a meeting of the Royal Prussian Academy of Sciences. During this event, Schmidt presented his research on the codex, which had been purchased in January of that year by Dr. Reinhardt from an antiquities dealer in Cairo. The manuscript, originally from Akhmīm, is now safely kept at the Berlin Egyptian Museum. Schmidt's announcement was a major moment in the study of Gnosticism. His first report appeared in the Academy's records, and in 1907, he published a more detailed study. I included a summary of his first report in my 1900 book, Fragments of a Faith Forgotten.

The Berlin Codex contains three major Gnostic works that were originally written in Greek but have survived in Coptic translations: The Gospel of Mary, The Apocryphon of John, and The Wisdom of Jesus Christ. It also includes a passage from The Acts of Peter, a Gnostic story about a miraculous healing performed by the apostle.

The Gospel of Mary describes visions seen by both John and Mary Magdalene, but Schmidt has not provided many details about its content. Similarly, he only briefly discusses The Wisdom of Jesus Christ and shares its introduction. In this text, the resurrected Jesus appears to twelve male and seven female disciples on a mountain in Galilee, which is similar to a scene from the fourth section of Pistis Sophia. Jesus, glowing like an angel of light, invites his followers to ask him questions, which he then answers. Schmidt does not go into much detail, but Harnack has suggested that this text could be the lost work known as Wisdom, which some believe was written by Valentinus.

Schmidt focuses most of his analysis on the second text, The Apocryphon of John. In two important papers, he examines its significance and shows strong evidence that the original Greek version of this text was already known to Irenaeus around 190 A.D. However, Schmidt argues that Irenaeus misrepresented the text in Adversus Haereses. His summary distorts the meaning and makes the system of beliefs seem less structured and serious than it actually is.

The Apocryphon of John highlights the role of Barbēlō, described as "the perfect Power" and "the Æon perfect in glory." Far from being random or confusing, this belief system is highly developed and reflects deep Gnostic philosophy. In the past, Irenaeus's misleading account has been used to define a group called the Barbēlō Gnostics. Because of this, scholars like Scott and Moffat have linked the Barbēlō Gnostics to Pistis Sophia. However, Irenaeus's version of events is unclear and places this group alongside other sects that Epiphanius harshly criticized two centuries later.

Schmidt, on the other hand, has proven that The Apocryphon of John actually belongs to the Sethian tradition. This same group is now believed to have written the untitled apocalypse found in the Bruce Codex. The Apocryphon of John also shares a deep philosophical style similar to the Valentinian school, suggesting a close connection between the two traditions. Schmidt has plans to do a detailed comparison of the Sethian and Valentinian systems to explore their relationship further. His upcoming translations of these texts are expected to provide important insights into early Christian Gnostic thought and help us better understand this complex tradition.

The Current State of the Inquiry

It's unclear how much Schmidt's upcoming publications will help solve the mystery of Pistis Sophia's origins and its place in history. However, his work will likely provide valuable insights into some of the biggest challenges and unanswered questions surrounding this text.

Based on what we know so far, the idea that Pistis Sophia is linked to Valentinian teachings should probably be set aside. However, there's no strong reason to believe it was written in the second half of the third century rather than the first half. Scholars like Lipsius and Bousset have pointed out that Pistis Sophia shares similarities with the teachings of Mani, but in a simpler, earlier form. Since Manichaeism appeared around 265 A.D., these similarities might suggest that both traditions came from a common source rather than Pistis Sophia borrowing directly from Manichaeism. However, figuring out exactly what Manichaeism originally looked like remains a challenge.

The New and Old Perspectives in Gnostic Studies

One thing is clear: the Askew Codex, along with the Bruce and Berlin Codices, gives us direct insight into what can be called "Gnosticism from the perspective of its followers." This is very different from the earlier accounts written by Church leaders who opposed Gnosticism. Those writings mainly presented "Gnosticism from the perspective of its enemies," focusing on criticism rather than understanding. These texts often exaggerated the strangest, most controversial, or morally questionable aspects of Gnostic beliefs. They also tended to mix together unrelated ideas—both good and bad—without recognizing the similarities between Gnostic and traditional Christian teachings.

Church leaders at the time had little reason to point out any common ground they shared with the Gnostics. They rarely acknowledged the Gnostics' deep faith in Jesus, their strong spirituality, or the strict moral discipline many of them followed. While some Gnostic groups did hold unusual beliefs or engage in questionable practices, most upheld high ethical values. Many were extremely devoted to self-discipline, and some of their philosophical ideas were profound, even resembling certain Catholic teachings that developed later.

Looking at the original Gnostic texts, which have survived in Coptic translations, we see a moral code that is admirable, even if some of their religious practices were extremely strict. These writings also show a deep and passionate devotion to Jesus. This challenges the negative image of Gnosticism that has long been shaped by its critics.

A New Perspective on Commentary

The goal of this translation is not to provide a full commentary, as that would require an entire book and might still leave many questions unanswered. Even with input from the most knowledgeable experts, some parts of the text would likely remain unclear. However, it is helpful to share a few general thoughts to set the stage for further discussion.

The discovery of these original sources gives us a chance to take a fresh look at Gnosticism and understand it in a more balanced way. While many questions remain, having direct access to Gnostic texts allows us to explore their deep spiritual beliefs and moral ideas with greater clarity.

The Role of the First Mystery

In Pistis Sophia, Jesus is the most important figure. He is shown as the Savior and the First Mystery, a being with complete knowledge who reveals all truths with endless kindness. His existence has no beginning or end, and his mission is not just on earth but extends throughout the universe and beyond. His role is the key part of the divine plan. Interestingly, the text never directly calls him "the Christ." If this was done on purpose, there is no clear reason given for it.

The text does not show any hostility toward Judaism or the Old Testament. In fact, the psalms and other scriptures it quotes are confirmed as true because they are believed to have been spoken through figures like David, Solomon, and Isaiah by the power of the Savior.

The events in Pistis Sophia take place after Jesus' resurrection, where he appears as a powerful and central figure, both as the Savior and the First Mystery. The story places his teachings in a time eleven years after his crucifixion, during which he has been sharing deep spiritual knowledge—also known as Gnosis—with his disciples, both men and women. At the beginning, the disciples are gathered with him on the Mount of Olives, where he teaches them vast spiritual truths. Later in the text, another scene takes place on the Mount of Galilee, where a sacred ritual is performed. However, the story does not stay on earth. The disciples are taken to hidden spiritual realms, both above and below, where they witness visions and learn their meanings.

At one point, Jesus promises to take his disciples into the heavens and different spiritual realms to show them their nature and the beings who live there. However, this promise does not seem to be fully carried out in the surviving parts of The Books of the Savior. Another section of the text focuses on earlier teachings about lesser mysteries, while the beginning of Pistis Sophia is more concerned with revealing the highest mysteries. These greater revelations only become possible after a major event in Jesus' spiritual journey.

This turning point happens in the twelfth year of his ministry, when Jesus completes his mission on earth and is clothed in a brilliant triple robe of glory, symbolizing the full power of the universe. He rises into heaven, glowing so brightly that his disciples are temporarily blinded. After thirty hours, he returns, dimming his radiance so they can see him again, and continues teaching them in a more familiar form. The text claims to include not only teachings given after the resurrection but also deeper revelations that go beyond what he taught during his time on earth or even right after he rose from the dead.

These teachings describe a complex system of spiritual realms and beings. The structure suggests that what was once thought to be the highest level of existence is actually just a step toward even greater heights. This idea creates a vision of endless spiritual progress, where new layers of mystery and divine knowledge are constantly revealed.

The story of Sophia is one of the most important parts of Pistis Sophia. It tells a cosmic tale similar to ideas found in Valentinian teachings, which include the concept of a "tragic myth" about the soul of the world. Sophia's journey of sorrow and repentance is filled with symbolism and mystical explanations, leading many scholars to see it as central to the text's message. However, Pistis Sophia stands out because of its strong ethical focus. Instead of just exploring the structure of the universe, it emphasizes personal transformation, faith, and salvation. Sophia represents the soul that has strayed but seeks forgiveness. The story is not just about cosmic forces but about sin, its causes, the process of purification, and the unlimited mercy of the Savior.

In Pistis Sophia, salvation comes from true repentance, turning away from worldly distractions, and having complete faith in the Savior as the Divine Light. The teachings focus on morality and are closely tied to discussions about sin, where it comes from, and how forgiveness works. While the text also explores hidden spiritual worlds, different levels of existence, the soul's journey, and the nature of light and spirit within people, these ideas are secondary to the main goal—seeking salvation and redemption.

The mysteries in Pistis Sophia are not just rituals or sacred words, as seen in older traditions. Instead, they are deeply connected to the Savior, who represents both the First and Last Mystery. His robe of light is called the "mystery of mysteries," and those who receive the highest mysteries are transformed into beings of pure light when they leave their physical bodies. These mysteries are not just abstract ideas but are described as real, divine forces, directly linked to the Savior's glory and power.

Astral Lore

One of the key ideas in Pistis Sophia is its use of ancient astral beliefs, which were based on the idea that the movements of the stars and planets influenced both divine and human events. These beliefs had been important for centuries, but the Gnostics of Pistis Sophia took a different approach. While they still used astrological ideas in their teachings, they placed them at a lower level in their spiritual system. They acknowledged that astrology may have once held some truth, but they believed that the Savior's mission changed the entire cosmic order, making astrological predictions unreliable. They compared astrology to a game of chance, like flipping a coin, showing that they considered it meaningless in the new spiritual reality.

Transcorporation
(Reincarnation)

Another major belief in Pistis Sophia is the idea of the soul passing through multiple lifetimes, a process known as transmigration or transcorporation. This idea is fully woven into their understanding of salvation. Unlike early Christian teachings, which expected the world to end soon, the Gnostics saw life as an ongoing journey of rebirth. They interpreted certain sayings of Jesus in ways that supported reincarnation. They even described how Jesus, as the First Mystery, guided the rebirth of souls, including John the Baptist and his followers. They also claimed that Jesus himself arranged the conditions for his own birth on Earth. In this way, Pistis Sophia provides one of the most detailed ancient explanations of reincarnation, offering insights not found in any other Western religious text from that time.

The Role of Magic

One of the most puzzling and mysterious parts of Pistis Sophia is its use of magical elements. This is most noticeable in the fourth section, which includes invocations and names similar to those found in Greek magical writings and other ancient texts. Scholars have struggled to understand this part, and its connection to Pistis Sophia is still unclear. The authors of this section, along with the first text in the Bruce Codex, placed great importance on magical formulas and the power of sacred names. However, this magical tradition is not entirely absent from earlier parts of Pistis Sophia. For example, five sacred words are said to be inscribed on the Savior's robe of light. The Gnostics who wrote this text clearly believed in a type of high-level magic, which they saw as fully aligned with their spiritual beliefs.

The Gnostics, in their effort to honor and elevate the Savior, incorporated elements from what they saw as the most respected traditions, including those related to magic. They seemed to have identified a mysterious figure—Aberamenthō—within magical traditions and associated him with their vision of the Savior. This name appears only a few times in other texts, and its exact meaning and origin remain unclear. However, it seems that the Gnostics attempted to take elements of ancient magical practices and reshape them into their spiritual system. By adopting what they considered the most powerful aspects of these traditions, they aimed to combine the best ideas of the ancient world into their understanding of divine truth. This reflects their larger goal of bringing together religious, philosophical, and mystical beliefs to enrich their view of salvation and the divine.

History and Spiritual Storytelling

To fully understand this text, it helps to consider the larger tradition of religious writings during that time. Many religious texts, both accepted and non-canonical, used storytelling methods that were not strictly historical but were designed to convey deeper meanings. Because this was a common practice, it is not surprising that the writers or compilers of Pistis Sophia presented their work in this way. What stands out, however, is their deep devotion to Jesus, expressed with the same passion as his most dedicated followers. This leads to the question: what kind of authority did they believe they had to tell their story in this way?

For the Gnostics, recording history with precise accuracy, as we expect today, was not their main concern. In fact, it didn't seem very important to them at all. Their focus was on deeper spiritual truths and cosmic revelations, often shared through visions and symbolic storytelling. They were not alone in this approach—many of their opponents also interpreted history in flexible ways. However, the Gnostics were more open about their beliefs, encouraging ongoing revelations and embracing visionary experiences as an essential part of their faith.

The idea that Jesus continued teaching after his resurrection was already a well-established belief in many Gnostic traditions. As Schmidt has recently shown, this idea had become so popular by the late second century that even a Catholic writer in Asia Minor used the same storytelling style to argue against Gnostic ideas. Ironically, this effort to disprove them actually showed how widespread the belief had become. It is likely that the writers of Pistis Sophia truly believed they were acting under divine inspiration. They saw themselves as guardians of sacred wisdom, not as part of a fading movement, as some modern critics suggest. Instead, they believed they were revealing deep spiritual truths that had never been fully understood before. To them, these revelations gave them the knowledge and authority to share their message with the world.

Pistis Sophia as a Private Text

Despite their passion for spreading their beliefs, it is clear that Pistis Sophia was never meant to be a public gospel. It was carefully structured, with certain teachings meant for a wider audience and others kept secret. Some mysteries were only to be shared under special conditions, while others were meant to remain hidden. In this way, The Books of the Savior fit the original meaning of the word apocrypha—writings that are "hidden" or "reserved" for specific people rather than shared with everyone.

The text follows the common practice of secrecy found in many spiritual traditions of that time. These traditions often kept certain teachings hidden, which was meant to protect their sacredness but could also lead to misunderstandings. Despite this, Pistis Sophia was clearly written for a specific group—disciples who were already familiar with its teachings, dedicated learners, and those training to become apostles. It was more than just a teaching guide; it served as a manual for spreading the Gnostic message. It contained the deeper teachings of a movement that believed it had discovered the ultimate truth and wanted to prepare its followers to share it with the world.

Its Overall Importance

If The Books of the Savior had survived in their complete form—instead of the sections that remain in Pistis Sophia—and if the higher mysteries and missing teachings had been fully preserved, we might have a clearer picture of what the text was meant to communicate. Additionally, some of the lower mysteries found in the fourth section seem to have been intentionally kept from the general public, possibly to prevent misuse. However, today, such concerns are no longer relevant. This section of the text remains difficult to interpret, and its complexity still acts as a natural barrier, keeping its meaning hidden even now.

Even so, much of the text remains challenging to understand. This is true even for those who have spent years studying the psychology of religious experiences and the deeper meanings behind spiritual beliefs. Despite these difficulties, Pistis Sophia is more than just a collection of mysteries. It contains passages of rare beauty, teachings with deep moral lessons, and moments of profound spiritual insight.

No matter how one chooses to interpret its combination of different beliefs and traditions, Pistis Sophia is undeniably an important historical document. Its significance goes beyond its role in Christian Gnosticism. It also helps us understand the broader development of religion in the Western world. This text not only reveals the spiritual ideas of its time but also sheds light on the evolution of religious thought and mystical practices, bringing together different traditions in a way that still fascinates and inspires today.

The First Book of Pistis Sophia

Chapter 1

After Jesus rose from the dead, he spent eleven years teaching his disciples. During this time, he instructed them about the First Commandment and its mysteries, leading up to the deeper truths hidden within it. These teachings were connected to the First Mystery, one of the greatest secrets of the divine order. This First Mystery contained twenty-four other mysteries, which existed in a special place before all others. It was represented by the Father in the form of a dove.

Jesus told his disciples, "I have come from that First Mystery, which is the twenty-fourth and final mystery." However, the disciples did not fully understand what this mystery contained. They believed it was the highest power in the universe, the source of everything, and the final truth. This belief came from Jesus' earlier teachings, where he described this mystery as surrounding the First Commandment, the five Impressions, the great Light, the five Helpers, and the entire Treasury of the Light.

Even though Jesus taught them many things, he did not reveal everything about what lay beyond this mystery. He did not explain the vast regions of the great Invisible, the triple powers, the twenty-four invisible beings, or the great Invisible's emanations. He also did not describe the different levels of existence, including the beings that were never created, those that created themselves, and those that were brought into existence. He left out details about the rulers, authorities, lords, archangels, angels, and the many other beings that existed within these realms.

Jesus also did not tell his disciples everything about the Treasury of the Light. He did not explain how its different levels worked, how each Savior played a role, or who guarded the entrances to this sacred place. He did not describe the Twin Savior, known as the Child of the Child, or the regions connected to the three Amens and their expansions. The disciples were also not taught about the five Trees, the seven Amens (also called the seven Voices), or the places where these divine forces extended.

Additionally, Jesus did not explain the role of the five Helpers or the places they inhabited. He did not tell them how the great Light spread, where it went, or how the five Impressions and the First Commandment were connected to different regions. While he taught that these things existed, he did not go into detail about how they were arranged or how they expanded.

Because of this, the disciples did not realize that there were even more regions beyond what they had learned. Jesus never told them, "I came from specific places before entering this mystery." Instead, he simply said, "I have come from that mystery." As a result, they believed this mystery was the ultimate truth—the highest power in the universe and the completion of everything.

Jesus had told them, "This mystery surrounds the entire universe. I have spoken to you about it from the first day I met you until now." Because of this, the disciples assumed that there was nothing beyond it. They believed it was the final reality, not knowing that even greater and deeper mysteries existed beyond what they had been taught.

Chapter 2

The disciples gathered on the Mount of Olives, talking about the words Jesus had spoken to them. They were filled with joy and excitement, amazed by what they had learned. They said to each other,

"We are truly blessed above all people on earth, for the Savior has shared with us these incredible mysteries. We have been given complete knowledge and understanding of all things."

As they spoke, they felt deeply grateful for the teachings they had received. They understood what a great privilege it was to be chosen by Jesus and trusted with such profound wisdom. Their hearts were full of awe and humility as they thought about the importance of what they had been shown. Jesus sat a short distance away, watching them in silence, his presence filling them with peace and strength.

Then, on the fifteenth day of the month of Tybi, when the moon was full and the sun shone brightly, something extraordinary happened. A brilliant, powerful light appeared behind Jesus, shining with a radiance beyond anything the disciples had ever seen.

This was no ordinary light. It was impossibly bright, far beyond the light of the sun or anything found on earth. It seemed to come directly from the highest realms of heaven, a reflection of the purest divine glory. The disciples were in awe, realizing that this light was a sign of something far greater than human understanding.

The divine light surrounded Jesus, wrapping him in its incredible glow. It was not just a random event but a deeply meaningful moment, showing the presence of the divine. The disciples were overwhelmed, their hearts filled with wonder and reverence as they gazed at the breathtaking sight. They knew they were witnessing something beyond anything they had ever imagined—a direct revelation of heaven through the Savior himself.

Chapter 3

A brilliant light completely surrounded Jesus.

As the disciples sat together, an incredible light came down from the heavens, wrapping around him. This light came from the last and highest mystery—the twenty-fourth mystery—located in a sacred space beyond all others. It shone so brightly that its radiance was beyond description. Jesus sat apart from his disciples, glowing with an unimaginable brilliance.

The disciples could not look at him directly because the overwhelming brightness made it impossible to see. They could only glimpse the dazzling light shining from him. This light wasn't just one color or form—it was made of countless rays, each different from the others. These beams stretched from deep below the earth to the highest heavens, forming a breathtaking display of divine energy. Each ray seemed even more magnificent than the last, creating an endless ocean of light.

The sight left the disciples stunned. They were filled with awe and fear, overwhelmed by what they were witnessing. The sheer power of the light left them speechless and trembling, for they knew they were seeing something far beyond human understanding.

As the light completely surrounded Jesus, he began to rise. He ascended into the sky, glowing with an unmatched radiance, his form disappearing into pure brilliance. The disciples remained still, unable to move or speak, watching as he lifted higher and higher until he vanished into the heavens. This miraculous event took place on the fifteenth day of the month of Tybi, under a full moon.

Three hours after Jesus entered the heavens, a great disturbance shook the universe. Every power in the celestial realms was thrown into chaos. The heavens trembled, and different spiritual forces collided with one another. The entire earth shook, and all living things felt a deep sense of fear. People everywhere, including the disciples, were filled with dread, wondering if the world itself was about to break apart and disappear.

From the third hour of the fifteenth day until the ninth hour of the following day, the turmoil did not stop. The sky roared with movement, and the heavenly powers continued to shake. Angels, archangels, and all the celestial beings lifted their voices in praise, singing hymns to the highest realms of the divine. Their songs echoed through the universe, their voices unbroken and unwavering, filling the heavens and the earth until the ninth hour of the next day.

Chapter 4

The disciples sat together, overcome with fear and confusion, shaken by the powerful earthquake they had just experienced. The tremors and chaos around them left them deeply unsettled. Their hearts were filled with worry, and they cried out in distress, "What is happening? Will the Savior destroy everything?" They turned to each other, their voices filled with sorrow, their fears spilling out in desperate cries.

As they sat in their fear and uncertainty, the hours passed. Then, at the ninth hour of the next day, something incredible happened—the heavens suddenly opened before them. They lifted their tear-streaked faces and saw an astonishing sight: Jesus descending from above. His presence was even more radiant than when he had first ascended. The light surrounding him was beyond anything they could understand, brighter and more glorious than any earthly light. No words could truly describe its brilliance.

Jesus glowed with an intensity that overwhelmed everyone who saw him. His light was not just one single glow but made up of countless rays, each different in shape and brightness. Some were soft and gentle, while others were sharp and piercing. Some carried a quiet beauty, while others shone with an indescribable brilliance. Together, they formed a breathtaking, endless display of light—so powerful and vast that it seemed impossible to measure or contain.

The light radiating from Jesus spread in all directions, stretching across the sky and reaching down to the earth. It was not just an ordinary brightness; it was a divine sign, revealing the heavenly glory of the Savior. This light reflected the infinite depth of his being, filling the air with a presence that left the disciples in awe.

As they gazed at him, their fear began to fade, replaced by a sense of wonder. This light did not just illuminate the world around them— it also filled their hearts, allowing them to glimpse something far greater than themselves. In that moment, Jesus returned to them, not just as their teacher but as the very essence of divine power and wisdom. The disciples watched in amazement, their tears of fear turning into awe. They knew they were about to witness something extraordinary, ready to listen, to learn, and to uncover the mysteries that were still to come.

Chapter 5

The meaning of His greatness. Jesus speaks to them.

Chapter 6

He pulled the light back into himself.

The light surrounding Jesus was unlike anything seen before. It had three distinct layers, each one brighter and more powerful than the one below it. The first, at the lowest level, looked like the light that had surrounded him before he ascended to heaven. It was unique, shining with its own special glow. The second, in the middle, was even more brilliant, and the third, at the highest point, outshone them all with a radiance beyond human understanding. Though each layer was different in brightness and nature, together they formed a breathtaking display of divine power.

The disciples, seeing this incredible sight, were filled with fear and uncertainty. The overwhelming light was too much for their human senses to handle. Noticing their distress, Jesus spoke gently, reassuring them, "Do not be afraid. It is I."

Hearing his voice, the disciples felt comforted but were still shaken by the dazzling light. They pleaded with him, "Lord, if it is truly you, please dim your light so we can stand before you. It is too bright for our eyes, and even the world around us trembles because of it."

Understanding their weakness, Jesus pulled the powerful light back into himself, softening its glow so they could bear his presence. As the brightness faded, the disciples found the strength to come closer. Overcome with emotion, they knelt before him in worship, their hearts filled with awe and gratitude. "Teacher, where have you been? What was the purpose of your journey? Why have there been so many disturbances and earthquakes?" they asked.

With kindness, Jesus answered, "Rejoice! From this moment forward, I will no longer speak in parables or hidden messages. I have returned from where I first came, and now I will tell you everything clearly, from beginning to end. Nothing will be kept secret anymore. I will reveal the mysteries of the highest realms and the truths of the light beyond. The power to share these mysteries has been given to me by the One above all and by the First Mystery. Listen carefully, for I am ready to tell you everything."

He continued, "When I was sitting alone on the Mount of Olives, I was thinking about my mission and what was left to be completed. I realized that there was just one final step remaining. The last mystery, the twenty-fourth in order, belonging to the second space of the First Mystery, had not yet sent me my Vesture—the divine robe I had left behind in that higher realm. It was not yet the right time for it to be returned to me.

"So I sat apart from you, waiting for this final step to be fulfilled. Now, the time has come, and I will reveal everything to you."

Chapter 7

When the sun rose in the east, something extraordinary happened. Through the power of the First Mystery—the eternal source from which the entire universe was created, and from which I myself have now come—my Light Vesture was sent to me. This did not happen before my crucifixion, but now, at this moment, as commanded by that great mystery. This Vesture is the same one that was given to me from the very beginning. I had left it in the final mystery, the twenty-fourth mystery, within the second space of the First Mystery, until the right time came for me to wear it again. Only when I put it on could I begin to teach humanity everything—from the very start to the very end, from the deepest truths to the most distant reaches, and then back again.

Be joyful, for I have come to reveal these things to you first. You were chosen from the very beginning by the First Mystery. Rejoice, for when I entered the world, I brought with me twelve great powers from the very start. As I have told you before, these powers came from the twelve Saviors of the Treasury of the Light, as commanded by the First Mystery. When I came into the world, I placed these powers into the wombs of your mothers, and now they are within you.

These powers were given to you even before the world was created because you are meant to bring salvation to it. They give you the strength to face the rulers of this world, to endure hardship, and to overcome suffering. I have reminded you many times that the power within you comes from the twelve Saviors of the Treasury of the Light. That is why I told you from the beginning that you do not belong to this world—just as I do not. While most people's souls come from the rulers of the lower realms, the power inside you comes from me. Your souls are from the higher realms.

The twelve powers I brought come from the twelve Saviors of the Treasury of the Light, and they are part of the power I first received. When I entered the world, I took the form of Gabriel, the angel of the æons. The rulers of these realms did not recognize me; they thought I was truly Gabriel.

When I entered their domain, I looked down upon the world of humanity, following the command of the First Mystery. I found Elizabeth, the mother of John the Baptizer, before she had conceived him. I placed a power within her, one that I had received from the Good One in the Midst, Iaō. This was so that John could announce my coming, prepare the way, and baptize people with the water of forgiveness. That power now lives within John.

Also, instead of allowing John to be born with the soul originally assigned to him by the rulers, I found the soul of the prophet Elijah in the higher realms. I took that soul and placed it into the care of the Virgin of Light, ensuring that it would be given to John the Baptizer. In this way, John became the reborn Elijah.

As for my own birth into the world, it was also arranged through the Virgin of Light. At the right time, I prepared everything so that I could enter the world and complete my mission—to reveal all the hidden truths and guide humanity back to the light.

Chapter 8

She placed it in the care of her receivers, and they carried it to the realm of the rulers, where they placed it into Elizabeth's womb. This is how the power of the little Iaō, who dwells in the Midst, was united with the soul of the prophet Elijah inside John the Baptizer. That is why, in the past, you were confused when I told you, 'John said: I am not the Christ,' and you asked me, 'Doesn't scripture say that before Christ comes, Elijah must appear first to prepare the way?'

When you asked this, I told you, 'Yes, Elijah has already come and has done what was foretold, but people treated him however they wanted.' You did not realize that I was speaking about the soul of Elijah, which was within John the Baptizer. So I spoke even more clearly and told you directly, 'If you can accept it, John the Baptizer is Elijah, the one I said would come.'

Then Jesus continued, saying, "By the command of the First Mystery, I turned my attention to the world of humanity and found Mary, who is called 'my mother' in a physical sense. I spoke to her in the form of Gabriel. When she looked toward the heavens and saw me, I placed within her the first power I had received from Barbēlō—this was the heavenly body I had in the higher realms. Instead of placing a regular soul within her, I gave her the power I had received from the great Sabaōth, the Good, who dwells in the region of the Right.

At the same time, I took the twelve powers of the twelve Saviors of the Treasury of the Light, which I had received from the twelve ministers of the Midst, and cast them into the realm of the rulers. The rulers and their servants mistook these powers for ordinary souls belonging to their domain. Their servants carried these powers and placed them into the bodies of your mothers. That is why, when you were born, you did not have souls created by the rulers of this world. Instead, you carried a portion of the divine power that had been placed into the Mixture by the last Helper.

This power exists within all things—within the unseen realms, the rulers, the aeons, and the entire world of imperfection known as the Mixture. From the very beginning, the power that I carried within me was given to the First Commandment. The First Commandment passed a portion of this power to the great Light, and the great Light shared it with the five Helpers. The last of these Helpers took part of its portion and placed it into the Mixture. Now, this power lives within all who are part of the Mixture, just as I have told you.

Jesus shared these words with his disciples as they sat with him on the Mount of Olives. Then he continued, saying, "Rejoice and be glad, for the time has come for me to put on the Vesture that has been prepared for me since the very beginning. This Vesture, which I left behind in the last mystery, has been waiting for the right time. That time has now come, as the First Mystery has commanded me to reveal the truth to you from beginning to end."

Chapter 9

[Missing]

Chapter 10

The mystery of the five words on the vesture

The solution thereof

Jesus said to his disciples, "Be joyful, for the time of completion has arrived. From now on, the secrets of the universe will no longer be hidden from you. You will come to understand everything, from the most visible things to the deepest truths. Through you, the world will be saved, and you are blessed above all people on earth. You are the ones who will bring salvation to humanity."

After saying this, Jesus continued, "Now that I have put on my Vesture, I have been given full authority through the First Mystery. Soon, I will reveal the mystery of the entire universe to you—the fullness of all that exists. From this moment, I will hold nothing back.

You will be made complete, gaining full understanding and perfection in every way. These mysteries are the highest form of knowledge, the ultimate truth, and they are all written within my Vesture.

"I will share everything, from the outermost reaches of creation to the deepest secrets. Listen carefully as I explain what has taken place. When the sun rose in the east, a powerful light descended upon me. Inside this light was my Vesture, the same one I left behind in the twenty-fourth mystery, as I have told you before. When I received my Vesture, I saw that a sacred message was written on it in five words: zama zama ōzza rachama ōzai.

"These words carry a powerful meaning: 'O Mystery, the one who is above all things, the source for whom the universe was created and through whom all things exist—come to us, for we are one with you. We are part of you, and you are the First Mystery. You existed before anything else, in the presence of the Ineffable, before you revealed yourself. We all bear your name, and now we come to meet you at the outer boundary, the final mystery within, which is also a part of us.

"'We have sent you your Vesture, the one that has belonged to you since the beginning. It has waited at the final boundary until the time was right, as commanded by the First Mystery. Now, that time has arrived, and you must put it on.

"'Come to us, for we are ready to clothe you in the glory of the First Mystery and the brilliance it gives. By the command of the First Mystery, we bring you two more Vestures to complete your splendor. These are given to you because you are worthy of them. You existed before us, and you are greater than us. This is why the First Mystery has sent us to bring you the fullness of its light.'

"The first of these Vestures," Jesus explained, "contains the complete glory of all sacred names, the mysteries of all creations, and the essence of all existence."

He paused, allowing his disciples to absorb the depth of what he had just revealed, as the mysteries began unfolding before them.

The Divine Vestures and the Order of the Universe

"The second Vesture holds the full brilliance of the names of all mysteries and all created things in the structure of the two spaces of the First Mystery. It contains the essence of these higher truths, bringing light and understanding to all who receive it.

"The third Vesture, the one just sent to me, holds the name of the Revealer, the mystery of the First Commandment. It carries the secret of the five Impressions and the great Messenger of the Ineffable, who appears as the great Light. It also contains the mystery of the five Leaders, known as the five Helpers.

"Additionally, within this third Vesture is the brilliance of the names of all the mysteries of the Treasury of the Light, including its Savior figures and the many levels of divine order. These include the seven Amēns, the seven Voices, the five Trees, the three Amēns, and the Twin-Savior, who is the Child of the Child. It also holds the mystery of the nine guardians who stand at the three gates of the Treasury of the Light.

"This Vesture also reveals the names of all who dwell within the Right and the Midst. It holds the full glory of the name of the great Invisible, known as the Forefather, and the mysteries of the three triple-powers, along with their realms and unseen forces. It contains everything within the thirteenth aeon, the names of the twelve aeons, their rulers, archangels, and angels. It also includes the secrets of everything within Fate and the heavens, as well as the names and mysteries of everything within the sphere, its firmaments, and all its many realms.

"This Vesture," Jesus continued, "is unlike anything known below the First Commandment. Its light was hidden, and none of the lower realms had knowledge of it. The brilliance of its glory remained a secret.

"The words written on the Vesture called to me: 'Hurry, put on this radiant garment and come to us. We are prepared to clothe you with two additional Vestures that have been with you since the beginning. These Vestures have been waiting for their time to be revealed, as determined by the Ineffable.

"'Come quickly so that we may dress you in them. Only then will you complete the mission of the First Mystery as ordained by the Ineffable. The time is near for you to leave the world and return to us. We are waiting to bring you into your full glory—the complete brilliance of the First Mystery.'

"When I read these words written within the Vesture that was sent to me," Jesus said, "I immediately put it on. As I did, my entire being began to shine with incredible brightness, radiating a light beyond anything measurable. I ascended into the heights.

"As I reached the first gate of the firmament, my light became so powerful that the gates of the firmament trembled and opened all at once.

"All the rulers, powers, and angels in the firmament were shaken by the brilliance coming from me. They stared in amazement at the dazzling Vesture I now wore, and the power of its light filled the heavens.

"The time had come for the words written on the Vesture to be fulfilled. They had called me to ascend and receive the full glory of the First Mystery. 'Come to us,' the message declared, and wrapped in the shining light of the Vesture, I rose to meet my destiny."

Chapter 11

Jesus puts on his garments.

He enters the sky above.

The forces of the heavens are amazed, and they bow down in worship.

Chapter 12

When I entered the first sphere, the light surrounding me shone with such brilliance that it illuminated the entire region. The powers within this realm were filled with awe, overwhelmed by the mystery revealed in the radiance of my presence. They saw the sacred names inscribed within the light, names that held them in their places. Trembling with fear, they could not understand how the Lord of the universe had passed among them unnoticed.

As my light spread throughout the sphere, their chains and bindings—things that had kept them fixed in their positions—were suddenly released. No longer restrained, they abandoned their stations, overcome by the presence of the divine mystery. They bowed before me, though they could not see my form—only the dazzling brilliance of my vesture. In astonishment, they cried out, "How has the Lord of the universe come among us without our knowing?" Their voices trembled as they sang praises to the highest realms, filled with reverence and awe.

They were not worshipping me as a person, but the radiant light— the pure presence of the divine mystery, which revealed their true nature and purpose. Their amazement could not be contained as they witnessed a glory beyond their understanding.

Leaving this region behind, I ascended further into the first sphere. My light now shone forty-nine times brighter than it had in the firmament. As I approached, the gates of the sphere shook violently and opened on their own, welcoming me into their domain.

As I entered the dwellings of the first sphere, my radiance filled every space. The rulers and beings within were thrown into confusion, unable to comprehend the overwhelming brilliance surrounding me. When they saw my vesture, they became even more unsettled, for it bore the mysteries of their own names—the very essence of their existence.

Fear took hold of them as they realized the immense power contained within the mystery unfolding before them. They cried out once more, "How has the Lord of the universe passed through us without our knowing?" Their terror loosened their bonds, and the order of their realm was shaken. One by one, they abandoned their places, unable to resist the overwhelming force of the light and the divine mystery it carried.

Together, they fell in reverence—not before me, but before the brilliant light of my vesture. They lifted their voices in praise, their hymns resonating in harmony with the deepest parts of creation. Though they were confused and shaken, their devotion was pure, as they bore witness to a glory far beyond anything they had ever known.

In surrendering to the light, they recognized the supreme mystery that governs all things. Their voices blended into a celestial symphony, their praises filling the sphere as it trembled with the presence of the divine.

Chapter 13

As I left that realm, I approached the gate of the second sphere, known as Fate. As I drew near, the gates trembled violently and, as if moving on their own, swung open before me. I entered the vast domain of Fate, and the light surrounding me became even more powerful. It was beyond measure, shining forty-nine times brighter than it had in the first sphere. Its brilliance filled every space, stretching beyond all limits and understanding.

The rulers and beings of Fate were overcome with fear and confusion. They stumbled over one another in panic, unable to comprehend the overwhelming light that surrounded me. Its radiance pierced through them, revealing mysteries beyond their understanding. When they looked at my shining vesture, they saw that their own sacred names—the very essence of who they were—were written within its brilliance.

This discovery unsettled them even more. The light of the vesture was not just a display of power; it was a revelation of their true existence within the divine plan. Terrified and bewildered, they cried out, "How has the Lord of the universe passed through us without our knowing?" The light exposed their weakness, leaving them unable to understand how such a presence could move through their realm unnoticed.

At that moment, the bonds holding their realms, ranks, and positions together were broken. The complex structures of power that had once kept them in place dissolved as if they had never existed. Their stations were abandoned, and the hierarchy that had once ruled them fell apart under the weight of the overwhelming truth. One by one, they stepped forward, drawn toward the source of this divine light.

They fell to the ground, bowing in deep reverence. They could not look at me directly because the light was too pure and too powerful, but they saw the radiance of the vesture, and before it, they worshipped. With trembling voices, they lifted their praises, their hymns filled with awe and wonder. Their songs echoed throughout the entire sphere, a united expression of surrender to the mystery they had just witnessed.

Their fear was not of punishment or destruction but of the immense power of the truth revealed before them. The divine light had shaken the very core of their existence, dissolving the limits of what they had believed to be unchangeable. Their worship came naturally and without restraint, a recognition of the vastness of the universe's true order.

Leaving the realm of Fate behind, I prepared to ascend even higher. The mystery within me grew even stronger, and I knew that with each step, the next sphere and its inhabitants would witness the unfolding of the divine plan. Their understanding would be shaken and reshaped by the powerful truths revealed before them.

Chapter 14

I moved forward into the vast regions of the great aeons, where powerful rulers resided. As I neared their veils and gates, my light grew so intense that it could not be measured. When I reached the twelve aeons, the very fabric of their barriers trembled, shaking against each other. The veils parted on their own, moving aside in awe, and the gates swung open without resistance, clearing the way for me to enter.

As I stepped into the aeons, my radiance increased beyond all understanding, shining forty-nine times brighter than when I passed through the realms of Fate. This was no ordinary light—it was divine and overwhelming, filling every space and surpassing all limits.

The beings of the aeons—angels, archangels, rulers, gods, lords, authorities, tyrants, powers, sparks of light, givers of light, solitary beings, the unseen ones, the Forefather, and the triple powers—gazed at my presence. The brilliance surrounding me shook them to their very core. Confusion and fear spread among them as they struggled to understand what they were witnessing. Overwhelmed by terror, they fled, retreating toward the region of the great invisible Forefather and the three mighty triple powers.

Even these highest beings, the Forefather and the triple powers, were shaken. They moved restlessly within their own domains, unable to contain their fear. Their regions, which had remained firm for ages, could not hold steady, and their order began to break apart. The aeons, their realms, and all the systems within them fell into turmoil. Nothing like this had ever happened before. This was not the kind of light that the world had known, something that human eyes could withstand— it was a supreme brilliance. If this true light had appeared on earth, the world and everything in it would have been destroyed instantly. The radiance surrounding me in the twelve aeons was 8,700 myriad times greater than the light I had carried during my time on earth.

All who dwelled in the twelve aeons were frozen in fear and confusion. They scattered in all directions, unsure of how to react. The heavens themselves, once perfectly aligned, shook and clashed against one another. The order of the universe had been disrupted—not by destruction, but by the sheer mystery and power of what was unfolding before them.

Then Adamas, the great Tyrant, along with the other rulers of the aeons, rose up to resist the light. They launched an attack against its brilliance, but their efforts were useless. The light was beyond their understanding, and they could not even grasp what they were fighting against. Their attacks struck nothing but the endless radiance, which they could neither harm nor diminish.

As they struggled against the light, their strength began to fade. Their power drained away as they fought in vain, until they collapsed, completely defeated. They lay still within the aeons, as powerless as mortals, without breath or life. These once mighty rulers, feared by so many, had been subdued by the divine force.

In that moment, I took away a third of their power, ensuring that they could no longer carry out their corrupt deeds. This meant that if people on earth tried to summon these fallen rulers through the dark teachings of rebellious angels—using sorcery and forbidden practices—their efforts would fail. The tyrants could no longer act as they once had, their influence now greatly reduced.

I also changed the workings of Fate and the celestial sphere ruled by these fallen powers. Their movements were altered—now, for six months they would turn to the left, carrying out their influences, and for six months they would turn to the right, completing their cycle with reduced strength. These changes ensured that their control would never again be unchecked, restoring balance to the universe.

Chapter 15

[Missing]

Chapter 16

Mary Magdalene asks for permission to speak and is allowed to do so.

Chapter 17

They would still exist, but they could no longer control humanity through their dark practices and sorcery. Isaiah's vision predicted this change, my Lord, as a symbolic prophecy. His words spoke of a time when these rulers' influence over the heavens and the earth would be broken, making their horoscopes, predictions, and mystical powers useless. This prophecy revealed your divine authority and your mission to free humanity from their grip.

Mary Magdalene, her voice steady and full of conviction, continued her explanation. "When Isaiah said, 'Where then, O Egypt, are your advisors and those who cast horoscopes?' he was speaking about the rulers and their followers who once controlled people's fate through deception. Many relied on them, believing their predictions were absolute. But you, my Lord, have put an end to their schemes. You have disrupted their cycles, broken their power, and ensured that their influence fades as your light prevails."

She paused, her eyes lifted as if drawing strength from above. "The six-month turning of the sphere—first to the left and then to the right—represents their weakened control. They are now limited, their power restrained. This shift is part of the divine plan, ensuring that humanity is no longer trapped by their illusions and false prophecies. Their hold over both the physical and spiritual realms has been broken."

Mary's voice softened, yet her determination remained strong. "But my Lord, this change is not simply a punishment—it is also a form of redemption. By taking away a third of their power, you have not destroyed them, but you have stopped them from leading people astray. Now, instead of using their power for harm, they can no longer interfere with those who seek the truth. Humanity has been given a chance to rise above darkness and walk in the light."

Jesus listened with deep compassion, his radiant presence filling the space with warmth. "Mary, your understanding is great," he said gently. "You have spoken wisely. The words of Isaiah were indeed a prophecy of this moment, foretelling the freedom of humanity from these rulers and their deception."

The other disciples, who had been listening closely, looked at Mary with admiration and respect. Her ability to interpret these mysteries with such clarity and depth filled them with a renewed sense of purpose. They now understood that the Savior's actions were not just about restoring balance but also revealing the ultimate truth—a truth meant to guide them in their mission.

Jesus then turned to all of them and spoke. "Rejoice, for the time has come for the hidden mysteries to be revealed. What has been concealed from the beginning will now be made known to you. Through you, the world will find its salvation. You are the ones chosen to carry this truth, the light that will shine in the darkness. Take courage, for the task ahead is great, but the reward is eternal."

The disciples bowed their heads, feeling the weight of their mission. But within their hearts, a new strength and joy burned brightly. They knew they had been chosen for a purpose far beyond themselves—a purpose that would echo through eternity.

Chapter 18

Jesus praises Mary for her understanding. She then asks him more questions about the changes in the spheres.

Chapter 19

Mary continued asking questions, her voice calm but filled with respect for the deep mysteries being revealed. "Lord," she said, "your words have made many things clearer, but they also bring new questions. If the rulers of the aeons and spheres have lost much of their power, what about those who still try to use their remaining strength? Will people still be able to practice magic and call upon these rulers, or has their influence been completely broken?"

Jesus looked at Mary with approval, recognizing her desire to understand the full plan. "Mary," he said, "I have taken away a third of the rulers' power so they can no longer spread evil as they once did. Those who try to use the magic connected to the aeons and Fate will find that it is much weaker now. The rulers' influence has been greatly reduced, and they can no longer interfere in the world as before."

He paused for a moment, his expression serious as he prepared to share a deeper truth. "However," he continued, "there are those who may try to use the higher mysteries, especially those belonging to the thirteenth aeon. I have not taken any power from that realm because I follow the command of the First Mystery. Anyone who learns and uses the magic of the thirteenth aeon may still find success, as its power has not been diminished."

Mary listened carefully, trying to understand the full meaning of his words. "Lord," she asked, "what happens to those who misuse these higher mysteries? Will they create obstacles for those following the path of salvation?"

Jesus nodded, his gaze sharp as he answered. "Yes, Mary, the misuse of these mysteries can be dangerous. Their power is great, and their secrets run deep. But the path to such knowledge is not easy, nor is it given freely. Only those who truly understand and are guided by divine purpose can access the highest mysteries. Even then, they carry a great responsibility. Those who use this knowledge for selfish or harmful reasons will eventually be trapped by their own greed and ambition. The light cannot be used for darkness without consequences."

Mary thought deeply about his words, feeling both awe and responsibility. She knelt before him again, her voice filled with gratitude. "Lord, your wisdom has no limits, and your kindness is endless. Thank you for revealing these truths to us. They strengthen our commitment to walk the right path and serve the divine will with all our hearts."

Jesus reached out his hand and gently lifted her up. "Rise, Mary," he said. "You are a vessel of understanding and a guiding light for those seeking truth. Keep asking, keep searching, for the mysteries of the universe will continue to be revealed to you. And remember this: the power of the First Mystery protects all who walk in the light, ensuring that darkness will never overcome them."

Chapter 20

When Jesus finished speaking, Mary stepped forward again, her eyes filled with wonder and curiosity. "Lord," she asked, "since you have changed the rulers of Fate and the spheres, does this mean that astrologers and those who consult them will no longer be able to predict the future for people on earth?"

Jesus looked at Mary and answered calmly but firmly. "Mary, the accuracy of astrology depends on the way Fate and the sphere are positioned. If these forces remain turned to the left, as they were before I changed them, then astrologers will be able to make correct predictions, and their words will come true. But if Fate and the sphere are turned to the right, their predictions will fail because I have changed the patterns, calculations, and influences that once guided them."

He paused, giving his disciples a moment to take in this teaching, then continued. "From the beginning, these forces—whether in square, triangle, or octagon formations—were always aligned to the left. But now, I have altered their movement. For six months, they remain turned to the left, keeping their old influences, and for six months, they shift to the right, where everything is different. This change has confused those who rely on their past knowledge. Only those who understand this transformation and carefully track the new movements from the moment I made this change will be able to recognize the truth and predict what Fate and the sphere will bring."

Mary listened closely as Jesus explained further. "The same is true for those who call upon the rulers' names in their rituals. If they summon these rulers when they are turned to the left, they will receive correct answers because the rulers remain in their original state. But if they try to reach them when the rulers are turned to the right, their efforts will be useless. The rulers will not respond the way they once did. Their names, forms, and very nature have been altered when they shift to the right, no longer following the patterns that Yew established from the beginning."

He continued, "When the rulers are turned to the right, their responses will be chaotic, filled with confusion and threats instead of clear answers. Those who try to understand their future without recognizing these changes will be misled. They will be trapped by their own misunderstandings, as the rulers' formations in their squares, triangles, and octagons now follow an entirely new pattern."

Jesus's voice grew stronger as he explained the impact of this transformation. "For ages, these rulers have been using their influence, always aligned to the left. But now I have set a new order, forcing them to shift to the right for half of the year. This change was not just to disrupt their actions, but to throw them into confusion. They no longer understand their own paths, their positions, or their influence over the heavens and the earth."

Mary's face showed both awe and gratitude as she absorbed his words. Seeing her deep faith and eagerness to understand, Jesus continued with kindness. "Mary, this change was not only to weaken the rulers but to free those who have been under their control for so long. The rulers of the aeons, the spheres, and the heavens will remain lost in their own confusion. Their paths are no longer clear to them, and they will struggle to keep their power over the world. In this way, the forces of darkness are being undone, allowing the light of truth to shine even brighter."

With these words, Jesus reminded his disciples of the great transformation happening in the heavens and on earth, encouraging them to remain strong and trust in the divine plan that was unfolding before them.

Chapter 21

When Jesus finished speaking, Philip, who had been carefully writing down everything he said, felt moved in his heart. He stood up with humility and stepped forward, bowing at Jesus' feet with deep respect. "My Lord and Savior," he said, his voice both reverent and sincere, "please allow me to speak and ask a question about your teaching before you continue revealing the places you visited during your ministry."

Jesus, always patient and kind with his disciples, looked at Philip warmly. "Philip," he said, "you are free to speak. Ask whatever is in your heart, and I will answer."

Encouraged by Jesus' words, Philip stood and asked, "Lord, there is something I truly want to understand. When you changed the rulers, their aeons, Fate, the sphere, and all their regions, what was your purpose? You caused them to lose their way, become confused in their movements, and fall from the paths they once followed so precisely. Did you do this to save the world, or was there another reason?"

Philip's question hung in the air, and the disciples remained silent, eager for Jesus' response. They, too, were filled with wonder, amazed at the great changes that had taken place in the heavens and beyond. They longed to understand the true meaning behind the Savior's actions—the deeper purpose of his mission and the great mysteries that were unfolding before them.

Jesus paused, looking at each of his disciples, who watched him with anticipation. The moment felt heavy with meaning, for they knew his answer would reveal another piece of the divine plan that shaped all things. They waited as their compassionate teacher prepared to share wisdom that only he could reveal—wisdom that would bring clarity to his actions and a deeper understanding to their hearts.

Mary asks him another question.

Chapter 22

Jesus, filled with both kindness and wisdom, looked at Philip and the other disciples. They waited in silence, eager to understand the mysteries he was about to reveal. With a voice both strong and gentle, Jesus began to answer, speaking not just to Philip but to everyone gathered.

"I changed the paths and movements of the rulers and their aeons," he said, choosing his words carefully, "so that all souls might be saved. If I had not done this, many would have been lost forever, trapped in suffering without a way out. The rulers of the aeons, with their full power and control over their realms, would have continued to capture souls under their rule. Their influence would have remained unchecked, leaving countless beings stuck in endless cycles of confusion and despair, unable to find their way back to the light."

The disciples leaned in, hanging on every word. Jesus continued, his tone filled with both urgency and reassurance. "If I had left things as they were, many souls would have remained bound to their Fate, unable to escape the rulers' grip. Their power would have continued to dominate the universe, keeping souls lost and leading them further from the truth. The light within them would have remained hidden, buried under the weight of these forces, and their journey toward salvation would have been delayed beyond measure."

Jesus looked at his disciples, his eyes full of compassion. "This change was not made without purpose," he explained. "It was commanded by the First Mystery, the source of all mysteries, to bring balance to the heavens and the aeons. By shifting the course of the rulers and breaking their control, I have made a way for souls to rise above them, to escape the darkness and find the path to the light. This was done for the good of all creation, so that the divine plan could unfold and the power of the light could reach every corner of existence."

The disciples exchanged glances, feeling the weight of what Jesus had just revealed. They could sense the great struggle behind his words—the battle to bring salvation to all souls. Jesus continued, his voice steady and filled with certainty.

"The rulers are now confused," he said. "Their paths have changed, their power has weakened, and they no longer control the spheres and Fate as they once did. This was done so that the light could shine brighter, breaking through the darkness that once trapped souls. Because of this, the way to salvation has been opened wider. Now, those who seek the truth can find it, and those who were lost can return to the path."

As Jesus finished speaking, the disciples felt a deep sense of wonder and gratitude. They understood the magnitude of what had been accomplished and the depth of his love for every soul. In the quiet that followed, they reflected on his words, realizing they were witnessing something greater than they had ever imagined. Through his actions, Jesus had ensured that the path to salvation was not only possible but clearly lit, guiding all who sought the truth toward eternal light.

Chapter 23

All living things on earth are made from this material. The rulers take it, purify it slightly less than before, and shape it into different forms depending on the type of soul they want to create. These souls are then placed into human bodies and other living creatures, continuing the cycle of life in the physical world.

Jesus continued, his voice carrying the weight of his revelation. "Before I came into the world, the rulers of the aeons, Fate, and the sphere controlled this entire process. The souls they created were tightly bound to their influence, preventing them from progressing toward the light. These rulers constantly drew from the material world, increasing their power and creating more souls to serve their rule. Because of this, the completion of the number of perfect souls meant for the Treasury of the Light was delayed again and again, keeping them trapped in this cycle for endless ages."

He paused to let his disciples absorb his words before continuing. "This is why I intervened. I changed the movements of the spheres and disrupted the rulers' authority. By creating disorder among them, their power weakened, and the light they had trapped within matter began to break free. Now, the souls meant to ascend can be purified faster, freed from the rulers' control, and lifted toward the Treasury of the Light. Meanwhile, those souls that are not destined for salvation dissolve more quickly, returning to their source."

Mary, always thoughtful and full of wisdom, leaned forward, her voice respectful yet eager. "My Lord, you have explained so much, but how does this change speed up the purification of souls? And in what way do they now find their release?"

Jesus looked at her with deep approval, his compassion evident. "Mary, your understanding is great, and your desire to know is a blessing. Before I revealed the mysteries to the rulers of the aeons and changed their paths, they had complete control over the spheres and Fate. The purification of souls was a slow and difficult process because the rulers held onto the light trapped within matter. But now that their power has weakened, this process has become much faster.

"Melchisedec, the great Receiver of the Light, plays an important role in this. When he enters the realms of the aeons and Fate, he removes the pure light that has been trapped inside the rulers' matter. Once freed, this light is carried into the Treasury of the Light, where it becomes part of the divine fullness. The rulers and their servants, no longer able to use this purified light, are left with only the remaining material, which is weaker and less powerful than before. Because the rulers no longer receive the same nourishment from this light, their influence continues to fade, allowing more souls to be freed."

Mary and the disciples listened closely as Jesus concluded, "Now, the souls that are meant for salvation are released from the rulers' grasp much more quickly. Their purification is no longer slowed down by the power of the aeons and the spheres. They are able to rise to the Treasury of the Light, where they become part of the eternal glory of the divine. This is the fulfillment of the plan established by the First Mystery, ensuring that all things are returned to their rightful place and that the light is restored to its source."

The disciples were filled with awe and gratitude, realizing that they were witnessing the unfolding of a divine plan. Mary, deeply moved, knelt before Jesus, her spirit uplifted by his teachings. "My Lord," she said, "your words bring light to the greatest mysteries, and your compassion for all souls is beyond measure. May we continue to learn from you and serve the divine plan with all our hearts."

Jesus looked at her and the disciples with love and said, "Rejoice, for the time of fulfillment is near, and the light of truth will shine upon all who seek it."

Chapter 24

The keepers of the sun and moon watch the movements of the aeons, Fate, and the sphere. They gather the light energy that flows through these celestial paths, carefully storing it until it is ready to be given to Melchisedec, the Light Purifier. Any remaining material that cannot be turned into light is sent down to a lower sphere beneath the aeons. There, it is shaped into human souls, as well as the souls of animals, reptiles, cattle, wild beasts, and birds. This process follows the cycles set by the rulers of that sphere, matching the patterns of its rotations. These newly formed souls are then sent into the world, entering life according to the design of the universe.

For a long time, this cycle continued without change, as the rulers had full control over their realms. But as their strength began to weaken, their ability to keep this process going started to fade. The light in their domains grew dim, their power crumbled, and their kingdoms began to fall apart. This marked the beginning of a great shift, bringing the universe closer to its divine purpose.

When the rulers realized they were losing power, they became desperate. At the appointed time, when the number of Melchisedec's cipher was reached, the Receiver of the Light descended once more into the realms of the rulers, the aeons, Fate, and the sphere. His arrival threw them into chaos. He disrupted their cycles, forcing them to release the light energy they had been holding. This energy was expelled from their bodies in the form of breath from their mouths, tears from their eyes, and sweat from their skin.

As he had done many times before, Melchisedec purified this light and carried it to the Treasury of the Light. Meanwhile, the rulers of the aeons, Fate, and the sphere turned to what was left—the matter that could not be purified. Out of desperation, they consumed this leftover material, trying to hold onto what little power remained.

This act of consuming their own matter was their way of surviving. The rulers feared losing all their strength, which would bring about the complete collapse of their kingdoms. By feeding on the remaining material, they delayed their downfall, stretching their influence for as long as possible. Their goal was to maintain their rule until the full number of perfect souls meant for the Treasury of the Light had been gathered.

In doing so, their refusal to let go of this matter served two purposes. It kept them from losing power completely, while also allowing the universe to continue its path toward completion. As the purified light returned to its source, the rulers' control slowly faded, even though they fought to hold on. This delicate balance ensured that the divine plan continued as it was meant to, guiding all of creation closer to its final reunion with the light.

Chapter 25

As the rulers of the aeons, Fate, and the sphere continued their work, they focused on consuming the leftover remains of their own matter instead of allowing new souls to be born into the world. Their goal was clear—they wanted to delay their downfall and hold onto their power for as long as possible. By feeding on this matter, they kept the souls created from their energy trapped in their regions, preventing them from rising toward the light. This allowed them to extend their control, slowing down the divine plan for salvation. They repeated this process constantly, cycling through it twice without interruption.

When the time came for me to ascend and fulfill my mission, as commanded by the First Mystery, I entered the realm of the rulers who controlled the twelve aeons. I was clothed in my light vesture, shining with a brilliance beyond measure. As I approached, the great tyrant Adamas and all the rulers of the twelve aeons rose against the light. They tried to overpower it and trap it within their domain, believing that doing so would delay their end and keep them in power. But in their ignorance, they did not realize who I was or what they were truly fighting against—they opposed me without understanding the true nature of the light.

Following the command of the First Mystery, I acted. I changed the movements of the aeons, Fate, and the sphere, disrupting their paths. I forced them to continue their cycles for six months to the left, as they had done before, but then altered their course, making them turn to the right for another six months, shifting their influence. This threw their entire system into disorder. Their cycles became unstable, and confusion spread among them. No longer able to understand their own movements, they lost control. In this state of chaos, they could no longer consume the leftover matter they depended on. Their regions, which once seemed unshakable, could no longer function as they had, and their rule began to crumble.

I took away a third of their power, reducing their ability to control the world. I also changed the speed of their spheres, making their cycles move faster so their purification could happen more quickly. I shortened their timeframes and disrupted their precise patterns, making them disoriented and unable to feed on the matter they once relied on. Without this source of energy, their regions could no longer sustain themselves indefinitely.

I did this to make sure that the perfect number of souls, those meant to receive the mysteries and enter the Treasury of the Light, could reach their destiny without delay. If I had not changed their paths, the rulers would have continued consuming the matter of purification, preventing new souls from entering the world. Many would have been lost, never given the chance for salvation. This is why I told you before: 'I have shortened the times for the sake of my chosen ones, or no soul would have been saved.' By speeding up their cycles and limiting their power, I ensured that the perfect number of souls—those who would embrace the truth—would be completed. Without this intervention, material souls would have been destroyed, consumed by the very rulers who sought to maintain their rule.

Hearing these revelations, the disciples were filled with awe. They fell to the ground in unison, worshiping me, and said, "We are truly blessed above all people, for you have revealed these great mysteries to us."

Chapter 26

Jesus kept speaking to his disciples and said, "Listen carefully to what happened when I entered the place ruled by the leaders of the twelve realms, along with their followers, lords, and angels. When they saw the bright robe of light I was wearing, they were amazed. Each of them noticed that their own name was written within the light of my robe, and they were completely overwhelmed. They fell to the ground together, worshiping the shining light around me. In shock, they cried out, 'How did the Lord of the universe pass through our realm without us even noticing?'

They all began praising the deepest of mysteries. The powerful rulers of their worlds—including their elders, ancient beings, and gods—watched in awe. They saw that the once-mighty rulers of the twelve realms had lost their strength. These rulers, who had always been powerful, suddenly felt weak. A deep and immeasurable fear overtook them.

They stared at the robe of light surrounding me and realized that their own names were written on it. Because of this, they wanted to come closer and bow before their own names, but the powerful brightness of the light kept them back. They didn't dare get too close, so they bowed from a distance, honoring the robe itself. From where they stood, they worshiped, their voices rising together in praise of the great mystery.

As all this happened, the rulers of the twelve realms lost their power. They collapsed, falling as if they were dead. It was like they had lost all strength, just as they had before when I had taken power from them. Everyone who saw them could tell they were weaker than before.

After this, when I left their realms, order was restored. Each ruler and their domain returned to their places and continued their tasks. I had arranged their movements so they would follow their paths— spending six months facing one way as they worked within their patterns, then another six months facing the other way, continuing their tasks.

In the same way, those in charge of fate and the stars returned to their proper movements. They followed the paths I had set for them, keeping the balance of their regions and continuing their work according to the new order I had created."

Chapter 27

After this, I rose up to the barriers of the thirteenth realm. As I reached them, they opened on their own, moving aside completely to let me pass. When I entered the thirteenth realm, I saw Pistis Sophia sitting just below it, completely alone, with no one by her side.

She stayed there, filled with sorrow and grief because she had not been allowed to return to the thirteenth realm, the place where she truly belonged. She was also suffering because of the harm caused by Self-Willed, one of the three great powers. But I will explain the full story, along with the deeper meaning behind it, when I talk about how everything was arranged and how it all works.

When Pistis Sophia saw me, she noticed the enormous and brilliant light surrounding me—so powerful that its brightness couldn't be measured. She was amazed, and as she looked at the incredible light shining from me, she was deeply moved. The overwhelming presence of the light stirred something inside her.

Chapter 28

Mary wanted to understand Sophia's story.

Sophia longed to enter the Realm of Light. She was restless and completely focused on the light shining from my robe. As she looked closely, she saw her own name written within the light and understood its full meaning. In the past, she had lived in the highest regions, within the thirteenth realm. Back then, she would often sing praises to the greater light she had seen shining through the veil of the Treasury of Light.

As Sophia continued to praise this higher light, all the rulers connected to the two great triple powers, along with the invisible being linked to her and the other twenty-two invisible beings, turned their attention toward it. Pistis Sophia, her companion, and the twenty-two others together made up the twenty-four emanations created by the great invisible Forefather and the two great triple powers.

When Jesus finished explaining this, Mary stepped forward and asked, "My Lord, earlier you said that Pistis Sophia was one of the twenty-four emanations. Why is she no longer in their realm? And why did you find her below the thirteenth realm?"

[The Story of Pistis Sophia]

Jesus answered his disciples, saying,

"When Pistis Sophia lived in the thirteenth realm with the other unseen beings—the twenty-four emanations of the great Invisible—something happened because of a command from the First Mystery. She looked up toward the heights and saw a bright light shining from the veil of the Treasury of Light. She felt a deep longing to reach that divine place, but she was unable to ascend. Still, she stopped performing the rituals of the thirteenth realm and instead began singing praises to the light she had seen.

"As she worshiped the higher light, the rulers of the twelve realms below her began to resent her. They despised her for abandoning their ways and wishing to rise above them. This made them furious, especially Self-Willed, one of the powerful beings of the thirteenth realm. He had already disobeyed the divine order by refusing to purify himself when the other rulers had made their offerings. His true desire was to gain control over the entire thirteenth realm and everything beneath it.

"When the rulers of the twelve realms turned against Pistis Sophia, Self-Willed joined them. He was filled with rage because she wanted to reach the higher light, a place he believed she did not deserve. Overcome by his anger, he created a powerful force in the form of a lion's face. From his own material essence, he formed an army of violent and destructive beings. He sent these forces down to the lower regions, into the depths of chaos, where they would wait in ambush for Pistis Sophia."

Chapter 29

Sophia mistook the lion-faced power of Self-Willed for the true light. Believing it was the same light she had seen before, she left the thirteenth realm and descended first to the twelve realms, then even further into chaos.

The rulers of the realms turned against her because she had rejected their ways and wanted to rise above them toward the higher light. Instead of following their mysteries, she spent her time grieving and searching for the light she had seen earlier. The rulers who remained loyal to their practices resented her deeply, and even the gatekeepers of the realms grew hostile toward her.

Following the command of the First Commandment, the powerful being known as Self-Willed—one of the three great triple-powered rulers—went after Sophia in the thirteenth realm. His plan was to make her look downward, toward the lower regions where his lion-faced power waited. He wanted to lure her there so he could steal her light.

Eventually, Sophia did look down and saw the lion-faced power of Self-Willed. She didn't realize it belonged to him; instead, she believed it was the same light she had glimpsed shining from the veil of the Treasury of Light. Thinking it was part of the true higher light, she decided to descend to that place, leaving behind her partner. Her plan was to take the light and use it to create new light realms for herself so that she could ascend to the highest Light of all.

With this thought, Sophia left the thirteenth realm and descended into the twelve realms below. The rulers of those realms became furious and chased after her. She then left the twelve realms entirely and entered the chaotic regions, drawing closer to the lion-faced power, hoping to absorb its light. But instead, the material forces of Self-Willed surrounded her. The great lion-faced power drained all of Sophia's light, taking her strength away. What was left of her matter fell into chaos, where it formed a being called Yaldabaoth, a ruler with the face of a lion, made of both fire and darkness. This is the being I spoke of before.

With her light taken away, Sophia was left weak and powerless. The lion-faced power continued to strip away what little light she had left, while the material forces of Self-Willed pressed in on her from all sides, increasing her suffering.

Desperate and filled with sorrow, Pistis Sophia cried out in pain.

Chapter 30

She cried out to the Light of Lights, the one she had trusted from the very beginning, and spoke her plea:

"O Light of Lights, the one I have always believed in, please hear me now. Save me, for dark thoughts have entered my mind.

I looked down at the lower regions and saw a light. I thought to myself, 'I will go there and take that light.' But when I did, I became trapped in the darkness of chaos. I can no longer return to my place, because the forces of Self-Willed have surrounded me, and the lion-faced power has taken away my light.

I cried out for help, but my voice could not escape the darkness. I looked up, hoping the Light I had trusted would come to rescue me. But when I looked, I saw the rulers of the realms watching me. There were many of them, and they rejoiced in my suffering, even though I had never harmed them. They hated me for no reason. Seeing their joy, the forces of Self-Willed grew stronger, knowing the rulers would not step in to help me. They attacked me even more fiercely, stealing the last of my light.

Now, O Light of Truth, you know that I acted in innocence. I believed the lion-faced light belonged to you. My mistake is before you.

Do not leave me in this suffering any longer, Lord, for I have trusted in your light from the beginning. O Lord, O Light of Power, do not let me remain without my light.

Because I longed for your light, I have fallen into this suffering, and shame has covered me. I was deceived by something that only looked like your light. Now I am a stranger to my own companions, the unseen beings, and the great emanations of Barbēlo.

This has happened to me, O Light, because I was devoted to your dwelling place. Self-Willed's anger has come upon me because he refused to follow your command. This all happened because I lived in his realm and did not follow his ways.

All the rulers of the realms mocked me.

I wept in that place, searching for the light I had once seen above. The gatekeepers of the realms looked for me, and those who still followed the old ways laughed at me.

But I never stopped looking up to you. I kept my faith in you. O Light of Lights, I am trapped in the darkness of chaos. If you come to save me now, let your great mercy prevail. Hear me and rescue me.

Save me from this material darkness so that it does not consume me. Free me from the forces of Self-Willed that oppress me and from their wicked plans.

Do not let this darkness swallow me completely. Do not let the lion-faced power drain me of all my strength. Do not let the chaos take away my power.

Hear me, O Light, for your mercy has no limits. Look upon me with kindness and grace.

Do not turn away from me, for my suffering is unbearable. Please answer me quickly and restore my strength.

Save me from these rulers who hate me. You see the depth of my pain and the harm they have done to me. You know how much light they have taken from me. These ones who have caused my misery are before you. Do with them as you see fit.

From the depths of chaos, I searched for my companion, hoping he would come to fight for me, but he never arrived. I waited for someone to strengthen me, but I found no help.

When I searched for light, I was given only darkness. When I looked for power, I was left with nothing but empty matter.

Now, O Light of Lights, let the darkness and material forces of Self-Willed become their own trap. Let them fall into it and stumble, unable to return to their master.

Let them be stuck in the darkness, never to see the light. Let them remain in chaos forever, unable to rise again.

Let them face the consequences of their own actions. Let your justice reach them.

Do not let them return to their places with their leader, Self-Willed. Do not allow his forces to return to their positions. Their god is selfish and unholy, believing he alone caused my suffering. But he did not understand that he had no power over me unless you had allowed it.

Yet even when I was brought low, they attacked me even more. They increased my suffering and humiliation. They stole my light and kept pressing on me to take away what little I had left. Because of this, let them never rise to the thirteenth realm, the place of righteousness.

Do not count them among those who cleanse themselves and their light. Do not include them among those who will repent quickly and receive the mysteries of the Light.

They stole my light from me, and now I am weak. I am left without my strength.

Now, O Light that lives within me, I will still sing praises to your name. I will glorify you.

May my song of praise be pleasing to you, O Light, like a great mystery that leads to the gates of the Light. Let it be the song of those who repent, a song that purifies them with its light.

Now, let all creation rejoice. Let everything seek the Light so that the power within them may live.

For the Light listens to all creation and will not leave anything in darkness.

Let every soul and all creation praise the Lord of all realms. Let all matter and everything in it give him glory.

For God will save souls from the grip of matter, and a place will be prepared in the Light. All the souls who are saved will live there and inherit it.

The ones who receive the mysteries will remain in that place, and those who have accepted the mysteries in his name will dwell there forever."

Chapter 31

After Jesus spoke to his disciples, he said, "This is the hymn of praise that Pistis Sophia sang in her first act of repentance. She admitted her mistake and described everything that happened to her. Let those who are willing to listen, hear."

Mary then stepped forward and said, "My Lord, the light within me understands, and I see clearly because of the power you have placed in me. Your spirit has brought wisdom to my mind. Let me speak about the repentance of Pistis Sophia, her mistake, and the suffering she endured. Your light, through the prophet David, foretold this in Psalm 68:"

"Save me, O God, for I am drowning in deep waters.

I am sinking in thick mud with nothing to hold onto. I have fallen into deep waters, and strong waves are sweeping over me.

I have cried out for so long that my throat is sore. My eyes are weary from waiting for you, my God.

Those who hate me for no reason are too many to count, more than the hairs on my head. My powerful enemies attack me without cause. They demand things from me that I did not take from them.

O God, you know my mistakes. Nothing I have done is hidden from you.

Do not let those who trust in you be ashamed because of me, Lord of power. Do not let those who seek you be disgraced because of me, O God of Israel.

For your sake, I have endured shame, and dishonor has covered my face.

I have become a stranger to my own brothers, an outsider to my own family.

My passion for your house has consumed me, and the insults of those who dishonor you have fallen upon me.

I humbled myself with fasting, but instead of respect, I was mocked.

I dressed in mourning clothes, and people laughed at me.

Those who sit at the gates gossip about me, and drunkards make songs about me.

But I turn to you, O Lord, pouring out my heart. In your great mercy, hear me and bring me salvation.

Rescue me from this pit so that I do not sink deeper. Save me from those who hate me and from the deep waters that surround me.

Do not let the flood sweep me away. Do not let the deep swallow me whole or let the pit close over me.

Hear me, O Lord, for your kindness is great. In your endless mercy, turn toward me.

Do not hide your face from me, your servant, for I am in distress.

Come quickly to help me. Listen to my cry and save my life.

Rescue me from my enemies, for you see my shame and suffering. All those who seek to harm me are before you.

My heart is broken by sorrow and humiliation. I hoped someone would comfort me, but no one did. I looked for someone to care, but I found no one.

They gave me bitter gall for food, and when I was thirsty, they gave me vinegar to drink.

Let their own table become a trap for them, a snare and a stumbling block.

Make their backs weak and bent forever.

Let your anger pour over them, and may your wrath consume them.

Let their homes be abandoned, and may no one live in their tents.

For they persecuted the one you wounded and added to the pain of the brokenhearted.

Let them be weighed down by their guilt. Do not count them among the righteous.

Erase their names from the book of life. Do not let them be listed among those who are saved.

But I am poor and suffering. O God, let your salvation lift me up.

I will sing praises to the name of God and honor him with thanksgiving.

This will please the Lord more than any sacrifice, more than a young bull with horns and hooves.

Let the humble see this and rejoice. Seek God, and let your hearts be filled with life.

For the Lord hears the cries of the needy and does not turn away from those who are suffering.

Let heaven and earth praise him, along with the seas and everything in them.

For God will save Zion and rebuild the cities of Judah. People will live there and inherit the land.

The children of his servants will receive it, and those who love his name will dwell there."

When Mary finished speaking, she paused.

Chapter 32

As Mary finished speaking to Jesus in front of the disciples, she turned to him and said, "My Lord, this is the meaning and explanation of the mystery behind Pistis Sophia's repentance."

When Jesus heard Mary's words, he looked at her with kindness and said, "Well spoken, Mary. You are truly blessed, the one who holds all blessings in fullness. Every generation will call you blessed, and your name will be honored for all time."

His voice was filled with warmth and deep respect, recognizing her wisdom and the great understanding she had shown in explaining Sophia's repentance. The disciples, watching this moment, were amazed by Mary's insight and the way Jesus acknowledged her. It was clear that she was not only a faithful follower but also someone who truly understood the deeper mysteries of the divine truths he was revealing.

Chapter 33

Jesus continued speaking and said:

Pistis Sophia, filled with unwavering devotion, lifted her voice again in a second repentance, crying out to the Light:

"O Light of Lights, the one I have trusted since the beginning, do not leave me in this darkness. Stay with me until my time here is over, and rescue me from this place.

Help me, O Light, and save me through the power of your mysteries. Hear my cries, listen to me, and bring me salvation.

Let the strength of your light protect me and lift me up to the higher realms. Only you have the power to save me and lead me to the heights of your divine kingdom.

Save me, O Light, from the grasp of this fierce lion-faced power and from the hands of the forces of Self-Willed, who seek to harm me.

For you are the Light—the one I have always trusted. From the beginning, I have placed my faith in you, and your radiance has always been my hope.

I have believed in you since the moment you brought me into being. You are the one who created me, and from the start, I have placed my trust in your eternal light."

Though her heart was heavy with sorrow, Sophia's words were filled with faith and hope. Her prayer was a testament to her deep trust in the divine Light, her only source of comfort in the chaos and suffering she endured. She continued her praises, holding onto the belief that the Light would hear her and bring her salvation.

Chapter 34

"When I placed my trust in you, the rulers of the realms mocked and laughed at me, saying, 'She has abandoned her path.' But you, O Light, are my Savior, my Deliverer, and the very source of my purpose. You are the one who will rescue me and restore my power.

"My mouth was filled with praises, and I could not stop speaking of the greatness of your mystery. I declared it at all times.

"So now, O Light, do not leave me stranded in this chaos until my time here is complete. Do not abandon me to the darkness, for you are my only hope.

"The forces of Self-Willed have stolen all my light. They have surrounded me and cut me off from my strength. They tried to take away everything I had and placed guards over what little power remains.

"They plotted together, saying, 'The Light has abandoned her. Let's take everything from her until there is nothing left.'

"But O Light, do not turn away from me. Hear my cries and save me from the hands of those who show no mercy.

"Let those who seek to steal my power fail. May those who try to take my light fall into darkness themselves, losing all their strength and becoming powerless."

"This is the second repentance of Pistis Sophia, as she sang praises to the Light and pleaded for rescue."

After Jesus finished sharing these words with his disciples, he turned to them and asked, "Do you understand the way I am speaking to you?"

Peter, unable to hold back, stepped forward and said, "My Lord, we cannot handle this woman! She always speaks first and never gives the rest of us a chance. She has spoken so many times and does not let us share our thoughts."

Jesus looked at his disciples calmly and said, "Let the one who understands step forward and speak. But Peter, I see that you have the ability to grasp the meaning of Pistis Sophia's repentance. So now, Peter, share your understanding with your brothers."

Eagerly, Peter responded, "Lord, I will explain the meaning of her repentance, for your power spoke of her long ago through the prophet David, writing these words in Psalm 70:"

"O God, my God, I have put my trust in you. Let me never be put to shame—now or ever.

In your righteousness, save me and set me free. Hear my cry and rescue me.

Be my strength and my unshakable refuge. For you are my protector, my only shelter.

My God, save me from the hands of sinners, from those who are cruel and without mercy.

For you are my hope, O Lord. From my earliest days, you have given me strength.

I have trusted you since the moment of my birth. You brought me into this world from my mother's womb. I have always remembered you.

Many people look at me as if I am lost, but my trust in you has made me an object of ridicule."

Peter paused, his voice heavy with meaning, preparing to reveal the deeper message hidden within Pistis Sopia's repentance.

Chapter 35

The Savior turned to Peter with warmth and approval and said, "Well done, Peter. You have understood and explained the meaning of her repentance correctly. You are blessed, and all of you are blessed before all the people of the earth, for I have revealed these deep mysteries to you. Truly, I tell you, I will lead you to perfection in every way, from the most hidden mysteries to those that are known. I will fill you completely with the Spirit so that you will be called 'spiritual ones,' perfected in every way.

"And truly, I tell you, I will give you the knowledge and power of all the mysteries belonging to every realm of my Father, and to the entire domain of the First Mystery. With this authority, you will have power on earth—so that whoever you accept will be welcomed into the Light of the Heights, and whoever you reject will be turned away from my Father's kingdom in heaven. Listen carefully now and pay attention to all the repentances of Pistis Sophia, for she continued and spoke her third repentance, saying:

'O Light of all powers, hear me and save me.

'May those who try to take my light find themselves lost and empty. May those who seek to steal my power be thrown into chaos and filled with shame.

'May those who oppress me and claim, "We have defeated her, now we rule over her," fall quickly into darkness.

'But may all who seek the Light be filled with joy and celebrate. May those who long for your mystery always proclaim, "Let the mystery be praised forever."

'Now save me, O Light, for my light has been taken from me, and I am weak without the power they have stolen.

'You alone, O Light, are my Savior. You are the one who can rescue me. Come quickly and deliver me from this chaos. Restore me and make me whole again.'"

Chapter 36

When Jesus finished explaining the third repentance of Pistis Sophia to his disciples, he said, "If anyone feels moved in their spirit, let them come forward now and share the meaning of her repentance."

Before Jesus had even finished speaking, Martha stepped forward. Overcome with emotion, she fell at his feet, holding them tightly and kissing them with deep respect. With a trembling voice, filled with humility, she cried out, "My Lord, please have mercy on me. Allow me to share the meaning of Pistis Sophia's repentance."

Jesus looked at Martha with kindness and understanding, granting her permission to speak. Taking a deep breath, she carefully gathered her thoughts and began to explain the third repentance, using the sacred words of the Psalm that had foretold it:

"O God, rescue me, for the waters have risen and are overwhelming my soul.

Save me, for I am sinking into deep mud, with no solid ground beneath me. The flood is pulling me under."

Martha's voice carried the weight of the repentance, her humility shining through every word. As she spoke, the disciples listened closely, eager to understand the deeper meaning behind Sophia's repentance and the eternal truth hidden within it.

Chapter 37

When Jesus heard Martha's words, he reached out and gently held her hand, saying, "Blessed are those who humble themselves, for they will receive mercy. Martha, you are truly blessed. Now, share the meaning of Pistis Sophia's repentance as it has been revealed to you."

With great humility, Martha stood among the disciples and spoke to Jesus. "My Lord Jesus," she began, "the repentance that Pistis Sophia offered was foretold through your light-power in Psalm 69, which says:

'Lord God, come to my aid.

Let those who wish to harm me be put to shame and confusion.

Let those who mock me, saying 'Ha, ha,' turn back in disgrace.

May all who seek you rejoice and find happiness in you.

And may those who love your salvation always say, 'The Lord be praised.'

But I am weak and in need. Lord, help me.

You are my helper and protector. Lord, do not delay.'

"This is the meaning of Pistis Sophia's third repentance, as she lifted her praises to the Light."

When Jesus heard Martha's explanation, he replied, "Well said, Martha. Your words are true and filled with wisdom."

Then Jesus continued teaching his disciples. "After completing her third repentance, Pistis Sophia began a fourth, knowing that she was about to face even greater hardship. She understood that the lion-faced power and the forces of Self-Willed in the chaos were determined to steal the last of her light. To protect herself, she cried out in the following repentance:

'O Light, in whom I have trusted, hear my plea and let my voice reach your holy place.

Do not turn away from me; instead, listen to my cry and save me when I call to you.

My time is slipping away like a passing breath, and I have become like mere matter.

The light within me has been stolen, and my strength is drained. I have forgotten the mysteries I once knew.

Because of the power of fear and the might of Self-Willed, my strength has faded.

I have become like a lifeless being, trapped in matter, with no light left within me. I am like one of the false spirits bound in material form, without power.

I am like a lost star, wandering alone in the sky.

The forces of Self-Willed have tormented me harshly, and my partner has abandoned me.

Instead of being filled with light, I am surrounded by chaos. I have had to consume my own sweat and tears just to prevent my oppressors from taking what little I have left.

All of this has happened by your command, O Light. It is by your decree that I am here.

You have allowed me to fall, sending me into chaos, making my strength fade away.

But you, O Lord, are eternal Light, always watching over those who suffer.

Now, O Light, rise up and seek the strength that remains within me. My suffering is complete, and the time has come for you to restore me. This is the moment you promised—to search for my power and save my soul.

Your messengers have come to seek the strength within my soul because the appointed time has arrived. My being is ready to be rescued.

When that moment comes, all the rulers of the material world will tremble before your Light. The forces of the thirteenth realm will fear the mystery of your Light, and because of this, others will begin to purify their own light.

For the Lord will seek the power within the soul and reveal his mystery.

He will show mercy to those who repent in the lower realms and will not ignore their cries.

This promise is for future generations, and those who come after will sing praises to the heavens.

For the Light has looked down from its highest dwelling and will watch over all matter.

It will hear the cries of those who are trapped and will free the souls bound in darkness.

So that it may place its name within them and its mystery within their power.'"

Chapter 38

As Jesus finished speaking to his disciples, he said, "This is the fourth repentance of Pistis Sophia. Let those who can understand, understand."

At that moment, John stepped forward, bowed respectfully, and rested his head against Jesus' chest. With a voice full of humility, he said, "My Lord, please allow me to speak and share the meaning of Pistis Sophia's fourth repentance."

Jesus looked at John and said, "You have my permission. Speak and explain her repentance."

John, his voice steady and filled with reverence, began, "My Lord and Savior, this repentance from Pistis Sophia was foretold by your divine light-power through David. It was prophesied long ago in Psalm 102:

'Lord, hear my cry and let my voice reach you.

Do not turn away from me. Listen to me in my time of suffering. Answer me quickly when I call out to you.

For my days have vanished like smoke, and my bones have become dry like stone.

My heart is scorched like grass, and my strength has faded because I have forgotten to eat.

Because of my endless sorrow, my bones cling to my flesh.

I am like a lonely bird in the desert, like an owl in a desolate place.

I lie awake at night, like a sparrow alone on a rooftop.

My enemies mock me all day long, and those who once respected me now speak against me.

I have eaten ashes like bread and mixed my drink with tears.

This has happened because of your anger and your judgment. You lifted me up, only to cast me down again.

My days fade like a passing shadow, and I am dried up like withered grass.

But you, O Lord, live forever, and your name will be remembered for generations.

Rise up and show mercy to Zion, for the time has come to bring her favor.

Your servants hold her stones dear and care for her dust.

The nations will fear the name of the Lord, and the kings of the earth will see your glory.

For the Lord will rebuild Zion and reveal his glory.

He will listen to the prayers of the humble and will not ignore their cries for help.

This will be written down for future generations so that those yet to be born may praise the Lord.

The Lord looks down from his holy heights, watching over the earth.

He hears the groans of prisoners and sets free those condemned to death.

He proclaims his name in Zion and his praise in Jerusalem.'

"This, my Lord, is the meaning of the mystery within Pistis

Sophia's fourth repentance."

When John finished speaking, he stood before Jesus in silence, waiting for his response.

Chapter 39

When John finished speaking, Jesus turned to him and said, "Well spoken, John, the Virgin, who will one day reign in the kingdom of the Light." His words carried deep recognition, acknowledging John's wisdom and spiritual understanding.

Then, Jesus continued speaking to the disciples:

"This is what happened: The forces of Self-Willed, filled with hatred, attacked Pistis Sophia again while she was trapped in chaos. They tried to steal the last of her remaining light. But the time for her rescue had not yet come because the command to free her had not yet been fulfilled. The First Mystery had not yet sent the order for me to bring her out of the chaos.

"As the material forces of Self-Willed surrounded her, pressing down on her, she cried out in pain and poured her soul into a fifth repentance, saying:

'O Light of my salvation, I sing to you both in the heights and now here in the depths of chaos.

I offer the same hymn of praise that I once sang in the heights, now again in the chaos. Let my cry reach you, O Light, and hear my repentance.

For my power has faded, and darkness has filled me. My light has fallen into the lowest depths of chaos.

I have become like the rulers of chaos, thrown into the deepest darkness. I feel like nothing more than a material body, abandoned, with no one in the heights to save me.

I am like scattered matter from which power has been taken, cast into chaos, left unsaved, and condemned by your command.

Now, they have placed me in the deepest darkness, among lifeless things, where no power remains.

Your command has been fulfilled upon me, and everything you decreed has come to pass.

Your spirit has left me, and I am alone. Even those from my own realm have turned away from me, rejecting and separating themselves from me. Yet, I am not completely destroyed.

My light has faded within me, and I cry out to you, O Light, with what little light I have left. I lift my hands toward you in desperate hope.

Will you not fulfill your promise even here in the chaos? Will the saviors, who follow your command, not rise in the darkness and call themselves your disciples?

Will they not declare your mystery even in this place?

Or will your name only be spoken over the things in chaos that you have chosen not to purify?

Still, I have continued to praise you, O Light, and my repentance will reach you in the heights. Let your light come to me now.

They have taken my light, and I suffer greatly because of it. This suffering has been with me since I first came into being.

When I looked up to the heights, longing for the Light, I also looked below at the light trapped in chaos. I rose up but ended up falling into it.

Your command was upon me, and the terrors you allowed have overwhelmed me, filling me with confusion.

They have surrounded me like endless waters, and they have consumed all my time.

And by your command, you have not allowed my companions to help me, nor have you permitted my partner to rescue me from my suffering.'

"This is the fifth repentance that Pistis Sophia spoke while trapped in chaos, surrounded and constantly attacked by the material forces of Self-Willed."

Chapter 40

When Jesus finished speaking, he turned to his disciples and said, "Let those who are willing to listen, truly hear. And let those whose spirit is moved come forward to explain the meaning of Pistis Sophia's fifth repentance."

As Jesus spoke, Philip stood up. He was the disciple responsible for writing down everything Jesus said and did. Carefully, he set aside the book in which he had been recording all of Jesus' teachings and actions. Then he stepped forward and said, "My Lord, surely this responsibility of caring for the world and writing down your words is not mine alone."

Jesus looked at Philip with kindness, understanding the weight of his role. He said, "Philip, you have been given a great responsibility, but you are not carrying it alone. The duty of recording my words and deeds is shared with others who have been chosen for this purpose. Along with you, Thomas and Matthew have also been given this task. The three of you will preserve my teachings so they may be passed down for the sake of the world and future generations."

These words reassured Philip and the other disciples. The task of writing down Jesus' teachings was a serious and sacred duty, one that required care, devotion, and humility. It was clear that those entrusted with this role had been chosen because of their faithfulness and understanding.

Then Jesus continued, saying, "Philip, you have worked faithfully as a scribe, carefully recording all that has been revealed. Now, if your spirit is moved, speak. Share the meaning of Pistis Sophia's fifth repentance. Let wisdom flow through you so that the mysteries may be revealed and understood by everyone here."

Encouraged by Jesus, Philip prepared to speak. He felt the weight of the moment, but also the light of understanding that had been given to him. He knew that by sharing this interpretation, he was helping to reveal the deeper truths that those who sought wisdom longed to understand.

Chapter 41

When Jesus finished speaking to his disciples, he said, "Let those who are willing to listen, truly hear. And if anyone feels their spirit stirred, let them step forward and explain the meaning of Pistis Sophia's fifth repentance."

After Jesus spoke, Philip stood up. He carefully set down the book in which he had been recording all of Jesus' teachings and actions. Then he said respectfully, "My Lord, you have given me the responsibility of writing down all your words and everything we do. Because of this, I have not been able to step forward and explain the mysteries of Pistis Sophia's repentance. Many times, I have felt a strong desire to share my understanding, but I held back, knowing my role as a scribe."

Jesus listened to Philip and responded kindly, "Philip, listen closely to what I am about to say. You are truly blessed. But this responsibility is not yours alone. Along with you, Thomas and Matthew have also been chosen by the First Mystery to record everything I say and do, as well as all that you witness. However, your task is not yet complete. When you have finished your part, you will be free to step forward and share whatever is in your heart. For now, the three of you must focus on writing down the teachings of the kingdom of heaven so they may be passed on to others."

Then Jesus turned to his disciples and said, "Let those who are willing to listen, truly hear."

At that moment, Mary stepped forward and stood beside Philip. She looked at Jesus and said, "My Lord, the light within me allows me to hear and understand. I have listened to your words, and I see their deeper meaning. Please allow me to speak openly about what you have said. You told Philip, Thomas, and Matthew that they are the three witnesses chosen to record the words of the kingdom of Light and bear witness to them. Let me explain the meaning of this. Your divine power spoke through Moses, saying, 'Every matter shall be established by the testimony of two or three witnesses.' In this case, the three witnesses are Philip, Thomas, and Matthew."

When Jesus heard Mary's explanation, he nodded and said, "Well said, Mary. You have understood my words correctly. Now, Philip, step forward and explain the fifth repentance of Pistis Sophia. After that, return to your role as a scribe and continue recording everything I say and do until your work is finished. Once you have completed your task, you will be free to share your understanding whenever you wish. But for now, come forward and explain the meaning of the fifth repentance."

Philip respectfully stepped forward and said, "My Lord, allow me to share the meaning of Pistis Sophia's fifth repentance. Your divine power spoke of this moment through David in Psalm 88:

'Lord, God of my salvation, I cry out to you day and night.

Let my prayer come before you; listen to my cry.

My soul is full of suffering, and my life is close to the grave.

I am counted among those who go down into the pit; I have no strength left.

I am abandoned among the dead, like those who lie in their graves—those you have forgotten, cut off from your care.

You have placed me in the lowest pit, in the darkest depths.

Your anger weighs heavily upon me, and your waves have overwhelmed me.

You have taken my closest friends from me and made them turn away from me. I am trapped with no escape.

My eyes are weak from sorrow. I call to you every day, Lord; I lift my hands to you.

Do you show your wonders to the dead? Do their spirits rise up and praise you?

Is your love declared in the grave, your faithfulness in the place of destruction?

Are your miracles known in the darkness, or your righteousness in the land of forgetfulness?

But I cry out to you, Lord; in the morning, my prayer reaches you.

Why, Lord, do you reject me and hide your face from me?

From my youth, I have suffered and been close to death. I have faced your terrors and am in despair.

Your wrath has swept over me; your terrors have destroyed me.

All day long, they surround me like a flood; they have completely engulfed me.

You have taken from me my friends and my companions—darkness is my only company.'

"This, my Lord, is the meaning of the fifth repentance of Pistis Sophia, which she spoke while being oppressed in chaos."

Jesus listened to Philip's explanation and responded with approval, "Well done, Philip. You have explained it well. Now, return to your work as a faithful scribe of the kingdom of Light."

Chapter 42

When Jesus finished listening to Philip, he spoke kindly, saying, "Well done, Philip, my beloved. Now, return to your place and continue writing down all the teachings I will share, the actions I will perform, and everything you will witness." Without hesitation, Philip sat down and resumed his task, carefully recording everything that took place.

Soon after, Jesus continued teaching his disciples, saying, "In her sorrow, Pistis Sophia cried out to the Light, which forgave her for leaving her rightful place and falling into the darkness. In her plea for mercy, she spoke her sixth repentance, saying:

'I have sung praises to you, O Light, even from the depths of this darkness.

Hear my repentance, and may your light listen to my cries.

O Light, if you count my mistakes against me, I will not be able to stand before you, and you will surely turn away from me.

But you, O Light, are my Savior. Because of the power of your name, I have placed my faith in you.

My soul has also believed in your mystery. It trusted in the Light when it dwelled in the heights, and it continued to trust even when it was cast down into chaos.'

"This was the desperate cry of Pistis Sophia as she sought forgiveness from the Light, knowing of its mercy and endless compassion. She longed to be saved and restored, believing that the Light would not abandon her in her time of struggle."

Chapter 43

Andrew explained the meaning of the sixth repentance using Psalm 129:

"Let all the powers within me trust in the Light while I am in the darkness, and let them trust in it again if they rise to the higher realms. The Light is full of mercy and is the one who saves. A great and mysterious salvation is found within it. It will rescue all powers from the chaos that came from my mistakes, for I left my rightful place and fell into darkness."

"Let those who understand, think carefully about this."

When Jesus finished speaking, he asked his disciples, "Do you understand the way I am speaking to you?"

Andrew stepped forward and said, "My Lord, regarding the meaning of Pistis Sophia's sixth repentance, your Light-Power spoke about this long ago through David in Psalm 129:

'Out of the depths, I have cried to you, O Lord.

Hear my voice; let your ears be open to my cry for mercy.

If you, O Lord, counted sins, who could stand before you?

But with you is forgiveness, so that you may be honored.

I have waited for you, O Lord, because of your name.

My soul has waited for your word.

My soul has placed its hope in you from morning until night.

Let Israel also hope in the Lord from morning until night.

For the Lord is full of grace, and with him is great redemption.

He will save Israel from all their sins.'"

Jesus responded, "Well said, Andrew, my blessed one. This is the meaning of her repentance. Truly, I tell you, I will make you perfect in all the mysteries of the Light. From the deepest mysteries to the farthest reaches of existence, all evil rulers and their powers will be destroyed by the purifying fire. You will be made whole in every way— from the highest Light to the lowest levels of the world, from all gods to demons, from every ruler to the least servant, from humanity to every living creature. You will be completely perfected.

"Truly, I tell you: In the place where I will dwell in my Father's kingdom, you will also dwell with me. When the perfect number is complete and the Mixture is undone, I will command all the tyrant gods who refused to give up their light to step forward. Then, I will order the wise fire, through which the perfected ones pass, to consume these rulers until they surrender every last bit of their light."

After Jesus finished speaking, he asked his disciples again, "Do you understand what I am telling you?"

Mary stepped forward and said, "Yes, Lord, I understand your words. Regarding what you said—when the Mixture is dissolved, you will take your place in the Light-Power, and your disciples will…"

Chapter 44

When Sophia cried out in her seventh repentance, her plea was still not accepted. The rulers of the realms mocked her, taking pleasure in her suffering. But the time would come when those who trust in the Light would sit beside it and judge the tyrant gods who refused to release their light. The wise fire would consume them until they gave up the last of it. Regarding this, the Light-Power had spoken long ago through David in Psalm 82:

"God will stand in the assembly of the gods and judge them."

Jesus turned to Mary and said, "Well spoken, Mary."

Then he continued teaching his disciples:

"When Pistis Sophia finished her sixth repentance, she looked up again, hoping her sins were forgiven and that she would be freed from the chaos. But by the command of the First Mystery, her plea was not yet accepted. She was not forgiven, nor was she led out of the darkness. When she looked up, she saw the rulers of the twelve realms laughing at her. They were pleased that her repentance had been rejected. Seeing their mockery, she felt deep sorrow and cried out again in her seventh repentance, saying:

'O Light, I lift my power to you, my true Light. I have trusted in you; do not let me be humiliated. Do not let the rulers of the twelve realms who hate me celebrate my downfall. All who trust in you will never be ashamed. But let those who have stolen my power remain in darkness, unable to benefit from it, and let it be taken away from them.

O Light, show me your ways so that I may be saved. Teach me your paths so that I may escape the chaos. Guide me in your light and help me see that you are my Savior. I will trust in you forever. Hear me and rescue me, O Light, for your mercy is endless.

Do not hold against me the sins I committed in ignorance. Instead, save me through your great mystery of forgiveness because of your goodness. The Light is kind and pure, and it will show me the way to escape my wrongdoings. It will come close to my weakened powers and teach them its wisdom, for they have been drained by the fear of Self-Willed's forces.

All knowledge of the Light leads to salvation and holds the mystery for those who seek to inherit it. For the sake of your mystery, O Light, forgive my sin, for it is great. To all who trust in the Light, it will reveal the mystery meant for them. Their souls will live in the regions of the Light, and their power will inherit its treasures.

The Light gives strength to those who believe in it, and its name belongs to those who put their trust in it. It will show them the place of their inheritance, which lies within the Treasury of the Light. I have always trusted in the Light, for it will free me from the chains of darkness.

Turn to me, O Light, and save me, for my name has been stolen in chaos. Because of the forces of darkness, my suffering and oppression have grown even greater. Rescue me from my sins and from this shadow. See my pain and forgive my mistakes. Pay attention to the rulers of the twelve realms who hate me out of jealousy.

Watch over my power and save me, so that I will not remain trapped in this darkness, for I have trusted in you. Yet they have mocked me for putting my faith in you, O Light. Now, O Light, save me from the forces of Self-Willed, who have brought me so much suffering.'

"Let those who are wise understand this."

When Jesus finished speaking, Thomas stepped forward and said, "My Lord, I am prepared. My spirit rejoices because you have revealed these teachings to us. I have waited patiently with my brothers so as not to cause conflict, and I have allowed them to come before you and explain the meaning of Pistis Sophia's repentance. Now, regarding her seventh repentance, your Light-Power spoke about this long ago through David in Psalm 25:

100

'O Lord, I lift my soul to you, my God.

I have placed my trust in you; do not let me be ashamed.

Do not let my enemies mock me.

For all who hope in you will not be shamed,

But let those who act unjustly be disgraced.

Show me your ways, O Lord, and teach me your paths.

Guide me in your truth and instruct me,

For you are my God and my Savior, and I will wait for you all day long.

Remember your mercy, O Lord, and your kindness, for they have existed forever.

Forget the sins of my youth and my mistakes made in ignorance.

Remember me in your great mercy, O Lord.

The Lord is gracious and pure; he teaches sinners the way.

He will guide the humble and instruct them in his wisdom.

All the ways of the Lord are filled with grace and truth

For those who seek his righteousness and follow his path.

For the sake of your name, O Lord, forgive my great sin.

Who is the one who fears the Lord?

He will lead them in the way they should go.

Their soul will live in peace, and their descendants will inherit the land.

The Lord strengthens those who fear him and reveals his covenant to them.

My eyes are always on the Lord, for he will free my feet from the trap.

Look upon me and have mercy, for I am alone and in distress.

The troubles of my heart have multiplied; rescue me from my suffering.

See my pain and my struggles, and forgive my sins.

See how my enemies have grown in number and hate me without cause.

Protect my soul and save me; do not let me be ashamed, for I have trusted in you.

The honest and the faithful will stay with me, for I have placed my hope in you, O Lord.

O God, save Israel from all its troubles.'"

When Jesus heard Thomas' words, he said, "Well spoken, Thomas. You have explained it beautifully. This is the meaning of Pistis Sophia's seventh repentance. Truly, I tell you, all generations on earth will bless you because I have revealed this to you, and you have received my Spirit. You have been enlightened and made spiritual, able to understand all that I have spoken.

"From now on, I will fill you with the complete light and power of the Spirit so that you will fully understand everything you hear and see. Soon, I will reveal to you even greater mysteries, the highest and deepest ones."

Chapter 45

Jesus continued teaching his disciples and said:

"After Pistis Sophia spoke her seventh repentance while trapped in chaos, the command from the First Mystery had not yet been given for me to save her and bring her out. However, because of my compassion, I decided to help her on my own, even without a command. I moved her to a more open space within the chaos. Though she was still trapped, this place was less restrictive.

"When the forces of Self-Willed saw that she had been moved to this slightly freer place, they stopped attacking her for a while. They thought she might soon be rescued from chaos completely.

"At that time, Pistis Sophia did not realize that I was helping her. She did not recognize me or understand that I had shown her kindness. Instead, she continued to sing praises to the Light of the Treasury—the Light she had seen before and believed in. She was convinced that this Light, which she had worshiped many times, was her true guide and protector. Because her faith in the Light of the Treasury was pure and unwavering, she would eventually be saved from chaos, and her repentance would be accepted. But the command from the First Mystery to accept her repentance had not yet been given.

"Now, listen closely as I explain everything that happened to Pistis Sophia.

"After I moved her to a more open space within the chaos, the forces of Self-Willed completely stopped attacking her for a while. They assumed she would soon be lifted out of chaos altogether. But when they realized she had not yet been fully rescued, they returned with even greater force, oppressing her even more than before.

"Seeing that they had resumed their attacks and were tormenting her more than ever, Pistis Sophia cried out again in her eighth repentance. In her pain and despair, she prayed:

'O Light, I have placed my hope in you. Do not leave me in this chaos. Save me and rescue me through your wisdom. Listen to my prayer and deliver me.

Be my Savior, O Light, and guide me into your radiance. You are my only salvation, and you will bring me into your presence. Because of the mystery of your name, lead me and give me your sacred mystery.

You will save me from the lion-faced power and from the trap they have set for me, for you are my Savior. Into your hands, I entrust the purification of my light. You have saved me, O Light, according to your wisdom.

You are angry with those who keep watch over me, and they will no longer have full control over me. Yet I have trusted in the Light. I will rejoice and sing praises because you have shown me mercy, heard my cries, and freed me from my suffering.

You will release my power from chaos. You have not left me in the grip of the lion-faced power, but you have guided me to a place where I am no longer constantly attacked.'

"This was her eighth repentance, a cry that came from her pain and her unwavering faith in the Light, even while she remained in the chaos."

Chapter 46

When Jesus finished speaking, he continued teaching his disciples:

"When the lion-faced power of Self-Willed saw that Pistis Sophia had not yet been completely freed from chaos, it returned, bringing all the other material forces of Self-Willed with it. Together, they attacked Pistis Sophia once again, this time with even greater force.

"As the oppression started again, Pistis Sophia cried out in the same repentance she had spoken before, saying:

'Have mercy on me, O Light, for they have come back to torment me. Because of your command, the light within me has become confused, and my power and understanding are in turmoil. My strength is fading as I continue to suffer, and my time in chaos feels endless.

My light is growing weaker because they have stolen my power, and everything within me is in disorder.

I am completely powerless in the presence of the rulers of the realms who hate me. I have no strength before the twenty-four emanations in whose region I once lived. Even my own companion, the one who was close to me, has not come to help me.'

Jesus paused for a moment before continuing, emphasizing the depth of Pistis Sophia's suffering and the cruelty of the forces that oppressed her. Her cries were not just pleas for mercy—they revealed the deep despair she felt, abandoned and powerless before the rulers and emanations that continued to attack her.

Jesus encouraged his disciples to reflect on her endurance and unwavering faith in the Light, even when faced with overwhelming hardship.

Chapter 47

I was afraid to ask for help because of the trap they had set for me.

All the rulers of the higher realms looked down on me and judged me as if I were nothing but empty matter, without light. They saw no value in me, as if I had fallen and been cast out like a useless force, rejected by the rulers themselves. Those in the realms above said, "She has become chaos." Then, all the ruthless powers surrounded me completely, plotting to take away every last bit of light within me.

But even as they worked against me, I placed my trust in you, O Light, and said, "You are my Savior." The command you have given for me remains in your hands. Rescue me from the forces of Self-

Willed, from those who endlessly oppress and persecute me. Let your light shine upon me, for without you, I am nothing. Save me, O Light, through your boundless mercy.

Do not let me be disgraced, for I have always sung praises to you. Let the chaos that threatens me fall instead on the forces of Self-Willed, and may they be thrown into the deepest darkness. Silence those who try to deceive me, those who plot to steal all the light within me, even though I have done nothing to harm them.

When Jesus finished speaking, Matthew stepped forward and said, "My Lord, your spirit has moved me, and your light has cleared my mind, preparing me to reveal the meaning of Pistis Sophia's eighth repentance. Your power spoke of this moment long ago through David in Psalm 31:

'In you, O Lord, I have placed my hope. Never let me be put to shame; save me through your righteousness.

Turn your ear to me and rescue me quickly. Be my strong protector and a safe shelter for me.

For you are my refuge and my strength; for the sake of your name, you will guide and sustain me.

You will pull me out of the trap they secretly set for me, for you are my defender.

Into your hands, I entrust my spirit, for you have redeemed me, O Lord, the God of truth.

You reject those who chase after worthless lies, but I have placed my trust in you.

I will rejoice and celebrate your mercy, for you have seen my suffering and saved my soul from affliction.

You have not handed me over to my enemies but have set my feet in a wide and open place.

Be merciful to me, O Lord, for I am in great distress. My eyes are filled with sorrow, my soul and body are worn down with pain.

My life is spent in sadness, my years filled with grief. My strength has faded in my misery, and my bones have grown weak.

I have become an object of scorn to all my enemies, a source of horror to my neighbors, even my friends are afraid of me.

When they see me, they turn away and flee.

I am forgotten, as if I were already dead, like a broken jar that has been thrown away.

I hear the whispers of many, the scorn they speak against me...'

Matthew paused, letting the weight of the Psalm settle in the hearts of those who listened. Jesus looked at him and said, "Well done, Matthew. Your understanding is true, and your words have captured the meaning of Pistis Sophia's eighth repentance. Let all who hear remember her unshakable faith in the Light, even when she faced overwhelming suffering. Her cries and her endurance will stand as a testimony for all who seek salvation."

Chapter 48

Jesus praised Matthew for his understanding and said, "Well done, Matthew. You have spoken with wisdom and insight. Truly, I tell you, when the perfect number is reached and the universe is restored, I will take my place in the Treasury of the Light. You, my disciples, will sit with me on twelve thrones of light. Together, we will guide and restore the twelve Saviors to their rightful places." He paused for a moment and then asked, "Do you understand what I am saying?"

Mary stepped forward and said, "Lord, you have spoken about this before in a parable: 'You have stood by me through my trials, and I will give you a kingdom, just as my Father has given me one. You will eat and drink at my table in my kingdom and sit on twelve thrones, judging the twelve tribes of Israel.'"

Jesus nodded and said, "Well said, Mary." Then he turned again to his disciples and continued:

"When the forces of Self-Willed saw that Pistis Sophia had still not been freed from chaos, they returned with even greater force. They attacked her again, trying to take every last bit of her power. Seeing this, Pistis Sophia cried out once more, offering her ninth repentance to the Light, saying:

'O Light, defeat those who have stolen my power. Take back from them the strength they took from me. For I belong to you, O Light— I am your power and your light. Come quickly and save me. Let great darkness cover my oppressors, and speak to my power, saying: I am here to rescue you.

Let all who try to steal my light become weak and powerless. Send them back into the chaos they tried to escape, and may they remain there, unable to harm me any longer. Let their strength crumble into dust, and send Yew, your angel, to strike them down. If they try to rise to the heights, let the darkness pull them back down, let them stumble and fall into chaos again. Let Yew chase them away and cast them into the depths.

For they set a trap for me, placing the lion-faced power before me, even though I did them no wrong. They sought to drain its light, and they have attacked my inner strength, though they cannot take it from me completely. O Light, take the purification from the lion-faced power without it knowing, undo the plans of Self-Willed, and take back the light they tried to steal from me. Let the light they wanted be taken from them instead.

But I will rejoice in the Light and celebrate my salvation. Every part of me will proclaim: There is no Savior but the Light! You will free me from the lion-faced power that tried to steal my strength. You will rescue me from those who robbed me of my light and power.

They have risen against me, spreading lies, claiming that I know the mysteries of the Light above—the very Light in which I placed my trust. They have pressured me to reveal the mysteries of the heights, mysteries I do not even know.

They have repaid my faith in the Light with cruelty, leaving me drained and empty. When they surrounded me, I sat in darkness, my soul weighed down with sorrow. But even then, I sang praises to you, O Light. I know you will save me, for I have followed your will from the beginning. In my realm, I obeyed your commands, just as the invisibles in my region have done, as has my companion. I have searched endlessly for your Light.

Now, the emanations of Self-Willed have surrounded me once again, rejoicing in my suffering and pressing me down even more. They left for a time, but they have returned, treating me even more harshly, grinding their teeth as they try to steal every last trace of my light.

How long, O Light, will you allow this? How long will you let them oppress me? Save my strength from their evil plans and free me from the power of the lion-faced one. I alone among the invisibles am in this place.

I will sing praises to you, O Light, even while surrounded by those who stand against me. I will cry out to you, even as they oppress me. Do not let those who hate me and seek to steal my power celebrate my downfall. Do not let those who despise me and glare at me with hatred have victory, for I have done nothing to harm them.

Even so, they have spoken kindly to me, pretending to be friendly while asking me about the mysteries of the Light—mysteries I do not know. They spoke with deceit and then became angry at me because I remained faithful to the Light of the heights. They opened their mouths against me, saying, "Now we will take her light."

But you, O Light, know their plans. Do not let them succeed. Do not let your help be far from me. Act swiftly, O Light, to protect me and bring me justice. Show your judgment upon me with your mercy.'

When Jesus heard Pistis Sophia's ninth repentance, he praised her strength and said to his disciples, "Remember this: the faith and cries of Pistis Sophia will not go unanswered. Her unwavering trust in the Light, even through such deep suffering, is an example for all who seek salvation. She has remained faithful, and in time, her light will be restored to her."

Chapter 49

James explained the meaning of the ninth repentance using words from Psalm 34.

After Jesus finished teaching and explaining Pistis Sophia's ninth repentance, he turned to his disciples and said, "Who among you is ready and clear-minded? Let that one step forward and share the meaning of her repentance."

James stepped forward respectfully, placed a devoted kiss on Jesus' chest, and said, "My Lord, your spirit has filled me with wisdom and understanding. I am ready to explain her repentance. Long ago, your power spoke through David in Psalm 34, foretelling the meaning of Pistis Sophia's ninth repentance. It says:

'O Lord, stand against those who treat me unjustly; fight against those who attack me.

Pick up your shield and armor, and come to my aid.

Draw your sword and turn it against those who oppress me, saying to my soul: I am your salvation.

Let those who seek to harm me be filled with shame and disgrace.

Let those who plot against me be humiliated and forced to turn away.

May they scatter like dust before the wind, and let the angel of the Lord chase them away.

Let their path be dark and slippery, and may the angel of the Lord drive them into fear.

Without cause, they set a trap for me, hoping to gain something for themselves.

They mocked me for no reason.

Let them fall into their own trap; let the net they secretly set for me catch them instead.

But my soul will rejoice in the Lord and celebrate his salvation.

All my bones will cry out: O Lord, who is like you?

You rescue the poor from those too strong for them, the weak from those who seek to take everything away.

False witnesses have risen against me, accusing me of things I do not know.

They repaid my kindness with cruelty, leaving me feeling abandoned.

Yet, when they suffered, I mourned for them. I humbled myself and fasted, praying from the depths of my heart.

I grieved for them as though they were my family.

But when I stumbled, they rejoiced. They gathered against me, attacking me without reason.

Strangers surrounded me, mocking and tormenting me endlessly.

They clenched their teeth in hatred toward me.

O Lord, how long will you stand by and watch?

Rescue me from their cruelty, my life from the jaws of the lions.

I will thank you in the great assembly; I will praise you among many people.

Do not let those who hate me without reason rejoice over me.

Do not let those who treat me unfairly celebrate my downfall.

They speak kindly to me, but in their hearts, they plan to harm me.

They open their mouths wide against me, saying, "Aha! Now we see what we wanted."

You have seen this, O Lord. Do not stay silent. Do not be far from me.

Rise up and defend me; bring justice to my cause, my God and my Lord.

Judge me according to your righteousness, O Lord, and do not let them celebrate my suffering.

Do not let them say to themselves, "Now we have what we wanted."

Do not let them say, "We have defeated him."

Let those who take joy in my pain be filled with shame and dishonor.

Let those who think they are better than me be covered in disgrace.

But let those who seek my justice celebrate and be glad.

Let them always say, "The Lord is great! He takes pleasure in the peace of his servant."

My tongue will speak of your righteousness and praise you all day long.'

When James finished speaking, Jesus looked at him with approval and said, "Well done, James. You have explained this with wisdom and accuracy. Truly, you have captured the meaning of this repentance."

Jesus then turned to the other disciples, encouraging them to think deeply about the powerful truths revealed in both Pistis Sophia's cries and the ancient prophecy that had been fulfilled through her struggles.

Chapter 50

This was the resolution of Pistis Sophia's ninth repentance. Jesus, full of kindness and understanding, said, "Truly, I tell you: You, my disciples, will hold the highest places in the kingdom of heaven. You will stand above all invisibles, all gods, and all rulers in both the thirteenth and twelfth realms. And not just you—anyone who follows my teachings and fulfills my mysteries will receive the same honor."

Then Jesus looked at his disciples and asked, "Do you understand what I am telling you? Do you see the meaning behind my words?"

Mary, always eager to learn, stepped forward and said, "Yes, Lord, I understand. You have told us before, 'The last shall be first, and the first shall be last.' The first ones created before humanity are the invisibles, the gods, and the rulers. They existed before us. But those who receive your mysteries, Lord, will be the first to enter the kingdom of heaven, even surpassing those who were created before."

Jesus smiled at her and said, "Well spoken, Mary. You have understood correctly." He then turned back to his disciples and continued teaching.

"After Pistis Sophia spoke her ninth repentance, the lion-faced power returned once again. It tried to steal what little strength she had left, draining her of all her remaining light. Weighed down by this attack, she cried out once more to the Light, saying:

'O Light, I have trusted in you since the beginning. I have endured unbearable suffering for your sake. Please, help me now.'

"At that very moment, her repentance was accepted. The First Mystery heard her cry, and I was sent to help her. I entered the chaos to rescue her because her faith in the Light had remained strong, even through her suffering. She had not been misled because of ignorance or rebellion—she had been deceived by Self-Willed, who had tricked her with a false light that resembled the true Light. Because of this, the First Mystery sent me to save her in secret.

"When I descended into the chaos, no other power saw me—not those in the deepest regions nor those in the outermost realms. No being knew I was there except for the First Mystery, who had sent me. I passed through unseen, hidden from all powers, both in the highest places and the lowest depths.

"When I arrived in the chaos, Pistis Sophia saw me for the first time. She recognized my wisdom and saw the great light that surrounded me. Unlike the lion-faced power, I was full of mercy and kindness. I was not like Self-Willed, who had taken her light and tried to steal what remained of her strength. My light was far greater than the lion-faced power—ten thousand times brighter. She realized that I had come from the highest place, the very Light she had trusted since the beginning.

"Seeing me, Pistis Sophia felt hope again. Her despair faded, and her heart grew strong. She lifted her voice once more and spoke her tenth repentance, saying:

'I have cried out to you, O Light of lights, from the depths of my suffering, and you have heard me. O Light, save my power from the hands of those who speak lies and from the traps they have set for me.

The light they tried to steal from me with their tricks and deceit will never reach you, O Light. The traps of Self-Willed and the snares of the merciless surround me.

Woe to me, for I am far from where I belong. I am stranded in the depths of chaos. My power is trapped in a place that is not my own.

I begged the merciless ones for help, but instead of mercy, they attacked me without reason. Even when I pleaded, they only sought to harm me.'

"With these words, Pistis Sophia began her tenth repentance. Though she was still in pain, she now had new hope because she had seen the Light that had come to rescue her. Her cries showed both her suffering and her determination to keep trusting in the Light.

"I tell you, my disciples, this is why faith and perseverance in the Light are so important. No matter how great the trials or how strong the darkness, those who remain steadfast will be saved."

Chapter 51

When Jesus finished speaking to his disciples, he turned to them again and said, "Now, if anyone feels moved in their spirit, let them step forward and explain the meaning of Pistis Sophia's tenth repentance."

Peter stepped forward and said, "Lord, long ago, your Light-Power spoke through David in Psalm 120, revealing the meaning of this repentance. The Psalm says:

'I cried out to you, O Lord, in my suffering, and you listened to me.

O Lord, save my soul from lying lips and deceitful tongues.

What will be your punishment, O deceiver? What more will be done to you?

Like sharp arrows in the hands of a warrior, tipped with burning coals from the desert, so is your judgment.'

After Peter finished, he paused, his voice filled with deep respect, and looked to Jesus for confirmation. Jesus nodded and said, "Well spoken, Peter. You have recognized the connection between David's prophecy and the repentance of Pistis Sophia."

Then Jesus turned to the other disciples and explained further:

"The words of this Psalm reflect the suffering of Pistis Sophia and her cries to the Light. She was tormented by the lies and deception of the forces of Self-Willed, who tried to take away her light through trickery and falsehoods. They were relentless and cruel, like sharp arrows piercing her, and their words, like burning coals from a barren desert, were full of malice, trying to consume her completely.

"Sophia's plea, 'O Lord, save my soul from lying lips and deceitful tongues,' was her desperate call to escape from those who twisted truth and tried to trap her. She knew her light was in danger and turned to the true Light, her only source of mercy and protection. Even as her enemies surrounded her with lies, she never lost faith.

"Peter, the verses you have shared do not speak only of Sophia's suffering, but of a struggle that all who seek the Light will face. Those who stand against truth and righteousness strike like arrows and burn like fire with their falsehoods. But the Light is the shield that protects the soul, the force that rescues the faithful from destruction."

Peter and the other disciples listened closely, reflecting on Jesus' words and the deep connection between the ancient prophecy and Pistis Sophia's suffering. They realized the power of her faith and perseverance in the face of so much deception and cruelty.

Jesus continued, encouraging them to see the greater lesson in Sophia's story.

"This is not just about her—it is a message for all who seek salvation. Even when faced with opposition as sharp as arrows or deceit as scorching as fire, one must hold on tightly to the Light, knowing that it will save and protect. Let Sophia's trust and courage be an example for all of you, as you cotinue on the path of truth."

Chapter 52

Pistis Sophia's eleventh repentance began with a cry of sorrow, filled with pain and longing:

"I am filled with sorrow! I am far from where I should be, living in a place that is not my home. My soul has traveled through many lands, always feeling like an outsider. I longed for peace, but I was surrounded by those who despise it. Whenever I spoke, they turned against me without cause."

This marked the conclusion of Pistis Sophia's tenth repentance, a desperate plea as she suffered under the forces of Self-Willed and his lion-faced power. They tormented her without mercy, trying to steal the last of her light and strength.

When Peter finished explaining the meaning of her tenth repentance, Jesus said, "Well done, Peter. You have interpreted Pistis Sophia's words clearly and wisely."

Then Jesus continued teaching his disciples:

"When the lion-faced power saw me approaching Pistis Sophia, shining with a light too powerful for it to withstand, it became furious. It sent out many violent forces, each stronger than the last, in a final attempt to overpower her. It tried to frighten and weaken her completely so that it could take all the light left within her.

"Seeing this, Pistis Sophia cried out once more in her eleventh repentance, pleading to the Light:

'Why has this mighty power risen up in wickedness? Its schemes never stop stealing my light, and its cruelty cuts into me like sharp iron. I chose to leave the thirteenth realm, the place of Righteousness, rather than remain in despair. But now they have turned against me with deception, trying to take everything I have left.

Because of this, the Light will take away their power. Their strength will disappear, and their matter will be reduced to nothing. Their light will be stripped from them, and they will no longer have a place in the thirteenth realm. Their names will not be remembered among those who live in the Light.

The twenty-four emanations will see what happens to you, O lion-faced power, and they will be filled with fear. They will no longer dare to disobey but will instead offer up their light to be purified.

They will rejoice at your downfall and say, "Look at what happens to those who refuse to cleanse their light! The one who boasted in its power, who tried to steal the light of Pistis Sophia, now has lost everything."'

When Jesus finished explaining Pistis Sophia's eleventh repentance, he turned to his disciples and said, "If anyone's spirit is moved, let them step forward now and explain the meaning of this repentance."

Salome stepped forward with great respect and said, "My Lord, your Light-Power spoke long ago through David in Psalm 52, revealing the meaning of this repentance. The Psalm says:

'Why does the mighty one boast in his wickedness?

All day long, your words bring harm; like a sharp razor, you spread deceit.

You love evil more than good, lies more than truth.

You take pleasure in words that destroy, your tongue full of trickery.

Because of this, God will bring you down to ruin.'

"These words describe the lion-faced power perfectly. It is filled with arrogance and deception. It wanted to take Pistis Sophia's light, believing itself to be stronger than all others. But in the end, it will be destroyed by the true Light."

Jesus listened to Salome and said, "Well spoken, Salome. You have explained Pistis Sophia's eleventh repentance with wisdom and understanding. Her cries and her trust in the Light are a lesson for everyone who seeks salvation. The fall of the lion-faced power is proof that no force can stand against the truth and justice of the Light."

Then Jesus turned back to his disciples and said, "This repentance is more than just one soul's cry for help—it is a message for all who follow the path of truth. No matter how strong or deceptive evil may seem, the Light will always overcome it. Let this give strength and hope to all who face struggles as they seek the mysteries."

Chapter 53

Self-Willed joined forces with his emanations, and their hatred grew even stronger. They no longer just wanted to harm Pistis Sophia—they wanted to completely destroy her. Their goal was to wipe out every last trace of her light and power. They didn't just want to keep her trapped; they wanted to cut her off from the Light forever and leave her in complete despair, separated from those who live in the Light.

The Psalm continues:

"The righteous will see this and be filled with awe. They will mock him, saying:

'Look at the one who refused to make God his helper, instead trusting in his own wealth and relying on his empty pride.

But I am like a healthy olive tree in the house of God. I have placed my trust in God's kindness forever, and I will give thanks for His goodness. I will wait for His name, for it is great and honored among His faithful ones.'"

Salome then spoke with confidence, saying, "Lord, this is the meaning of Pistis Sophia's eleventh repentance. Your Light has guided me, and I have spoken as you willed."

When Jesus heard Salome's words, he said, "Well said, Salome. Truly, I tell you, I will perfect you in all the mysteries of the kingdom of Light." Then he turned back to his disciples and continued teaching.

"After this, I came closer to the chaos, shining with an overwhelming brilliance, to reclaim the light stolen by the lion-faced power. My light was so great that the lion-faced power trembled with fear. In desperation, it cried out for help from Self-Willed. From his place in the thirteenth realm, Self-Willed looked down at the chaos with great fury, ready to defend the lion-faced power.

"Encouraged by this, the lion-faced power gathered all its forces and surrounded Pistis Sophia, determined to steal whatever light she had left.

"As they closed in on her, pressing down harder than ever, Pistis Sophia lifted her eyes to the heights and called out to me for help. But when she looked up, she saw the wrath of Self-Willed, and fear filled her heart. Overcome with anguish, she cried out once more, offering her twelfth repentance:

'O Light, do not forget the praises I have sung to you.

Self-Willed and his lion-faced power have opened their jaws against me with hatred, plotting in secret to trap me.

They have surrounded me, hoping to steal my strength.

They despise me because I have sung praises to you.

Instead of love, they spread lies about me, but still, I continue to sing to you.

They tried to take my strength because I have offered my songs to you, O Light.

They hate me because I love you.'

"In this twelfth repentance, Pistis Sophia did not just cry out for help—she declared her faith in the Light, even as her enemies plotted against her. She knew the evil of Self-Willed and his forces, but she refused to turn away from the Light. Even in her suffering, she chose to keep praising, turning her fear into trust and her pain into hope.

"Her song of faith, sung in the midst of darkness, became her greatest act of resistance against those who wanted to destroy her.

"Jesus paused, allowing his disciples to take in the weight of her words and the depth of her suffering. Then he continued:

"Even as she was surrounded by darkness, as her enemies worked against her, Pistis Sophia never lost faith. Her love for the Light and her dedication to praising it was stronger than the forces attacking her. Her repentance was not just a plea for help—it was a declaration of her unshaken loyalty to the Light.

"Let this twelfth repentance be a lesson to all who seek salvation. Even when facing overwhelming opposition, when surrounded by deception and cruelty, the faithful must keep their hearts turned toward the Light. Praise, when it comes from a sincere and devoted soul, cannot be destroyed by hatred or lies. Instead, it becomes a beacon that draws the Light closer, bringing rescue to those who endure with faith."

"Let the darkness take hold of Self-Willed, and may the ruler of the deepest abyss stand at his right side, serving as his eternal companion in his downfall.

When judgment is passed upon him, may his power be stripped away.

Let the very plan he made to steal my light be turned against him, and may the Light itself take his power away.

"May all the light in his forces fade away, and may another among the three great powers take his place.

Let his emanations lose all their light, and may his matter exist without any glow or strength.

May his emanations remain trapped in the chaos, unable to return to their realm.

Let all the light within them vanish, so that they may never again enter the thirteenth realm, the place from which they came."

May the Receiver, the Purifier of Lights, take all the light that still remains in Self-Willed and his forces, removing it completely. Let the rulers of the lower darkness have control over his emanations, and may no one offer them shelter or protection. Let their cries for help be ignored, and may no power in the chaos come to their aid. May their light be taken from them, erasing their names from the thirteenth realm and wiping out their memory forever.

Let the guilt of the one who created the lion-faced power be brought before the Light, and let the wrongdoing of the matter that gave birth to him remain unforgiven. May their sins stand before the Light for all eternity, and may they never again be able to see beyond the chaos. Let their names be erased from all places because they showed no mercy. They tried to destroy the light of someone who had put all their trust in the Light. With cruelty, they worked with those who trapped me, planning to take every last bit of light I had left.

They loved the darkness and will now remain there forever. They rejected the region of Righteousness, refusing it as their home, and they will never be allowed to enter it again. He covered himself in darkness like a robe, and now it has seeped into him like water, filling every part of his being as oil soaks into cloth. Let him be wrapped in chaos like a cloak and bound in darkness forever. Let this judgment fall upon all those who have harmed me for the sake of the Light and have declared, "We will take away all her power."

But you, O Light, show me mercy for the sake of the mystery of your name. Save me through the endless kindness of your grace. They have drained me of my light and strength, leaving me too weak to stand among them. I have become like fallen matter, thrown aside like a wandering spirit in the air. My power has faded because I lack the mystery to sustain it. My strength has been taken because they have stolen my light. They laugh at me, mocking and shaking their heads as they look upon me. Help me, O Light, in your great mercy.

After sharing this part of Pistis Sophia's twelfth repentance, Jesus turned to his disciples and said, "If anyone's spirit is moved, let them come forward now and explain the meaning of this repentance."

Andrew stepped forward and said, "My Lord and Savior, your Light-Power spoke about this long ago through David in Psalm 109. It is written:

'O God, do not stay silent while I cry out to you. Evil people and liars speak against me. They spread false stories and attack me with cruel words for no reason. Instead of kindness, they tell lies about me, but I keep praying to you. I showed them love, but they repaid me with hatred and treated me unfairly.

Let someone wicked rule over him, and let a deceiver stand at his side. When he is judged, let him be found guilty, and may even his prayers be counted as sins. Let his life be cut short, and may someone else take his position. Let his children become orphans and his wife a widow. May his children wander without a home, begging for food as they are driven from the ruins of their house. Let everything he owns be taken by others, and may strangers steal all he has worked for. Let no one be kind to him or feel sorry for his children. May his entire family line be cut off, and may their names disappear in a single generation.

Let the sins of his ancestors never be forgotten, and let the wrongdoing of his mother never be erased. May their guilt remain before you forever, Lord, and may their memory be wiped from the earth. This is because he showed no kindness to the poor and needy and tried to destroy those who were already suffering. He loved to curse others, so let his own curses fall upon him. He rejected blessings, so let them never come to him. He wrapped himself in curses like a coat, so let them soak into his body like water and into his bones like oil. Let curses surround him like a cloak and cling to him like a belt forever.

This is the fate of those who slander me before you, Lord, and speak falsely against me. But you, O Lord, be kind to me for the sake of your name. Save me with your goodness and grace. For I am poor and in desperate need, and my heart is full of sorrow. I am fading away like a shadow at sunset, tossed aside like a locust in the wind. My knees are weak from fasting, and my body has grown thin. I have become a joke to them; they see me and shake their heads in mockery. Help me, O Lord my God, and rescue me through your mercy. Let them see that this is your work, that you, O Lord, have done this.'

Andrew then said, "My Lord, this is the meaning of the twelfth repentance that Pistis Sophia spoke while she was trapped in chaos."

Chapter 54

Jesus continued teaching his disciples and said, "After everything that had happened, Pistis Sophia, filled with sorrow and longing for freedom, cried out to me:

'O Light of lights, I have made mistakes in the twelve realms and fallen from my rightful place. Because of this, I have spoken twelve repentances—one for each realm I left behind. Now, O Light of lights, please forgive me, for my mistake is great. I abandoned the higher places and ended up in chaos.'

After saying this, Pistis Sophia lifted her voice again and spoke her thirteenth repentance:

'Listen to me, O Light of lights, as I sing my praises to you. Hear my final repentance for the realm I left behind. Let this be the last repentance that makes up for my mistake so that I may return. O Light, hear my cry as I call from the place I abandoned. Save me by your great mystery, and forgive me through your endless mercy. Give me the baptism that washes away all sins, and make me pure again.

My greatest mistake was falling for the deception of the lion-faced power, which led me into chaos. I alone, among those from my realm, have fallen this far. Yet even in my fall, I tried to follow your will, so that your purpose would be fulfilled.'

After Pistis Sophia spoke these words, Jesus turned to his disciples and said, "Whoever understands her words, let them come forward and explain their meaning."

Martha stepped forward, her heart moved, and said, "My Lord, my spirit urges me to speak the meaning of what Pistis Sophia has declared. Your power spoke these very words long ago through David in Psalm 51:

'Have mercy on me, O God, because of your great kindness; in your endless love, erase my mistakes. Wash away all my wrongdoing, and cleanse me from my sins. My faults are always before me, so that you may be right in your words and just in your judgment.'

"This is the meaning of Pistis Sophia's thirteenth repentance."

Jesus responded, "Well said, Martha. You are truly wise and blessed." Then he turned back to his disciples and continued, "After these words were spoken, the time had come for Pistis Sophia to begin her journey out of the chaos. Without waiting for the command of the First Mystery, I chose to act on my own. I sent a light-power from myself into the chaos to help guide Pistis Sophia upward from the lowest depths. She would remain in a higher place until the time came for her full rescue.

"The light-power I sent reached Pistis Sophia and began leading her upward. When the forces of Self-Willed saw that she was escaping, they became furious and chased after her, trying to drag her back into the lower chaos. But the light-power I had sent was too bright for them, and they could not touch her. Though they tried to recapture her, Pistis Sophia lifted her voice once more, singing praises and crying out to me:

'I will sing to you, O Light, for my heart longs to return to you. You are my Savior, and I will praise you with all my soul. Do not leave me in chaos, O Light of the Highest; rescue me, for I have worshiped only you. You have sent your light to guide me, and it is leading me to safety.

May the forces of Self-Willed who chase after me fall into the lower chaos and remain there. Let deep darkness cover them so that they cannot reach me. Let their eyes be clouded in thick gloom, so they cannot see the light you have sent to save me. Let their plans to steal my power completely fail. Since they have spoken against me and tried to take my light, let their own light be taken from them instead.

Though they tried to steal all my light, they failed because your light-power was with me, protecting me. They acted without your command, O Light, so their efforts have led to nothing. I trust in you, O Light, and I am not afraid. You are my Savior, and I will not fear.'

After Pistis Sophia finished her song, Jesus turned to his disciples again and said, "Now let the one who feels led by the Spirit come forward and explain the meaning of her words."

Salome stepped forward and said, "My Lord, my heart urges me to share the meaning of these words. Your power spoke them long ago through Solomon in the Odes, saying:

'I will give thanks to you, O Lord, for you are my God. Do not abandon me, O Lord, for you are my hope. You have given me your salvation, and through you, I am saved. May those who chase after me stumble and fall, unable to catch me. Let a cloud of smoke cover their eyes, and let their vision be darkened by mist so that they cannot seize me. Let their own plans turn against them, and let all their schemes fail. They plotted against me, but they have been defeated.'

"This, my Lord, is the meaning of the song of praise spoken by Pistis Sophia."

Jesus said, "Well said, Salome. Your understanding is deep, and your words are filled with wisdom." He then reminded his disciples of the power of faith and persistence in seeking the Light, even in times of great struggle. The trials of Pistis Sophia and her eventual rescue stand as proof of the unshakable mercy and grace of the Light for all who remain faithful, no matter how dark their journey may be.

Chapter 55

The light-power sent by Jesus transformed into a shining wreath of light around Pistis Sophia's head, serving as both protection and renewal. This light-wreath not only kept the forces of Self-Willed away but also cleansed and strengthened her. As Jesus continued teaching his disciples, he explained:

"When Pistis Sophia finished praising the Light while trapped in chaos, I caused the light-power I sent to become a radiant wreath around her head. From that moment on, the forces of Self-Willed could no longer control her. This was not just a symbol—it was a true source of transformation. As it surrounded her, all the impurities within her were shaken loose and left behind in the chaos. The darkness that had clung to her was removed and could not follow her any longer.

"The forces of Self-Willed saw these remnants and felt a twisted kind of satisfaction, believing they had destroyed something. But they did not understand the true power and purity of the Light within Sophia. Now free from corruption, the pure Light within her merged with the power of the light-wreath, making it even brighter and stronger. This union gave Sophia the strength to resist the chaos completely.

"Her purified light did not leave her or become weak—it remained inside the light-wreath, safe and untouchable. No power of darkness could steal it from her again. Filled with this protection and strength, Pistis Sophia lifted her voice in praise once more, singing:

'The Light has become my crown, and I will never be separated from it. The forces of Self-Willed will never take it from me. Though the world around me may shake, I will remain steady. Even if parts of me are left behind in the chaos, seen by my enemies, I will not be lost. The Light is with me, and I am with the Light.'

"These were the words of Pistis Sophia as she rejoiced. Now, let the one who understands the meaning of her song step forward and explain it."

Hearing this, Mary, the mother of Jesus, stepped forward with deep respect and humility. She spoke to Jesus, saying, "My son, who I am connected to by the world, and my Lord and Savior, who I am connected to by the higher realms, please allow me the blessing of explaining the meaning of Pistis Sophia's words."

Jesus answered, "Mary, you, too, have received a form from Barbēlō in the material world and a likeness from the Virgin of Light in the spirit. You and the other Mary, the blessed one, are deeply connected to the divine mystery. Because of this, the forces of darkness have opposed you, for through you, my earthly body was brought into the world—a body that I have cleansed and perfected. Now, I ask you to reveal the meaning of Pistis Sophia's words."

Mary, the mother of Jesus, bowed and said, "My Lord, your light-power spoke about this long ago through Solomon in the nineteenth Ode, saying:

'The Lord is upon my head as a crown, and I shall never be separated from Him.'

She paused, reflecting for a moment before continuing, "This prophecy speaks of the unbreakable connection between the Light and those who remain faithful. The light-wreath on Sophia's head is not just a shield—it represents her complete purification, her renewal, and her unshakable bond with the Light."

When Mary finished speaking, Jesus looked at her with great approval and said, "Well said, Mary, my mother. You have spoken wisely and explained the truth clearly. Your understanding is blessed, and your words reflect the true mysteries of the Light."

Jesus then turned to his disciples once more and said, "Let the words of Pistis Sophia and the interpretation given by Mary serve as a lesson for all who seek the Light. Faith and true repentance have the power to overcome any darkness, cleanse the soul, and bring it back into unity with the Light. Sophia's journey is proof that no matter how far someone has fallen, the Light is always present, ready to restore and save those who return with a sincere and faithful heart."

Chapter 56

The command of the First Mystery was finally fulfilled, bringing Pistis Sophia's rescue from the chaos. This marked the end of her struggles and the acceptance of her repentance.

Jesus continued teaching his disciples, describing the moment of her deliverance. "After Pistis Sophia completed her thirteenth repentance, the time set by the First Mystery for her trials came to an end. It was time to bring her completely out of the chaos and save her from the darkness. The First Mystery, in its great mercy, accepted her repentance and sent a powerful light from above to help her. This light was sent to assist me in lifting Pistis Sophia from the depths of the chaos and leading her to safety."

Jesus paused for a moment, allowing his disciples to take in the importance of what he was saying. Then, he continued, "I looked toward the higher realms and into the Mystery of the heights. There, I saw the light-power descending. It had been sent by the First Mystery to help me save Pistis Sophia. The light moved quickly, coming down from the higher realms toward me as I hovered above the chaos. At that same moment, another light-power emerged from within me. It joined with the one sent from above. When these two light-powers met, they became one brilliant stream of light, united in purpose and radiance."

The disciples listened carefully, amazed by the way these divine forces worked together to save Sophia. Then, Jesus asked, "Do you understand what I am telling you?"

Mary Magdalene, full of wisdom, stepped forward and said, "My Lord, I understand. Your light-power spoke about this long ago through David in the eighty-fourth Psalm, which says:

'Grace and truth met together, and righteousness and peace embraced. Truth sprang forth from the earth, and righteousness looked down from heaven.'

"'Grace,' my Lord, is the light-power sent by the First Mystery. The First Mystery, in its kindness, heard the cries of Pistis Sophia and sent this power to help her in her suffering. 'Truth' is the power that came from you because you fulfilled your mission to save her from the chaos. 'Righteousness' is the power sent by the First Mystery to guide her on her path. And 'peace' is the power that came from you, working against the forces of Self-Willed to take back the light they had stolen from Pistis Sophia. Through this, her light was restored, bringing balance and harmony."

Jesus nodded in agreement, recognizing her wisdom, and said, "Well said, Mary. Your understanding is deep, and your words reveal the truth of these mysteries."

He then turned back to his disciples, emphasizing the meaning of the unity between the light-powers. "The meeting of these two lights— the one from the First Mystery and the one from within me— represents the coming together of grace, truth, righteousness, and peace. Together, they formed an unstoppable force, a great stream of light that brightened the chaos and lifted Pistis Sophia upward. This union is a symbol of the divine order that exists in the mysteries of the Light. It proves that no darkness, no power, can stand against the Light when it moves in unity."

As Jesus finished speaking, the disciples reflected deeply on the incredible mercy of the Light and the wisdom hidden in these mysteries. Pistis Sophia's rescue was more than just her salvation—it was proof of the endless grace and power of the Light. Her story encouraged all who heard it to remain faithful and strong on their own paths toward the Light.

Chapter 57

Mary, the mother of Jesus, stepped forward to explain more about the scripture and the events surrounding the power sent to help Pistis Sophia. With wisdom and respect, she said:

"My Lord, regarding the words your power spoke through David—'Grace and truth met together; righteousness and peace embraced. Truth rose from the earth, and righteousness looked down from heaven'—this prophecy was spoken about you long ago.

'Grace' refers to the power that came down from above through the First Mystery. This grace has shown mercy to the world and opened a path for salvation. 'Truth' is the power that came from you, entering the chaos to complete the divine plan. That is why the scripture says, 'Truth rose from the earth,' because you came to guide the lost back to the Light. 'Righteousness' is the power that came down through the First Mystery to enter Pistis Sophia, helping her find her way back."

When Mary finished speaking, Jesus looked at her and said, "Well spoken, Mary, blessed among all. Truly, you will inherit the entire Light Kingdom for your wisdom and faith."

Encouraged by his words, Mary continued with a request. "My Lord and Savior, allow me to repeat these words and explain them further."

Jesus answered, "For those who are moved by understanding, I place no limits. Instead, I encourage them to speak and share what is in their hearts. Now, Mary, my mother in the physical world, the one who gave me my earthly body, I invite you to share your understanding of this teaching."

With great respect, Mary began to speak. "My Lord, the prophecy from David—'Grace and truth met together; righteousness and peace embraced. Truth rose from the earth, and righteousness looked down from heaven'—speaks directly about you.

There is a story from when you were a child, before the Spirit had fully come upon you. You were with Joseph in the vineyard, tending to the work, while I was in the house. Suddenly, a spirit from above appeared inside. It looked exactly like you, so much so that I thought it was you. The spirit spoke, saying, 'Where is Jesus, my brother? I have come to meet him.'

At first, I was confused. I thought it might be a trick, so I tied the spirit to the foot of the bed and quickly went to find you and Joseph in the field. When I arrived, I saw you standing with Joseph as he worked in the vineyard. I told you what had happened and described the figure I had seen. When you heard my words, you were filled with joy and said, 'Where is he? I will wait for him here.'

Joseph was surprised by your words, and together we returned to the house. When we arrived, we found the spirit still tied to the bed. To our amazement, when we looked at you and the spirit, we saw that the two of you were identical. Then, the spirit was set free, and it approached you. It embraced you and kissed you, and you did the same. In that moment, the two of you became one, revealing a great mystery about grace and truth."

Mary paused for a moment before continuing. "This event helps us understand the prophecy. 'Grace' is the spirit that came down from above through the First Mystery. It was sent with mercy to bring forgiveness and reveal the mysteries to humanity so they could inherit the Light Kingdom. 'Truth' is the power within you, the divine essence that came from Barbēlō. It is the truth that entered the chaos to guide and save."

With conviction, Mary concluded, "The meeting of grace and truth shows the connection between the spiritual and physical parts of your mission, my Lord. Through this union, the sins of the world are forgiven, and the mysteries are revealed so that all may return to the Light."

Jesus looked at his mother with deep admiration and said, "Well spoken, Mary, my blessed mother. Your understanding of these mysteries is profound. You have explained the truth with clarity and wisdom. Truly, you will shine in the Light Kingdom forever."

Then, he turned to his disciples and said, "Let this be a lesson for all of you. The union of grace and truth is the foundation of the mysteries. It is through this harmony that salvation comes to the world, allowing all who seek the Light to find their way back to the divine source."

Chapter 58

Mary, the mother of Jesus, stepped forward to explain more about the scripture and the events surrounding the power sent to help Pistis Sophia. With wisdom and respect, she said:

"My Lord, regarding the words your power spoke through David—'Grace and truth met together; righteousness and peace embraced. Truth rose from the earth, and righteousness looked down from heaven'—this prophecy was spoken about you long ago.

'Grace' refers to the power that came down from above through the First Mystery. This grace has shown mercy to the world and opened a path for salvation. 'Truth' is the power that came from you, entering the chaos to complete the divine plan. That is why the scripture says, 'Truth rose from the earth,' because you came to guide the lost back to the Light. 'Righteousness' is the power that came down through the First Mystery to enter Pistis Sophia, helping her find her way back."

When Mary finished speaking, Jesus looked at her and said, "Well spoken, Mary, blessed among all. Truly, you will inherit the entire Light Kingdom for your wisdom and faith."

Encouraged by his words, Mary continued with a request. "My Lord and Savior, allow me to repeat these words and explain them further."

Jesus answered, "For those who are moved by understanding, I place no limits. Instead, I encourage them to speak and share what is in their hearts. Now, Mary, my mother in the physical world, the one who gave me my earthly body, I invite you to share your understanding of this teaching."

With great respect, Mary began to speak. "My Lord, the prophecy from David—'Grace and truth met together; righteousness and peace embraced. Truth rose from the earth, and righteousness looked down from heaven'—speaks directly about you.

There is a story from when you were a child, before the Spirit had fully come upon you. You were with Joseph in the vineyard, tending to the work, while I was in the house. Suddenly, a spirit from above appeared inside. It looked exactly like you, so much so that I thought it was you. The spirit spoke, saying, 'Where is Jesus, my brother? I have come to meet him.'

At first, I was confused. I thought it might be a trick, so I tied the spirit to the foot of the bed and quickly went to find you and Joseph in the field. When I arrived, I saw you standing with Joseph as he worked in the vineyard. I told you what had happened and described the figure I had seen. When you heard my words, you were filled with joy and said, 'Where is he? I will wait for him here.'

Joseph was surprised by your words, and together we returned to the house. When we arrived, we found the spirit still tied to the bed. To our amazement, when we looked at you and the spirit, we saw that the two of you were identical. Then, the spirit was set free, and it approached you. It embraced you and kissed you, and you did the same. In that moment, the two of you became one, revealing a great mystery about grace and truth."

Mary paused for a moment before continuing. "This event helps us understand the prophecy. 'Grace' is the spirit that came down from above through the First Mystery. It was sent with mercy to bring forgiveness and reveal the mysteries to humanity so they could inherit the Light Kingdom. 'Truth' is the power within you, the divine essence that came from Barbēlō. It is the truth that entered the chaos to guide and save."

With conviction, Mary concluded, "The meeting of grace and truth shows the connection between the spiritual and physical parts of your mission, my Lord. Through this union, the sins of the world are forgiven, and the mysteries are revealed so that all may return to the Light."

Jesus looked at his mother with deep admiration and said, "Well spoken, Mary, my blessed mother. Your understanding of these mysteries is profound. You have explained the truth with clarity and wisdom. Truly, you will shine in the Light Kingdom forever."

Then, he turned to his disciples and said, "Let this be a lesson for all of you. The union of grace and truth is the foundation of the mysteries. It is through this harmony that salvation comes to the world, allowing all who seek the Light to find their way back to the divine source."

[The Note of A Scribe]

(These are the sacred names I will now reveal, starting from the Boundless. Write them with care and mark them with a sign, so that the true followers of the Light may be recognized and revealed from this moment forward. The power and mysteries within these names are important, and understanding them is necessary for those who seek the Light.)

The name of the Immortal One is aaa, ōōō. This name represents the eternal nature of the Immortal One, the source of all life and light. The name of the Voice, the force that set the Perfect Man into motion, is iii. These names are not just words; they hold deep meanings that reveal the structure of divine mysteries.

Here is the meaning of these sacred names:

• The first name, aaa, means fff, representing the first breath of creation, the foundation of existence.

• The second name, mmm or ōōō, is interpreted as aaa, symbolizing the never-ending flow of divine energy.

• The third name, ps ps ps, is understood as ooo, reflecting the harmony that fills all things.

• The fourth name, fff, is interpreted as nnn, representing the power of transformation that moves through the worlds.

• The fifth name, ddd, means aaa, showing the return to the original source, the Boundless.

The One who sits on the throne of divine power is called aaa, because this name holds the endless light and unity of all things. This interpretation of the second mystery—aaaa, aaaa, aaaa—reveals the full meaning of the sacred name, expressing eternal grace, strength, and wisdom.

Each of these names is a key to understanding the higher mysteries. They offer insight into how the divine realms work and the forces that shape them. Those who reflect on these names with pure hearts will come closer to the Light and align themselves with the truth of the Boundless. Through these revelations, the true followers of God are made known, their purpose and path revealed in the grand plan of the Light Kingdom.

The Second Book of Pistis Sophia

Chapter 59

John stepped forward with respect and said to Jesus, "Lord, please allow me to explain the meaning of the words your light-power prophesied long ago through David."

Jesus turned to him and said, "John, you may speak. Explain the meaning of the prophecy my light-power revealed through David:

'Grace and truth came together,

righteousness and peace embraced.

Truth has sprung up from the earth,

and righteousness has looked down from heaven.'"

Filled with understanding, John began to explain, "Lord, these words speak about you and the mission you came to fulfill. You once told us, 'I came from the highest place and entered into Sabaōth, the Good, joining with the light-power within him.'

'Grace and truth came together' speaks of you, Lord. You are 'Grace,' sent from the highest regions by your Father, the First Mystery. Through his will, you came to bring mercy and salvation to the whole world.

'Truth' refers to the power of Sabaōth, the Good, which united with you and was then sent to the lower realms. This truth, which came from the First Mystery, was passed to Sabaōth, the Good, and entered into the material world. There, it proclaimed the mysteries of truth to those in the lower regions. The very body you now have, Lord, comes from the matter of Barbēlō, where truth was revealed.

'Righteousness and peace embraced' represents a deep connection. 'Righteousness' is you, Lord, because you brought all the mysteries from your Father, the First Mystery. You purified the power of Sabaōth, the Good, and made holy the places where you entered. You went to the realm of the rulers and gave them the mysteries of the highest Light, helping them become righteous.

'Peace' represents the power of Sabaōth, which is also your soul. It entered the material world and united with it, bringing harmony. Because of this, even the rulers of the lower realms were able to connect with the Light and accept its mysteries.

'Truth has sprung up from the earth' speaks of the power of Sabaōth, the Good, which came from the Right, just outside the Treasury of the Light. It traveled to the Left and entered the material world, bringing the mysteries of truth to those in darkness.

'Righteousness has looked down from heaven' refers to you, Lord, the one sent by the First Mystery. You came down from the highest Light, bringing with you the wisdom of the divine mysteries. You shared these teachings with the lower realms, offering them the chance to become righteous and enter the Light-Kingdom."

John paused, speaking with clarity and devotion, then continued, "This prophecy is about how different forces of the divine come together in you, Lord. Grace, truth, righteousness, and peace are not just ideas; they are living powers that united in your mission. You came from the highest Light, brought the mysteries together, and showed the path to salvation to all. This fulfills the will of the First Mystery, bringing harmony between the Light and the lower realms, guiding all toward salvation."

When John finished, Jesus looked at him with approval and said, "Well said, John, inheritor of the Light. You have explained these deep mysteries with wisdom and accuracy. You have revealed how these divine forces work together to bring salvation to the world."

Turning to the other disciples, Jesus said, "Let this teaching remind you of how everything in the divine plan is connected. Through grace and truth, righteousness and peace, the Light changes the chaos, bringing everything into harmony. These forces do not work separately but together, fulfilling the plan of salvation and leading all toward eternal life in the Light-Kingdom."

Chapter 60

Gabriel and Michael were sent on an important mission to restore and save what had been lost. Jesus continued teaching his disciples, explaining:

"When John spoke, he revealed the deep truth that I was the power sent from the highest place by my Father. I came down to help Pistis Sophia escape the chaos. My Father, the First Mystery, sent me, and I united with the power that came from me and the soul I received from Sabaōth, the Good. These forces came together, forming a single stream of brilliant light, shining brighter than anything else.

Following my Father's command, I called upon Gabriel and Michael from the higher realms. I gave them this powerful light and told them to take it down into the chaos. Their task was to recover the light-powers that the forces of Self-Willed had stolen from Pistis Sophia and return them to her.

When Gabriel and Michael carried this light into the chaos, it filled the entire region with incredible brightness. The light spread everywhere, touching every part of the chaotic realms. When the emanations of Self-Willed saw this great light, they were filled with fear. They were shocked and overwhelmed, unable to resist its power. As the light spread, it began pulling back the stolen light-powers from Self-

Willed and his forces. No matter how hard they tried to fight back or hold onto what they had taken, they were powerless against the divine light.

Gabriel and Michael then directed the light over Pistis Sophia, allowing it to flow into her. The light filled her completely, restoring all the powers that had been taken from her. Her weakened body, once drained and dim, now shone with renewed energy. The powers within her, which had lost their strength, were fully restored. They regained their brilliance, and nothing was missing anymore because the light had replenished everything. This restoration was possible because of me, the one who had sent the light in the first place.

Gabriel and Michael also carried with them the sacred mysteries of the Light. These mysteries were part of their mission, but they did not take anything for themselves. Every bit of light returned to Pistis Sophia belonged to her alone. It was taken back from the forces of Self-Willed and placed where it truly belonged.

As the light-stream completed its purpose, Pistis Sophia's entire being became radiant. The light-powers within her, which had never been stolen, celebrated and shone even brighter. The new light not only restored her but also strengthened her material body, which had been close to fading away. The light brought her back to life, giving her energy and power once more. Her strength returned, and she was restored to her original, complete form.

Through this powerful light, all of Sophia's inner forces recognized one another again. Their unity was restored, and they were saved by the very light that had come to rescue them. This light-stream brought balance back to her and reconnected her to the divine. Once it had finished its work, the light withdrew, leaving behind everything it had given to Pistis Sophia. Everything that had been stolen from her was now hers again.

When the light-stream's mission was complete, Pistis Sophia stood renewed, shining with a brilliance that could not be taken away. She had regained all her power, and the light within her was now whole and strong. Her transformation showed the incredible mercy and power of the Light."

Jesus paused, letting his disciples take in the meaning of these events. Then he said, "Let this be a lesson about the unstoppable power of the Light. No force of chaos, no deception from Self-Willed, can resist the divine will when it acts to restore and redeem. The Light does not simply rescue—it changes, heals, and makes new all that has been lost or broken."

Chapter 61

Peter stepped forward respectfully and said, "Lord, allow me to explain the meaning of the words your light-power spoke long ago through Solomon. These words reveal the deep mysteries you have shared with us and connect to the story of Pistis Sophia's rescue."

Jesus nodded and said, "Speak, Peter, and explain the meaning of the prophecy."

Peter began, "Lord, the prophecy from Solomon's Odes says:

'A stream flowed out and became a wide river.

It swept everything with it and turned toward the temple.

No walls or barriers could hold it back, nor could anyone control its waters.

It spread across the whole land and touched everything.

Those who stood on dry ground drank from it; their thirst was satisfied when they received the drink from the hand of the Highest.

Blessed are those who serve that drink, the ones entrusted with the

Lord's water.

They have refreshed thirsty lips; those who had lost their strength now rejoice.

They have breathed life into souls, so they would not perish.

They have raised those who had fallen; they have given strength and light to their eyes.

For all have come to know themselves in the Lord, and they are saved through the water of eternal life.'

Now, Lord, let me explain how these words relate to the rescue of Pistis Sophia.

When the prophecy says, 'A stream flowed out and became a wide river,' it refers to the great stream of light that was sent into the chaos. This light spread throughout the realm of Self-Willed's forces, shining into the darkness.

'It swept everything with it and turned toward the temple' means that the light-stream gathered all the stolen light-powers that had been taken from Pistis Sophia. It didn't stop until it had returned everything to her.

'No walls or barriers could hold it back' shows that the forces of Self-Willed had no power to block or resist the light. No structure or trick could stop it from restoring what was lost.

'It spread across the whole land and touched everything' describes how Gabriel and Michael carried the light-stream over Pistis Sophia's body. As they did, the stolen light returned to her, making her shine once again.

'Those who stood on dry ground drank from it; their thirst was satisfied' speaks of the parts of Pistis Sophia that had been drained of light. When the light returned, their need was fulfilled, and their suffering ended.

'The drink from the hand of the Highest was given' means that this light-stream, coming from you, Lord, and the First Mystery, was the divine power that restored everything she had lost.

'Blessed are those who serve that drink' refers to Gabriel and Michael, who carried out the mission without keeping anything for themselves. They faithfully returned all the light to Pistis Sophia.

'They have refreshed thirsty lips' means that Pistis Sophia's lost light returned to her completely. Gabriel and Michael ensured that nothing was left behind.

'Those who had lost their strength now rejoice' refers to the parts of Pistis Sophia's being that were not stolen. These parts celebrated when the missing light was restored, making them whole again.

'They have breathed life into souls, so they would not perish' speaks of how the light-stream revived Pistis Sophia's body, which had been close to fading away. It saved her from being lost forever.

'They have raised those who had fallen' shows how the light-stream brought back the powers that had nearly dissolved. It gave them new strength.

'They have given strength and light to their eyes' means that the light restored Sophia's awareness. It allowed her inner powers to recognize one another and be whole again.

'For all have come to know themselves in the Lord' means that all the parts of Pistis Sophia, through the return of light, understood their divine origin and connection to the Light.

'They are saved through the water of eternal life' means that the light-stream, which represents the life-giving power of the Light, was the force that saved them.

'The light-stream swept everything with it and returned to the temple' concludes the prophecy by describing how the light-stream, after gathering all the stolen light-powers, left the chaos and returned to you, Lord, the source of truth and Light."

When Peter finished, his words brought clarity to the prophecy's meaning. Jesus looked at him with approval and said, "Well done, Peter, inheritor of the Light. You have shown how the prophecy and the mysteries work together, revealing the divine plan. The light-stream, representing the limitless grace of the Light, restores, unites, and saves all who seek the truth."

Jesus then turned to the disciples and said, "Let this teaching strengthen your understanding. The Light never abandons its own. It sends forth its power to gather, restore, and make whole all who belong to it. Through the water of eternal life, the lost are saved, and those who seek the Light will always find their way home."

Chapter 62

The First Mystery continued revealing what happened in the chaos, speaking clearly and seriously to the disciples to help them understand.

"This is the explanation of all the words spoken through the Ode of Solomon by my light-power," he said. Then, turning to Peter, he acknowledged his understanding by saying, "Well said, Peter. Your explanation has revealed the true meaning of these words."

Then, the First Mystery continued, saying, "Before I was commanded to bring Pistis Sophia completely out of the chaos— before my Father, the First Mystery who looks inward, gave the order—many things happened. When the forces of Self-Willed realized that my light-stream had taken back the stolen light-powers and returned them to Pistis Sophia, they were furious. When they saw her shining again with the light she had from the beginning, they were filled with anger and called out to their master, Self-Willed, begging him to help them steal her light once again.

Self-Willed, who ruled in the highest part of the thirteenth realm, sent down a powerful force of light, filled with violent energy, like a flying arrow. This force entered the chaos to help his servants take the restored light from Pistis Sophia. As soon as it arrived, the forces of Self-Willed, now encouraged by its presence, renewed their attack. They changed into terrifying forms: one became a huge serpent, another a seven-headed creature, and another a great dragon. The lion-faced power of Self-Willed and many other dark forces joined them, surrounding Pistis Sophia. They pulled her back down into the lower parts of chaos, filling her with deep fear and hopelessness.

At the same time, Adamas, the Tyrant, who ruled over the twelve realms, looked down at Pistis Sophia. He, too, was angry because she was trying to rise toward the Light, far beyond his control. Filled with jealousy and rage, Adamas sent his own power into the chaos to join in the attack against Pistis Sophia. His dark force descended and worked with the emanations of Self-Willed to strip all the light from her once again. Together, they pushed her down even further, trapping her among the lion-faced power, the serpent, the dragon, and all the other dark forces. Their only goal was to take her power and completely defeat her.

Overcome with fear and pain, Pistis Sophia once again turned to the Light, crying out desperately for help. She lifted her voice in prayer, saying:

'O Light, you are my helper; let your light surround me.

For you are my protector, and I trust in you.

You are my Savior from the forces of Self-Willed and Adamas, the Tyrant.

Save me from their threats and attacks.'

Hearing her cry, my Father, the First Mystery who looks inward, gave me the command to act. I sent Gabriel and Michael once again, along with the powerful light-stream, to help Pistis Sophia. I told Gabriel and Michael to carry her so that she would not fall further into darkness. They were to lead her carefully through the chaos, guiding her to safety.

When Gabriel, Michael, and the light-stream entered the chaos, their brilliance was greater than anything seen before. The entire realm was filled with their radiant light. The dark forces of Self-Willed and the power of Adamas trembled with fear at the sight of this overwhelming brightness. They could not resist it and fled from Pistis Sophia, unable to harm her. The great light-stream surrounded her completely, forming a shining shield around her head and filling her with divine protection.

In this light, Pistis Sophia found new strength. The light-stream never left her side. She no longer feared the forces of Self-Willed, the dark power sent down like an arrow, or even the evil power of Adamas. The Light became her refuge, shielding her from all harm.

At my command, the light-stream grew even brighter, shining with a radiance beyond all understanding. Pistis Sophia stood in the middle of this brilliant light, safe and secure. The forces of Self-Willed, blinded and overpowered by the brightness, collapsed on both sides, defeated and powerless. They could not come near her or touch her again. The most powerful of them, the seven-headed beast, was crushed beneath her feet, unable to fight against the strength of the Light.

Then, following the command of my Father, the First Mystery who looks inward, I descended into the chaos myself, shining with a light no darkness could overcome. I faced the lion-faced power of Self-Willed and took all its light, making it weak and powerless. I bound the dark forces of Self-Willed so that they could never return to their realm in the thirteenth æon. Stripped of their power, they fell into the chaos, unable to rise again.

Finally, I led Pistis Sophia out of the chaos, with Gabriel and Michael at her side. The great light-stream poured into her once more, completely restoring her. As we ascended, she looked back at her enemies, now empty and defeated, without the stolen light they had once taken from her. Standing over the seven-headed beast, the greatest of her oppressors, she had won the victory. I took away the remaining power of the beast and all the other dark forces, leaving them with nothing. Their strength was gone, and they could never rise again.

Pistis Sophia, now fully restored, rose out of the chaos, her faith in the Light proven true. All that had been lost was returned to her. The forces of Self-Willed were destroyed, and the will of the Light was fulfilled. At last, she entered the Light's eternal embrace, safe and free forever."

Chapter 63

When the First Mystery finished speaking to the disciples, he turned to them and asked, "Do you understand what I have told you?" His question encouraged them to think deeply about his words and reflect on their meaning.

James, feeling the power of the teaching, stepped forward and said, "My Lord, I understand. Your light-power spoke of this long ago through David in the ninetieth Psalm. Allow me to share its meaning."

Then he recited the Psalm:

"Whoever dwells under the protection of the Most High will rest in the shadow of the Almighty.

They will say to the Lord, 'You are my helper and my safe place, my God in whom I trust.'

For He will rescue me from the trap of those who hunt me and from the power of destruction.

He will cover you with His wings, and under them, you will find safety; His truth will be your shield.

You will not fear the terror of the night nor the arrow that flies by day,

Nor the dangers that lurk in the darkness, nor the disaster that strikes at midday.

A thousand may fall at your left and ten thousand at your right, but you will remain unharmed.

With your own eyes, you will witness the punishment of the wicked.

For you, O Lord, are my refuge; you have made the Most High your home.

No harm will come to you; no plague will approach your dwelling.

For He will command His angels to watch over you in all your ways,

They will lift you up in their hands so you will not stumble over a stone.

You will walk over the serpent and the cobra, and you will trample the lion and the dragon.

Because you have placed your trust in Me, I will save you; I will protect you because you know My name.

You will call on Me, and I will answer you; I will be with you in times of trouble and will rescue and honor you.

I will give you a long life and show you My salvation."

James then explained, "This, my Lord, is the meaning of your words. Let me clarify each part.

'Whoever dwells under the protection of the Most High will rest in the shadow of the Almighty,' refers to Pistis Sophia. When she trusted in the Light, she was placed under the protection of the great light-stream that came down from you. This light surrounded her and kept her safe from the forces of darkness.

'I will say to the Lord: You are my helper and my safe place, my God in whom I trust,' reflects what Pistis Sophia declared in her own words: 'You are my helper, and I call out to you.' She put all her hope in the Light as her only source of safety and protection.

'My God, in whom I trust, you will save me from the trap of those who hunt me and from the power of destruction,' matches her own prayer: 'O Light, I believe in You, for You will save me from the forces of Self-Willed and Adamas the Tyrant, and from all who threaten me.' She knew that the Light would deliver her from those who wished to harm her.

'He will cover you with His wings, and under them, you will find safety,' describes the light-stream that surrounded Pistis Sophia. It wrapped around her completely, giving her a sense of peace and security. The light shining on both her left and right was like the protective wings of a great bird, sheltering her from harm.

James continued, "These words from David's Psalm show the promises of the Light—to provide safety, protection, and deliverance for all who trust in it, just as it did for Pistis Sophia."

When James finished speaking, the First Mystery looked at him and said, "Well said, James, faithful one of the Light. You have explained the connection between this prophecy and Sophia's rescue with wisdom and truth."

The disciples listened closely, amazed at how the ancient Psalm perfectly matched the events they had witnessed. Jesus then reminded them, "The Light will always protect those who put their trust in it. Every soul who seeks the Light with sincerity will be guided, guarded, and led into the eternal kingdom of peace and righteousness. Sophia's journey is proof of the power of faith and the endless mercy of the Light."

Then he continued, "The words of your light-power through David: 'Truth will surround you as a shield,' speak of the light-stream that completely enclosed Pistis Sophia, protecting her from all harm. This shield of light made her untouchable to the forces of darkness.

'You will not be afraid of the terror of the night,' refers to how Pistis Sophia overcame her fear of the chaos. The 'night' represents the suffering and danger she faced. But even when surrounded by darkness, her trust in the Light kept her strong, and she did not fall into despair."

"The phrase, 'He will not be afraid of an arrow that flies by day,' refers to the strongest and most powerful force that Self-Willed sent down from the thirteenth æon into the chaos. It came down like a flying arrow, meant to strike fear into Pistis Sophia. However, she was not afraid because she fully trusted in the Light. The mention of 'day' represents the thirteenth æon, which is above the twelve æons and shines its light over them.

The words, 'He will not be afraid of something lurking in the darkness,' describe the lion-faced power that tried to scare Pistis Sophia while she was trapped in the deep chaos, the realm of darkness. Even though it was terrifying, she stood strong and did not lose her faith.

'He will not be afraid of disaster and a demon at midday,' refers to the violent force sent by Adamas, the Tyrant. This force struck Pistis Sophia with great power and tried to destroy her. It came from the twelfth æon, called 'midday,' because it sits between the thirteenth æon (above) and the chaos (below, described as 'night'). But no matter how strong this attack was, Pistis Sophia remained fearless because of her trust in the Light.

'A thousand will fall at your left, and ten thousand at your right, but they will not come near you,' describes how so many of Self-Willed's forces were defeated by the power of the great light-stream. They collapsed all around Pistis Sophia, unable to touch or harm her.

'With your own eyes, you will see and witness the punishment of the wicked,' means that Pistis Sophia watched as her enemies were brought down. The beings that tried to steal her light ended up losing their own power instead. This was the work of you, my Lord, the First Mystery, who locked them in chaos and prevented them from ever returning to their original place. Not only did she see them fall, but she also understood that justice had been served. They had tried to steal her light, but in the end, their own light was taken away, fulfilling the prophecy.

'You have made the Most High your refuge; harm will not come near you, and no disaster will reach your dwelling,' describes the protection Sophia received because of her unshakable faith in the Light. Even though she was attacked and tormented, she continued to praise the Light. Because of this, her enemies could not harm her or enter the sacred place where she was kept safe.

'He will command his angels to guard you in all your ways; they will lift you up in their hands so that you will not strike your foot against a stone,' refers to the order you, Lord, gave to Gabriel and Michael. These loyal angels guided Pistis Sophia safely through the chaotic regions, carrying her so that she would not fall into the darkness. They protected her from being taken by the forces of chaos and made sure she did not stumble.

'You will walk over the serpent and the basilisk; you will trample the lion and the dragon. Because he has trusted in me, I will save him, and I will protect him because he knows my name,' symbolizes Pistis Sophia's victory. She rose from the chaos, standing above the defeated forces of Self-Willed. Because she kept her faith in the Light, she was protected and restored to her rightful place.

Pistis Sophia's story reveals the power of trust in the Light. Her struggles and triumph show that those who remain faithful will find protection, justice, and ultimately, salvation."

Chapter 64

Sophia sang a song of joy, celebrating her rescue from the chaos. She declared her victory over the serpent-faced, basilisk-faced, lion-faced, and dragon-faced beings that had tormented her. Because she never lost faith in the Light, she was saved, restored, and made whole again.

James, deeply moved by her words, stepped forward and said, "My Lord, I understand the meaning of what she has spoken." The First Mystery, pleased with his insight, replied, "Well said, James, my beloved one."

Then the First Mystery continued teaching the disciples, saying, "When I brought Pistis Sophia out of the chaos, she cried out in gratitude and sang this song of repentance and praise:

1. I have been rescued from the chaos and freed from the chains of darkness. I have come to you, O Light.

2. You surrounded me with your radiance, saving me and giving me strength.

3. The forces of Self-Willed tried to harm me, but your light stopped them. They could not get near me because your lightstream wrapped around me and protected me.

4. The emanations of Self-Willed trapped me, drained me of my power, and threw me into chaos until there was no light left in me. Compared to them, I felt as heavy as lead.

5. Then your lightstream came to me and saved me. It shined on both my left and right, surrounding me completely so that no part of me was left without light.

6. Your light covered me and cleansed all the evil from within me. Now I am free of my burdens because of your light.

7. Your light lifted me up and freed me from the oppression of Self-Willed's emanations.

8. I have placed all my trust in your light, and now I am purified within it.

9. The forces of Self-Willed that once attacked me have fallen back, and now I shine with your great power, for your salvation lasts forever.

"This is the song of repentance and gratitude that Pistis Sophia sang when she was finally freed from chaos. Let those who have ears to hear, listen and understand."

When the First Mystery finished speaking, Thomas stepped forward with respect and said, "My Lord, your words have awakened the light within me, and I now understand. Please allow me to explain the meaning of the song that Sophia sang."

The First Mystery replied, "I give you permission, Thomas. Speak and share the meaning of her song."

Thomas began, "My Lord, the words Pistis Sophia spoke in her song were already foretold by your light-power long ago through Solomon in his Odes:

1. I have been freed from my chains and have fled to you, O Lord.

2. You have stood at my right side, saving me and helping me.

3. You stopped my enemies and took away their power because your presence was with me, rescuing me through your mercy.

4. I was rejected and cast aside by many. To them, I was as heavy as lead.

5. But through you, I received strength. You placed light on my left and right, making sure no part of me remained in darkness.

6. You covered me with your grace, freeing me from my burdens.

7. Your right hand lifted me up and healed me from my suffering.

8. I have been strengthened by your truth and purified by your righteousness.

9. My enemies have been defeated, and I have been made whole by your goodness, for your peace lasts forever.

"This, my Lord, is the meaning behind the song that Pistis Sophia sang when she was saved from chaos. Allow me to explain it further."

Thomas continued, carefully explaining how each line of Sophia's song reflected her journey from suffering to salvation. He described how her words revealed the kindness and power of the Light and how faith and perseverance led to her ultimate redemption.

As he spoke, the disciples listened with great respect, gaining a deeper understanding of the divine mysteries.

Thomas then explained how the words spoken long ago in Solomon's Odes matched Sophia's own experience:

• "I have been freed from my chains and have fled to you, O Lord." These words align with Sophia's own declaration: "I am freed from the chains of darkness and have come to you, O Light." This shows her journey from captivity to freedom and her trust in the Light.

- "You have stood at my right side, saving me and helping me." This matches Sophia's words: "You have become light all around me, saving and helping me." It describes how the Light surrounded her completely, guiding and protecting her through all her struggles.

Thomas spoke with great wisdom, showing how Sophia's story was a powerful example of faith, endurance, and the limitless mercy of the Light.

Sophia sang a song of joy, celebrating her freedom from chaos. She declared victory over the serpent-faced, basilisk-faced, lion-faced, and dragon-faced beings that had tormented her. Because she remained faithful to the Light, she was saved, restored, and made whole again.

James, deeply moved by her words, stepped forward and said, "My Lord, I understand the meaning of what she has spoken." The First Mystery, pleased with his insight, replied, "Well said, James, my beloved one."

Then the First Mystery continued teaching the disciples, saying, "When I brought Pistis Sophia out of the chaos, she cried out in gratitude and sang this song of repentance and praise:

1. I have been saved from the darkness and freed from its chains. I have come to you, O Light.

2. You surrounded me with your brightness, saving me and giving me strength.

3. The forces of Self-Willed tried to harm me, but your light stopped them. They could not come near me because your light covered and protected me.

4.   The powers of Self-Willed trapped me, drained me of my strength, and threw me into chaos until I had no light left in me. I felt as heavy as lead compared to them.

5.   Then your light came to me and rescued me. It shined on both my right and left, surrounding me completely so that no part of me was left without light.

6.   Your light washed over me, cleansing all the darkness from within me. Now I am free of my burdens because of your light.

7.   Your light lifted me up and freed me from the oppression of Self-Willed's powers.

8.   I have placed all my trust in your light, and now I am made pure within it.

9.   The forces that once attacked me have fallen back, and now I shine with your great power, for your salvation lasts forever.

"This is the song of repentance and gratitude that Pistis Sophia sang when she was finally freed from chaos. Let those who have ears to hear, listen and understand."

When the First Mystery finished speaking, Thomas stepped forward with respect and said, "My Lord, your words have awakened the light within me, and I now understand. Please allow me to explain the meaning of the song that Sophia sang."

The First Mystery replied, "I give you permission, Thomas. Speak and share the meaning of her song."

Thomas began, "My Lord, the words Pistis Sophia spoke in her song were already foretold by your light-power long ago through Solomon in his Odes:

1.   I have been freed from my chains and have fled to you, O Lord.

2.   You have stood at my right side, saving me and helping me.

3. You stopped my enemies and took away their power because your presence was with me, rescuing me through your mercy.

4. I was rejected and cast aside by many. To them, I was as heavy as lead.

5. But through you, I received strength. You placed light on my right and left, making sure no part of me remained in darkness.

6. You covered me with your grace, freeing me from my burdens.

7. Your right hand lifted me up and healed me from my suffering.

8. I have been strengthened by your truth and purified by your righteousness.

9. My enemies have been defeated, and I have been made whole by your goodness, for your peace lasts forever.

"This, my Lord, is the meaning behind the song that Pistis Sophia sang when she was saved from chaos. Allow me to explain it further."

Thomas continued, carefully explaining how each line of Sophia's song reflected her journey from suffering to salvation. He described how her words revealed the kindness and power of the Light and how faith and perseverance led to her ultimate redemption.

As he spoke, the disciples listened with great respect, gaining a deeper understanding of the divine mysteries.

Thomas then explained how the words spoken long ago in Solomon's Odes matched Sophia's own experience:

- "You stopped my enemies, and they could not reach me." This mirrors Sophia's own words: "The forces of Self-Willed that fought against me were blocked by your light, and they could not come near me." This shows how the Light protected her from harm.

- "Your presence was with me, saving me through your mercy." This is reflected in Sophia's words: "Your light was with me, saving me through your lightstream." It demonstrates how the Light never left her, guiding her through her struggles.

- "I was rejected and cast aside by many." This aligns with Sophia's cry: "The powers of Self-Willed drained me of my strength and threw me into chaos, leaving me without light." This highlights her pain and isolation before she was saved.

- "I became as heavy as lead in their sight." Sophia's words echo this: "When they took my light, I became like heavy matter to them." This expresses how she felt burdened and powerless without the Light.

- "Through you, I received strength, and a great power came to my aid." Sophia's statement confirms this: "A light-power came to me through you and saved me." This shows that the Light renewed her strength.

- "You placed light on my right and left so that no part of me would be in darkness." This is reflected in Sophia's words: "Your power shined on all sides of me, so that no part of me was left without light." This illustrates how she was fully surrounded and protected by the Light.

- "You covered me with your grace." This matches Sophia's statement: "You covered me with the light of the stream." This shows that the Light acted as a shield, guarding her completely.

- "I have been purified and lifted up above my burdens." Sophia confirms this: "I have been cleansed of all darkness, and I have risen in your light." This highlights her transformation and renewal.

Each of these connections between Solomon's words and those of

Pistis Sophia shows how prophecy was fulfilled and how the Light brings healing and salvation.

Thomas then continued, "My Lord, the words Solomon spoke—'Your right hand has lifted me up and freed me from suffering'—are directly connected to Sophia's words: 'Your lightstream has lifted me up and taken the forces of Self-Willed away from me.' This shows how the Light rescues and strengthens those who trust in it."

He also pointed out, "Solomon said, 'I have become powerful in your truth and purified in your righteousness,' which matches Sophia's declaration: 'I have been made strong in your light and purified in your lightstream.' This shows how the Light brings both strength and purity."

Finally, he explained, "Solomon's words, 'My enemies have turned away from me,' are the same as Sophia's statement: 'The forces of Self-Willed that oppressed me have retreated.' This proves that the Light triumphs over darkness and sets its followers free."

When Thomas finished, the First Mystery said to him, "Well spoken, Thomas, blessed one. This is the true meaning of the song that Pistis Sophia has sung."

The First Mystery then told the disciples how Sophia continued to praise the Light:

"I sing to you, for you have guided me from the higher realms to the lower regions, showing me the mysteries hidden in the darkness.

You have rescued me from the lower regions and restored the light-powers within me.

You have cast away the forces of Self-Willed that held me captive and freed me from Adamas, who tried to overpower me.

You have destroyed the seven-headed basilisk through my hands

161

and placed me above its remains. You have removed its power completely so that it can never rise again.

You have always been with me, surrounding me with your presence and giving me strength. Through your mercy, I am renewed, and I will forever praise your name."

These words of Pistis Sophia show her deep gratitude for being saved and her endless praise for the Light that rescued her from darkness.

Chapter 65

The words spoken in the Ode of Solomon: 'The one who led me down from the higher realms has also brought me up from the lowest depths,' describe how Pistis Sophia recognized both her fall from the upper heavens and her rescue. It shows how the Light reached her in the chaos and lifted her back toward renewal and restoration.

The phrase, 'The one who has taken those in the middle has taught me about them,' means that the Light revealed the secrets and powers hidden in the chaos. Even while struggling, Pistis Sophia was given knowledge and understanding of the forces that controlled those lower regions.

The words, 'The one who scattered my enemies and gave me power to break my chains,' describe how the Light defeated the forces of Self-Willed and Adamas. The Light gave Pistis Sophia the strength to break free from the oppression and darkness that held her captive.

The passage, 'The one who struck down the seven-headed serpent with my hands and placed me above its roots so that I may destroy its offspring,' means that the Light empowered Pistis Sophia to overcome the most dangerous forces of darkness. She was given the authority to defeat them and ensure that their influence would never return.

The phrase, 'You were with me, helping me; your name surrounded me in all places,' expresses how Pistis Sophia knew that the Light was always by her side. No matter where she went, the Light's power guided and protected her.

The words, 'Your right hand destroyed the poison of the liar and cleared the way for your faithful,' describe how the Light removed the harmful influence of Self-Willed's forces. It opened a path of salvation for those who followed the Light's guidance.

The line, 'You freed them from the tombs and lifted them from the dead,' symbolizes how the Light awakened and restored the hidden powers within Pistis Sophia. The parts of her that were thought to be lost or trapped in chaos were given life again.

The phrase, 'You took dry bones and gave them bodies; you brought movement to those who were still,' shows how the Light has the power to transform and revive. What once seemed lifeless was renewed and made active again.

The words, 'Your way is eternal and unshakable, and so is your presence,' describe how the path of the Light is everlasting and cannot be destroyed. It is a constant source of life and guidance for those who seek it.

The phrase, 'You have raised your realm above decay, so that all may be freed and renewed, and your light may be their foundation,' explains how the Light brought restoration to Pistis Sophia. Her powers were freed from chaos, renewed, and placed on a strong foundation within the Light's grace.

The words, 'You have poured out your riches upon them, and they have become a holy dwelling place,' mean that the Light has abundantly blessed Pistis Sophia and her restored powers. She has been transformed into a vessel of the divine.

This, my Lord, is the meaning of the song that Pistis Sophia sang. Each verse shows her deep gratitude and the incredible power of the Light that saved her. Let me now explain its meaning more clearly.

The words spoken through Solomon: 'The one who led me down from the higher realms has also brought me up from the lowest depths,' reflect Pistis Sophia's own words:

'I sing praises to you! By your command, you led me down from the higher heavens and guided me to the lower regions. And by your command, you saved me and lifted me up from the lower regions.'

This shows that every moment of her journey—both her fall and her rescue—was under the guidance of the Light, leading her toward redemption.

The words spoken through Solomon: 'The one who took those in the middle and taught me about them,' match what Pistis Sophia said: 'Through your command, you purified the matter within my power, and I saw it.' This means the Light helped her understand and cleanse the forces within her.

The words, 'The one who scattered my enemies and opponents,' are the same as what Pistis Sophia said: 'You scattered all the forces of Self-Willed that trapped me and worked against me.' This shows how the Light removed those who tried to keep her in darkness.

The phrase, 'The one who gave me wisdom to break my chains,' is reflected in Pistis Sophia's words: 'You gave me wisdom to free myself from the bonds of these forces.' It highlights how the Light gave her the knowledge and strength to escape.

The words, 'The one who struck down the seven-headed serpent through my hands and placed me above its roots so I could destroy its offspring,' match Pistis Sophia's statement: 'You struck down the seven-headed serpent through me and placed me above its power. You destroyed it completely, so it will never rise again.' This shows her victory over the dark forces that once controlled her.

The phrase, 'You were with me, helping me,' is the same as Pistis Sophia's words: 'You were with me, giving me strength in all things.' It emphasizes that the Light never abandoned her.

The words, 'Your name surrounded me in all regions,' align with what Pistis Sophia said: 'Your light surrounded me in all their regions.' This highlights the constant presence and protection of the Light.

The phrase, 'Your right hand destroyed the poison of the slanderers,' matches Pistis Sophia's words: 'Through you, the forces of Self-Willed became powerless because you took their stolen light from them.' This shows how the Light weakened those who tried to harm her.

The words, 'Your hand cleared the way for your faithful,' are echoed in Pistis Sophia's statement: 'You made my path straight to lead me out of chaos because I put my trust in you.' This shows how her faith in the Light guided her to freedom.

The phrase, 'You freed them from the tombs and lifted them from the dead,' matches Pistis Sophia's words: 'You freed me from the chaos and took me out of the material darkness, removing the stolen light from those dark forces.' This speaks to how the Light rescued her from despair and brought back what was lost.

The words, 'You took dry bones and gave them bodies, bringing life to what was still,' align with Pistis Sophia's declaration: 'You restored my powerless forces by filling them with purified light, and you gave life to all my limbs that had no movement.' This shows how the Light revived what was weak and lifeless within her.

The phrase, 'Your path is indestructible, and so is your presence,' matches Pistis Sophia's words: 'You made my way straight, and the light of your presence has given me eternal life.' It emphasizes the strength and permanence of the Light's guidance.

The words, 'You raised your realm above decay, so that all could be freed and renewed,' are the same as Pistis Sophia's statement: 'You lifted me, your power, above the chaos and beyond decay, so everything in that region could be freed and my powers could be renewed in the Light.' This highlights how she was restored and how the Light can renew all things.

The phrase, 'Your light has become the foundation for them all,' aligns with Pistis Sophia's words: 'Your light has filled them all.' This speaks to the Light as the source of renewal and strength.

The words spoken through Solomon, 'You have poured your riches upon him, and he has become a holy dwelling place,' match what Pistis Sophia said: 'You have covered me with the light of your stream, and I have become pure light.' This shows how the Light completely transformed and sanctified her.

This, my Lord, is the meaning of the song Pistis Sophia sang, expressing deep gratitude for her salvation and renewal.

Chapter 66

When the First Mystery heard Matthew's explanation of the song, he responded with praise, saying, "Well said, Matthew, you have spoken wisely. This is truly the meaning of the song that Pistis Sophia has sung."

The First Mystery continued:

1. "I will declare: You are the highest Light, for you have saved me and brought me to you. You did not let the forces of Self-Willed, who were against me, take my light."

2. "O Light of lights, I sing praises to you because you have delivered me."

3. "O Light, you have lifted my power out of the chaos and saved me from those who have fallen into the darkness."

"These are the words that Pistis Sophia has spoken. Now, let anyone whose understanding has been enlightened and who comprehends these words step forward and explain their meaning."

When the First Mystery finished speaking, Mary stood with respect and said, "My Lord, my mind is always open to understanding. I am ready to step forward and explain the meaning of her words. However, I hesitate because Peter has threatened me before and looks down on women."

Hearing this, the First Mystery reassured her, saying, "Anyone who is filled with the spirit of light and steps forward to explain the mysteries of what I have spoken shall not be stopped by anyone. Now, Mary, go ahead and explain the meaning of Pistis Sophia's words."

Encouraged by his words, Mary began to speak before the First Mystery and the disciples:

"My Lord, concerning the meaning of Pistis Sophia's words, your light-power long ago prophesied through David, saying:

1. 'I will lift you up, O Lord, because you have raised me up, and you did not let my enemies celebrate my downfall.'

Chapter 67

When Mary spoke these words, "O Lord, my God, I called out to you, and you healed me. O Lord, you lifted my soul from the depths; you saved me from those who had fallen into the pit," the First Mystery responded with approval, saying, "Well spoken, Mary, you are truly blessed."

The First Mystery continued speaking to the disciples, saying, "Pistis Sophia continued her song and declared:

1. The Light has become my Savior.

2. It has turned my darkness into light, broken apart the chaos that surrounded me, and covered me in its brightness."

When the First Mystery finished speaking, Martha stepped forward and said, "My Lord, your power prophesied these very words long ago through David, who said:

3. The Lord has become my helper.

4. He has turned my sorrow into joy; he has taken away my mourning and clothed me with happiness."

After hearing Martha's explanation, the First Mystery said, "Well spoken, Martha, you have expressed this beautifully."

The First Mystery then continued speaking to the disciples, saying, "Pistis Sophia once again lifted her voice in song, proclaiming:

1. My power, sing praises to the Light, and never forget all the gifts the Light has given you.

2. Let the powers within you give praise to the name of its holy mystery.

3. The Light forgives all your wrongdoings and saves you from the suffering caused by the emanations of Self-Willed.

4. The Light has rescued your light from the forces of destruction. It has surrounded you with its compassion and set you free.

5. It has filled you with pure light, restoring you to your original state as one belonging to the invisible beings of the Height."

The First Mystery concluded, "These were the words of praise sung by Pistis Sophia as she celebrated her salvation, reflecting on all I had done for her and the great deliverance she had received."

Chapter 68

When the First Mystery finished speaking to the disciples, he asked, "Who among you understands the meaning of these words? Let that person step forward and explain."

Mary stepped forward again and said, "My Lord, the words that Pistis Sophia sang in her praise were foretold by your light-power through David, saying:

1. My soul, praise the Lord; let everything within me praise his holy name.

2. My soul, praise the Lord, and never forget all the blessings he has given.

3. He forgives all your sins; he heals all your illnesses.

4. He saves your life from destruction; he surrounds you with grace and kindness.

5. He fills your soul with good things; your strength will be renewed like an eagle's."

"This means that Pistis Sophia will become like the invisible ones who live in the highest realms. The mention of the eagle represents how, just as an eagle soars high in the sky, Sophia will regain her original brilliance and stand once more among those in the heights."

When the First Mystery heard Mary's words, he said, "Well spoken, Mary. You are truly blessed."

Then, the First Mystery continued teaching the disciples, saying, "I took Pistis Sophia and placed her in a region just below the thirteenth æon. There, I gave her a new mystery of the Light, one that does not belong to her former realm but instead to the region of the invisible ones. I also gave her a song of the Light, so that the rulers of the æons would no longer have any power over her. I placed her in this region temporarily, knowing that I would later return to guide her to her final destination."

"When I placed her in this region, Pistis Sophia sang this song:

1. With faith, I trusted in the Light; it remembered me and heard my song.

2. It raised my power from the depths of chaos and the darkness of matter. It lifted me up and placed me in a higher, stronger realm, secure and safe. It has changed my path, leading me toward the place I was meant to be.

3. It has given me a new mystery, one not from my former realm, and it has blessed me with a song of the Light. Now, O Light, all the rulers will see what you have done for me, and they will be afraid. They will place their trust in the Light."

"This song expresses the joy of Pistis Sophia after being saved from chaos and placed in a higher realm beneath the thirteenth æon. Now, let the one who understands the meaning of this song step forward and explain it."

Andrew then stepped forward and said, "My Lord, these words are the same as those spoken by your light-power through David:

1. I waited patiently for the Lord; he turned to me and listened to my cry.

2. He lifted my soul from the pit of misery, from the mud and filth; he set my feet on solid ground and guided me on a straight path.

3. He placed a new song in my mouth, a song of praise to our God. Many will see it, be in awe, and put their trust in the Lord."

4. "This song reflects the journey and rescue of Pistis Sophia."

5. When Andrew finished speaking, the First Mystery said to him, "Well spoken, Andrew. You are truly blessed."

Chapter 69

He continued speaking to his followers and said, "These are the experiences that Pistis Sophia went through. When I led her to the place just below the thirteenth realm, she came close to the Light. From there, she could see the brilliance of the higher realms, which filled her with new hope and strength to keep moving forward.

As she stood in that place, surrounded by the brightness of the realms above, she lifted her voice and spoke to the Light, giving thanks and reflecting on everything she had been through. She said, 'O Light, you have remembered me in my suffering and did not leave me alone in my struggles. You lifted me out of the chaos and brought me here, where I can finally see your glory. I will sing praises to you, O Light of lights, because you are my Savior, my guide, and my strength.'

She continued, 'Even when I was surrounded by darkness, and the forces of Self-Willed tried to steal my light and power, you were my refuge. You did not let them succeed, and you restored everything they had taken from me. O Light, you are faithful and just, and I will praise your mercy forever.'

In that moment, Pistis Sophia shared her heart with the Light, recognizing both the hardships she had faced and the salvation she had received. The Light answered her, saying, 'Do not be afraid, Pistis Sophia, for I am with you. You are precious to me, and I will lead you to your rightful place in the higher realms. Your faith has not been in vain, and your praises have reached the heavens. Stay strong, for the time is near when you will be fully restored, and everything will be made right.'

As they spoke, the power of the Light surrounded Pistis Sophia, filling her with strength and peace. The light around her grew brighter, breaking every chain of darkness that had once held her down. It was a moment of deep joy and renewal, as she stood firm in the promises of the Light and its unwavering guidance.

These are the continued experiences and revelations of Pistis Sophia as she moved closer to her final redemption. Each step of her journey reveals the limitless power of the Light and the faith that kept her strong through every challenge. Let those who understand come forward and explain the meaning of these words."

Chapter 70

The Light promises to protect the regions of Self-Willed.

As I prepared to return to the Light and leave Pistis Sophia behind, she spoke to me with concern, saying, "O Light of lights, you are about to leave and return to the Great Light. When Adamas the Tyrant realizes that you are no longer here with me, he will know that my Savior is gone. Then he, along with his rulers who despise me and Self-Willed, will send his lion-faced power against me. They will attack me, try to trap me, and attempt to steal all of my light until I am completely powerless and cast back into darkness. O Light, my salvation, take their power away so they can no longer harm me."

Hearing her words, I responded, "My Father, who sent me, has not yet commanded me to take away their light. However, I will seal the regions of Self-Willed and his rulers, who hate you because of your faith in the Light. I will also seal the regions of Adamas and his rulers, so they cannot harm you until the time comes when my Father commands me to take their power."

Then I told her, "Listen carefully, and I will explain when this will happen. The time I speak of will come when the three appointed periods are completed."

Pistis Sophia, eager to understand, asked, "O Light, how will I know when these three times are over? How will I know when the time has come for you to take me to my rightful place? And how will I know when you will strip the power of those who hate me? For I have placed my faith in your Light."

I answered her, "You will know when the gate of the Treasury of the Great Light, beyond the thirteenth realm, is opened. When this left gate is opened, it will be the sign that the three times are fulfilled."

Still wanting more clarity, Pistis Sophia asked, "O Light, since I am in this region, how will I know that the gate has opened?"

I replied, "When the gate opens, everyone in all the realms will know because the Light will shine brightly throughout every region. But for now, I have decreed that no harm will come to you until the three times are completed. You will have the freedom to move through the twelve realms whenever you wish and return to this place below the thirteenth realm where you now live. However, you will not yet be able to pass through the gate of the thirteenth realm and return to the place where you first came from.

"When the three times are completed, Self-Willed and his rulers will rise against you once more in anger. They will try to take your light again, believing that you trapped their power in the chaos and took its light. In their rage, they will attempt to steal your light and send it back into the chaos to strengthen their emanation once again. Adamas will lead this attack. But when that time comes, I will take back all your power from them and restore it to you.

"If they attack you, sing praises to the Light, and I will come quickly to help you. I will descend into the lower regions to confront them, take their light, and make you even stronger. Then I will return to this place below the thirteenth realm, where I have placed you, and from there, I will eventually lead you back to your true home."

When Pistis Sophia heard these words, she was filled with joy, hope, and relief. Then, I moved her to a safe place below the thirteenth realm and ascended to the Light, leaving her there.

The First Mystery later shared these events with the disciples, explaining everything that had happened to Pistis Sophia. Sitting with them on the Mount of Olives, he spoke of her journey and the challenges she had endured. He continued, saying, "This also took place while I was still among the people, seated here on this very mountain—the Mount of Olives—before my heavenly robe was sent down to me. This robe, which I had left in the twenty-fourth mystery of the inner realm, the first of the outer realm, awaited me. It belonged to the Great Uncontainable, the divine power that surrounds me. Before I ascended to the Heights to receive my second robe, the appointed time had come, just as I had told Pistis Sophia: 'Adamas and all his rulers will rise against you and try to trap you.'"

Chapter 71

When the time had come, while I was still here with you on the Mount of Olives, Adamas looked down from the twelve realms into the chaos. He saw that his dark power was trapped there, completely drained of its light because I had taken it away. His power had become weak and could no longer return to its place in the twelve realms. Overcome with rage, he turned his thoughts to Pistis Sophia and, in his fury, wrongly blamed her for trapping his power in the chaos. He believed that she had stolen its light, and his anger burned even stronger.

In his bitterness, Adamas created two dark and violent forces, sending them out to hunt down Pistis Sophia. He formed a shadowy place in his domain, planning to capture her and keep her trapped there forever. Gathering many of his rulers, he ordered them to go after her. He sent his dark forces to seize her, pull her into this shadowy chaos, and drain all her remaining light. His plan was to take whatever light she had left and transfer it to his dark creations, giving them power to carry that stolen light deep into the great chaos below. This was his desperate attempt to strengthen his dark power, which had been left weak and empty.

As these forces came after Pistis Sophia, she cried out to the Light for help. She remembered my promise: "If you are trapped and you sing praises to me, I will come quickly to save you." While she was being attacked, and I remained here with you on the Mount of Olives, she lifted her voice in praise and called upon the Light:

"O Light of lights, I put my trust in you. Save me from these rulers who are chasing me and come to my rescue.

Do not let them steal my light, as the lion-faced power did before. Without your Light to protect me, Adamas will become even more furious, blaming me for trapping his power in the chaos.

Now, O Light of lights, if I have truly imprisoned his power, or if I have done him any harm, or trapped him as he has trapped me, then let these rulers take my light and leave me with nothing.

Let Adamas take my power for himself, strip me of my light, and throw it into his dark forces in the chaos. Let me remain trapped there, powerless and lost forever.

But O Light, I beg you, rise in your justice and lift your power above these enemies who have risen so strongly against me.

Restore my strength, as you have promised, and come quickly to save me."

And so, Pistis Sophia sang this song, calling out to the Light to rescue her from the overwhelming forces that sought to destroy her.

Chapter 72

When the First Mystery finished speaking to the disciples, he looked at them and said, "If anyone understands the meaning of these words, step forward and explain them."

James stood up and said, "My Lord, the song that Pistis Sophia has sung was foretold long ago through David in the seventh Psalm. It is written:

'O Lord, my God, I have placed my hope in you. Save me from those who chase me and rescue me, so they cannot capture my soul like a lion, with no one to help.

O Lord, my God, if I have done wrong, if I have acted unfairly, if I have harmed those who were good to me, then let my enemies defeat me. Let them take my life and leave me powerless.

Let my enemies hunt me down, destroy my life, and leave my honor in the dust. (Pause and reflect.)

But rise up, O Lord, in your justice. Stand against my enemies and bring them to judgment. Act according to your command.'

"My Lord, these words reflect the prayer of Pistis Sophia as she calls upon the Light for protection and deliverance from those who want to destroy her."

When James finished, the First Mystery turned to him and said, "Well spoken, James, my beloved. You have explained the song with wisdom and understanding."

Chapter 73

The First Mystery then continued speaking to the disciples: "When Pistis Sophia finished her song, she turned to see if Adamas and his rulers had left, but she saw that they were still chasing her. She faced them and said:

'Why do you still come after me and say that I have no help, that the Light will not save me?

But my defender is the Light, and it is strong. It is patient, waiting for the right time to help me, just as it has promised. The Light will not hold back its judgment forever, but now is the time it has spoken of.

If you do not stop chasing me, then the Light will gather its power and prepare itself.

It will take away your light, and you will become dark. It will strip you of your strength, and you will be brought low.'

When Pistis Sophia finished speaking, she looked toward Adamas' region and saw the dark, chaotic place he had created. She also saw the two violent, shadowy forces that Adamas had sent after her. Their mission was to capture her, drag her down into the chaos he had made, and torment her until they could steal her light.

When Pistis Sophia saw the dark forces and the chaotic place that Adamas had created, she became afraid and cried out to the Light, saying:

'O Light, look! Adamas, the one who brings violence, is full of rage. He has created a dark force against me.

He has also made another deep chaos, dark and full of destruction, and he has prepared it to trap me.

Now, O Light, the chaos that he has built to throw me into and steal my light—let him fall into it himself.

The plan he made to take my light—let his own light be taken from him. The injustice he plotted against me—let him suffer the same fate and lose everything he tried to take from me.'

"These are the words Pistis Sophia spoke in her song. Now, let the one who is clear in spirit step forward and explain their meaning."

Martha stepped forward and said, "My Lord, I have a clear understanding of your words. Give me permission to explain their meaning openly."

The First Mystery answered, "Martha, I give you permission to explain the meaning of Pistis Sophia's song."

Martha said, "My Lord, these are the words your light-power prophesied long ago through David in the seventh Psalm:

'God is a just defender, strong and patient, who does not bring judgment immediately.'"

Chapter 74

Martha began to explain and said, "My Lord, these are the words that your light-power prophesied through David in the seventh Psalm:

'If they do not turn back, He will sharpen His sword; He has drawn His bow and made it ready. He has prepared His weapons of justice and set His arrows against those who do evil. Look, injustice works hard, gives birth to wrongdoing, and brings forth wickedness. It digs a pit and carves it out, but in the end, it will fall into its own trap. Its evil will return upon itself, and its wrongdoing will fall upon its own head.'

"These words show the justice of the Light, revealing how those who create harm and injustice will ultimately suffer from their own actions. This connects to the story of Pistis Sophia, who called on the

Light for help, while her enemies—Adamas and Selfwilled—fell into the very traps they had set for her."

When Martha finished speaking, the First Mystery said to her, "Well spoken, Martha, blessed one."

After this, Jesus, the First Mystery, spoke to the disciples about everything that had happened to Pistis Sophia while she was trapped in the chaos. He reminded them of how she sang praises to the Light for her rescue, how she was led out of chaos into the twelve realms, and how the Light protected her from the rulers who wanted to stop her from ascending.

Then Jesus said, "After all this, I took Pistis Sophia and brought her into the thirteenth realm. I was shining with incredible brightness, a light far greater than anything they had ever seen. When I entered the region of the twenty-four invisibles, my light was so strong that it caused a great disturbance among them. They recognized Pistis Sophia, who was with me, but they did not recognize me or understand who I truly was. They assumed I was an emanation from the world of Light.

"When Pistis Sophia saw her companions—the invisibles—she was overcome with happiness and joy. She wanted to share everything I had done for her while she was trapped in the chaos. In their presence, she lifted her voice and sang praises, saying:

'I give thanks to you, O Light, for you are my Savior, my eternal deliverer. I will sing this song to the Light, for it has rescued me from the hands of the rulers who were my enemies. You have protected me in every place, saving me from the heights, from the deep chaos, and from the rulers of the æons.

When I fell from the heights, I wandered through places without light, unable to return to the thirteenth realm, my home. I was left powerless, my strength completely gone. But the Light saved me from all my troubles. When I cried out in praise, it heard me in my suffering.

It led me through the created realms and brought me back to the thirteenth realm, where I belong.

I give thanks to you, O Light, for rescuing me and for the miracles you have shown to humanity. When I was weak, you gave me strength. When I lost my light, you restored me with pure light.

I was trapped in darkness, held down by the heavy chains of chaos, with no light left in me. I had gone against the command of the Light and sinned, leaving my rightful place and bringing judgment upon myself. When I fell, my light faded, and no one came to help me.

But in my suffering, I sang praises to the Light, and it rescued me from my pain. It broke all my chains and lifted me out of the chaos and darkness.

I give thanks to you, O Light, for saving me and for your miracles among humanity. You have broken the gates of darkness and shattered the mighty walls of chaos. You allowed me to leave the place where I had fallen, and even though my light was taken because of my mistakes, you restored me.

I had abandoned my mysteries and fallen to the gates of chaos. Yet, when I was trapped, I sang praises to the Light, and it freed me from all my suffering. You sent your stream of power, rescued me, and strengthened me.

I give thanks to you, O Light, for the wonders you have done for humanity.'

"This is the song Pistis Sophia sang among the twenty-four invisibles. She wanted them to understand the great things I had done for her. She also wanted them to know that I had descended into the world of humans and shared the mysteries of the higher realms with them. Now, if anyone understands the meaning of this song, let them step forward and explain it."

Chapter 75

When Jesus finished speaking, Philip stepped forward and said: "Jesus, my Lord, my mind has been enlightened, and I now understand the meaning of the song that Pistis Sophia sang. The prophet David spoke about this long ago in the one hundred and sixth Psalm, where he said:

'Give thanks to the Lord, for he is good; his kindness lasts forever. Let those who have been saved by the Lord say so, for he has rescued them from the hands of their enemies. He gathered them from all directions—from the east, west, north, and the sea. They wandered in the wilderness, in a barren land without water, unable to find a path to the city where they were meant to live. Hungry and thirsty, their strength faded within them. They called out to the Lord in their suffering, and he saved them from their troubles. He led them on a straight path so they could reach their home. Let them give thanks to the Lord for his goodness and the wonderful things he has done for people. He satisfies the hungry and fills those in need with good things.

Those who sat in darkness, trapped in misery and chains, had turned against the word of God and resisted the Most High. Their hearts were humbled through suffering; they became weak, and no one came to help them. They called out to the Lord in their distress, and he saved them from their troubles. He led them out of the darkness and broke their chains. Let them give thanks to the Lord for his kindness and the wonders he has done for humanity. He shattered the gates of bronze and broke apart the iron bars. He led them away from the path of wrongdoing because they had been brought low by their own actions. They lost the will to live and were close to death. They cried out to the Lord in their suffering, and he saved them from their troubles. He sent his word to heal them and free them from their pain. Let them give thanks to the Lord for his kindness and the miracles he has done for humanity.'

"This, my Lord, is the explanation of the song that Pistis Sophia sang. Listen closely, so I may explain further.

The words David wrote, 'Give thanks to the Lord, for he is good; his kindness lasts forever,' are the same as what Pistis Sophia declared: 'I will give thanks to you, O Light, for you are my Savior, and you are my deliverer forever.'

The words David wrote, 'Let those saved by the Lord say so, for he has rescued them from the hands of their enemies,' are the same as what Pistis Sophia said: 'I will sing this song to the Light, for it has saved me and delivered me from the rulers who were my enemies.'

The rest of the Psalm continues to express her gratitude and faith in the Light, showing how she was delivered from her suffering.

Thus, my Lord, this is the meaning of the song that Pistis Sophia sang among the twenty-four invisibles. She wanted them to know the great and wonderful things you have done for her. She also wanted them to understand that you have given the mysteries of the Light to the human race."

When Philip finished speaking, Jesus replied: "Well said, blessed Philip. You have correctly explained the meaning of the song sung by Pistis Sophia."

[End of The Story of Pistis Sophia]

Chapter 76

After all these things had happened, Mary stepped forward with respect, knelt before Jesus, and worshiped at his feet. She then said, "My Lord, please do not be upset with me for asking a question. We are committed to seeking true understanding in everything with clarity and certainty. You have told us before, 'Seek, and you will find; knock, and the door will be opened to you. For everyone who seeks will find, and to everyone who knocks, the door will be opened.'

"Now, my Lord, who should I seek, or where should we knock? Who can give us clear answers to the questions we ask? Who is able to understand the deep meaning behind these words? Truly, it is only you. You have given us the mind of the Light, the ability to perceive, and an enlightened understanding, which allows us to ask with wisdom and insight. That is why no one in this world or even in the heights of the æons can explain the mysteries we seek—except for you. You alone know everything in the universe, and you are perfect in all things.

"My Lord, we do not ask questions the way ordinary people do. We ask from the wisdom of the divine knowledge of the higher realms, which you have so generously shared with us. We have learned from you how to question with wisdom and careful thought, and we follow this way to seek the truth. So, my Lord, I humbly ask—please do not be upset with me, but reveal to me the truth about what I am about to ask."

When Jesus heard Mary's words, he answered her, "Ask your question, Mary, whatever is in your heart, and I will give you a clear and precise answer. Truly, I tell you: Be joyful and rejoice! For when you ask with such thoughtfulness and care, my joy is made complete. You are questioning in the best way possible. So, ask whatever you wish, and I will answer with happiness."

When Mary heard these kind words from Jesus, she was filled with great joy, and her heart overflowed with happiness. She then spoke again to Jesus, saying, "My Lord and Savior, I want to understand more about the twenty-four invisibles. What are they like? What kind of beings are they? What is the nature of their light, and how can we describe it?"

Chapter 77

Jesus answered Mary, saying, "What in this world could possibly be compared to them? What place here could resemble them? Tell me, how can I describe them using anything from this world? There is nothing here that even slightly reflects their true nature. No form, no structure, and no light in this world comes close to what exists in the higher realms. But listen carefully: I tell you the truth, each of the twenty-four invisibles is nine times greater than the heavens, far beyond the sphere above them, and even surpassing the twelve æons I have told you about before.

"The brightest light you know in this world is the light of the sun. But I tell you, the light of the twenty-four invisibles shines ten thousand times brighter than the sun's light. I have explained this before. Yet even this does not fully describe them, because the sun you see here is not shining in its true form. Its real light exists beyond this world, shining through many veils and realms before it reaches here. The sun in its true form, which exists in the region of the Virgin of Light, is ten thousand times brighter than the twenty-four invisibles. Its glory surpasses even the great invisible forefather and the mighty triple-powered god, just as I have told you before.

"Mary, there is nothing in this world—no shape, no light—that can compare to the twenty-four invisibles. Their nature is beyond anything you have ever seen or known. But in time, I will lead you, your brothers, and your fellow disciples into the highest realms. You will witness the three spaces of the First Mystery, but you will not see the space of the Ineffable, for it is beyond all things. There, you will see their true forms, beyond any earthly comparison.

"If I bring you into the Heights, their splendor will leave you speechless. If I take you to the region of the rulers of Fate, you will see how bright they are, and this world you live in will seem like pure darkness in comparison. The entire world of men will feel as small as a tiny grain of dust because of how far it is from their greatness and how superior their light is.

"If I lead you into the twelve æons, their light will completely outshine the rulers of Fate. The realm of Fate will seem as dark as night, and it will look as tiny as a speck of dust compared to their glory. Their greatness is beyond measure, just as I have told you before.

"If I take you into the thirteenth æon, its brilliance will surpass even the twelve æons. You will see the twelve æons as nothing but shadows, their brightness fading like the night. Their whole region will look like a tiny speck compared to the overwhelming light of the thirteenth æon.

"If I bring you to the region of the Midst, the brightness of that place will be even greater. The thirteen æons will look dim and unimportant, almost like shadows. The entire system of the twelve æons, the Fate, the spheres, and everything within them will seem as small as a single grain of dust, so far removed are they from the greatness of this higher realm.

"If I take you to the region of those of the Right, their brightness will surpass all the light of the Midst. To you, the Midst will seem no brighter than the darkest night of the world of men. Even if you look back at it, it will appear as nothing but a tiny speck of dust, so vast is the separation, and so overwhelming is the brilliance of the region of the Right.

"And if I bring you to the Lightland, the ultimate realm of pure and radiant glory..."

Chapter 78

"If I take you into the Treasury of the Light and you see its incredible brilliance, the region of those of the Right will seem as dim as a cloudy midday in the world of men, when the sun is hidden behind thick clouds. Even if you look directly at the region of those of the Right, it will seem no larger than a tiny speck of dust because of the vast distance between it and the Treasury of the Light, and because the Treasury is far greater in its splendor.

"And if I take you into the region of those who have inherited the Light and received its mysteries, and you see the amazing brightness in which they live, then even the Lightland itself will appear to you no brighter than the sun in the world of men. And if you look back at the Lightland from that higher place, it will seem like nothing more than a tiny speck of dust. This is because of the enormous distance between them and the incredible glory of those who have received the mysteries of the Light."

When Jesus finished speaking, Mary Magdalene stepped forward. With deep respect, she said, "My Lord, please do not be upset if I ask yet another question. We ask with great care because we want to fully understand everything."

Jesus replied, "Ask whatever is on your heart, and I will answer directly and clearly, without using comparisons or hidden meanings. Whatever you wish to know, I will explain with complete certainty. I will teach you everything, from the deepest mysteries to the highest truths, from the realm of the Ineffable to the lowest depths of darkness. In this way, you and your companions will be known as 'those who are perfected in all knowledge.' Now, Mary, ask freely, and I will answer with joy."

Hearing these words, Mary was filled with happiness and excitement. She asked, "My Lord, will the people in the world who have received the mysteries of the Light be greater than the emanations of the Treasury in your kingdom? I remember that you said, 'If I take you into the region of those who have received the mysteries of the

Light, then the Lightland—the region of the emanations—will seem like a tiny speck of dust compared to them because of the vast difference in their brightness.' This makes it seem like the Lightland, which belongs to the Treasury, is not the greatest. So, my Lord, does this mean that those who have received the mysteries of the Light will be even greater than the Lightland and its emanations in the kingdom of the Light?"

Chapter 79

Jesus answered Mary, saying, "Your question is thoughtful and well-asked. Listen carefully, Mary, and I will explain about the final time of the universe and how everything will rise to a higher place. This moment is not coming soon, but I have already told you: 'If I take you to the region where those who receive the mysteries of the Light will dwell, then the Treasury of the Light—the place of the emanations—will seem as small as a speck of dust, just like the sun shining in the sky during the day.'

"I said this because it will only happen at the final moment when everything ascends. At that time, the twelve Saviors of the Treasury, along with the twelve groups of emanations connected to them—who come from the seven Voices and the five Trees—will join me in the region where the Light's inheritance is given. They will rule with me in my kingdom. Each will lead over their own emanations, and their power and glory will match their greatness. Those with greater strength and majesty will have more authority, while those with less will govern in a way that fits their abilities.

"The Savior of the emanations of the first Voice will live in the place where the souls of those who have received the first mystery of the First Mystery will dwell in my kingdom.

"In the same way, the Savior of the emanations of the second Voice will rule over the souls of those who have received the second mystery of the First Mystery.

"Likewise, the Savior of the emanations of the third Voice will be in charge of the souls who have received the third mystery of the First Mystery within the region of the Light's inheritance.

"The Savior of the emanations of the fourth Voice of the Treasury of the Light will be in the place where the souls of those who have been given the fourth mystery of the First Mystery will live.

"And the fifth Savior, who is over the emanations of the fifth Voice of the Treasury of the Light, will be in the region where the souls of those who have been initiated into the fifth mystery of the First Mystery will reside in the Light's inheritance.

"The sixth Savior, who leads the emanations of the sixth Voice of the Treasury of the Light, will be in the place where the souls of those who have received the sixth mystery of the First Mystery will live. These souls will experience the glory of the mysteries they have learned and will be under the care of the sixth Savior.

"The seventh Savior, connected to the emanations of the seventh Voice of the Treasury of the Light, will guide the souls of those who have been given the seventh mystery of the First Mystery in the great Treasury of the Light. This Savior will help them grow even further in the mysteries of the Light.

"The eighth Savior, who is over the emanations of the first Tree of the Treasury of the Light, will take his place in the region where the souls who have received the eighth mystery of the First Mystery will dwell. He will lead them and help them continue on their path to greater enlightenment.

"The ninth Savior, connected to the emanations of the second Tree of the Treasury of the Light, will rule over the region set aside for the souls who have attained the ninth mystery of the First Mystery. These souls will continue to grow under the care of the ninth Savior.

"The tenth Savior, who belongs to the emanations of the third Tree of the Treasury of the Light, will lead the region where the souls who have received the tenth mystery of the First Mystery will live. This place will shine with the Light's glory, and the Savior will guide the souls in his care, helping them rise to greater understanding.

"In the same way, the eleventh Savior, connected to the emanations of the fourth Tree of the Treasury of the Light, will dwell in the place where the souls who have received the eleventh mystery of the First Mystery will be. This Savior will be their protector and teacher, ensuring that the light and wisdom they have received continues to grow as they progress in their spiritual journey."

"And the twelfth Savior, who leads the emanations of the fifth Tree in the Treasury of the Light, will rule over the souls who have reached the twelfth mystery of the First Mystery in the Light's inheritance. This Savior will guide them, helping them grow in understanding and ensuring that the mysteries they have received lead them closer to the Light.

"The seven Amēns, the five Trees, and the three Amēns will have their place of honor on my right, ruling as kings in the inheritances of the Light. Their glory will reflect the divine justice and order of the Light, with each one playing an important role in the great design. On my left, the Twin Saviors, also called the Child of the Child, along with the nine guards, will also reign as kings in the inheritances of the Light. Their power and authority will reflect the divine will.

"Each of the Saviors will continue leading their emanations in the inheritances of the Light, keeping their rank and glory just as they did in the Treasury of the Light. Their leadership will ensure that everything remains in harmony and follows the greater mysteries,

189

allowing the Light's kingdom to remain balanced and strong forever.

"The nine guards of the Treasury of the Light will have authority over the Saviors in the inheritances of the Light. The Twin Saviors will be placed above the nine guards, and even greater than them will be the three Amēns. The five Trees will stand above them all, reigning at the highest level in the inheritances of the Light.

"Yew, who guards the veil of the Great Light, the receiver of the Light, the two great guides, and the great Sabaōth, the Good, will rule as kings along with the first Savior of the first Voice of the Treasury of the Light. This Savior will dwell in the place where the souls who have received the first mystery of the First Mystery reside. Yew, the guard of the Right, Melchisedec—the great receiver of the Light—and the two great guides have all come from the pure and refined light of the first through the fifth Trees.

"Yew, as the overseer of the Light, has emerged from the purest light of the first Tree. The guard of the veil of those of the Right has come from the light of the second Tree. The two great guides have been formed from the refined light of the third and fourth Trees. Melchisedec, the great receiver of the Light, has come from the fifth Tree. Sabaōth, the Good—whom I have also called my father—was brought forth from Yew, the overseer of the Light.

"These six, under the command of the First Mystery, were placed in the region of those of the Right by the last Helper. Their role is to collect the higher Light from the æons of the rulers, the worlds, and all beings within them. Each of them has been given a great responsibility in the unfolding of the universe. Because of this, they will serve as co-rulers with the first Savior of the first Voice of the Treasury of the Light, dwelling in the place where the souls who have received the first mystery of the First Mystery reside.

"The Virgin of Light, along with the great guide of the Midst—

who is also known as the Great Yew by the rulers of the æons in honor of a powerful ruler in their domain—and his twelve ministers, from whom you have received your form and power, will also rule alongside the first Savior of the first Voice in the region where the souls who have attained the first mystery of the First Mystery now live in the Light's inheritance.

"Additionally, the fifteen helpers of the seven virgins of the Light, who reside in the Midst, will extend their presence and influence throughout the regions of the twelve Saviors, ensuring that all remains in divine order and harmony."

"All of these events and arrangements will only happen at the end of the age, when the divine order and the Light are fully revealed and completed.

Until then, the remaining angels of the Midst, each according to their glory, will reign with me in the inheritances of the Light. But above all of them, I will reign supreme in the inheritances of the Light.

Everything I have told you will not happen right now. These events will take place when the universe begins its final ascension—when the entire cosmos dissolves, and the perfect souls rise into the inheritances of the Light.

Until that final moment, these things will remain unfulfilled. Each being will stay in the place where they were originally assigned from the very beginning. This order will remain until all the perfect souls are gathered into the Light.

The seven Voices, the five Trees, the three Amēns, the Twin Saviors, the nine guards, the twelve Saviors, those in the region of the Right, and those in the region of the Midst will all remain in their appointed places. They will not move until all the perfect souls of the Light are gathered together.

Even the rulers who have repented and turned to the Light will remain where they were placed. They will not ascend until the final number of Light souls is complete, and all have been united in the inheritances of the Light.

Each soul will come in its own time, reaching the moment when they are ready to receive the mysteries of the Light. The rulers who have repented will also follow their destined path, eventually entering the region of the Midst. Once there, the beings of the Midst will baptize them, anoint them with spiritual oil, and seal them with the sacred marks of their mysteries.

From there, the souls will pass through the different regions of the Midst, then into the region of the Right. They will continue through the sacred spaces of the nine guards, the Twin Saviors, the three Amēns, the twelve Saviors, the five Trees, and the seven Voices. At each stage, they will receive the seal of the mysteries from the beings of that realm, marking their progress as they move closer to the Light.

Eventually, they will reach the inheritances of the Light, where they will dwell according to the mysteries they have received.

In the end, every human soul that comes to receive the mysteries of the Light will surpass the rulers who have repented. They will move beyond those in the region of the Midst, beyond all those in the Right, and beyond the entire Treasury of the Light. These souls will ascend higher than all who belong to the regions of the Treasury and even those of the first Commandment.

They will continue moving through these realms, advancing deeper and deeper until they reach the final Inheritance of the Light. There, each one will settle in the place that matches the mysteries they have received.

Meanwhile, those who belong to the Midst, the Right, and the Treasury of the Light will remain in their original places, exactly as they were from the beginning. They will not move until the entire universe has completed its ascension. Each one will continue fulfilling their role, carrying out the tasks they were given, especially in gathering and guiding the souls who are meant to ascend."

Chapter 80

Mary listens carefully and reflects deeply on the teachings, connecting them to the spiritual truths found in the scriptures. She explains how those who have received the mysteries play an important role in preparing and sealing the souls who will pass into the Inheritance of the Light. This is part of the divine plan, ensuring that every soul is fully ready before entering the eternal Light.

Jesus acknowledges her question and confirms her understanding. He says, "Mary, you have asked with clarity and wisdom. Let those who are able to understand listen carefully and grasp the truth of these words."

After Jesus finishes speaking, Mary Magdalene steps forward, filled with wisdom, and says, "My Lord, the light within me understands everything you have revealed. When you said that all souls who receive the mysteries of the Light will enter the Inheritance of the Light before the rulers who have repented and those of the higher realms, I recognize this as the fulfillment of your earlier words: 'The first shall be last, and the last shall be first.'"

She continues, explaining that humanity, which is considered "last," will enter the kingdom of the Light before those seen as the "first," meaning those from the higher realms. Her explanation shows a deep understanding of Jesus' teachings. She concludes, "My Lord, this is the meaning of your words, and it confirms your desire for us to fully understand the wisdom you share."

Jesus is moved by her insight and praises her, saying, "Well spoken, pure and spiritual Mary. You are completely of the spirit, and your understanding is deep and true."

Then, Jesus continues teaching the disciples, promising to reveal the glory of those in the higher realms. He speaks of the unimaginable greatness of the last Helper who surrounds the Treasury of the Light. "If you could see the glory of this last Helper," he explains, "you would see the Inheritance of the Light as no bigger than a small city on earth compared to his vast brilliance and power."

He goes on to say that the Helper above this last one is even greater, beyond anything that can be understood in this world. But he also points out that it is impossible to fully describe the regions of those who exist above all Helpers, because there is nothing in this world— no shape, no light, no comparison—that can reflect their greatness. Even among the highest realms of Righteousness, there is nothing that comes close to their endless glory. "This is why," he says, "human words and understanding cannot fully express the incredible majesty of those in the highest realms."

Chapter 81

Mary continues asking Jesus questions with deep respect and kindness, hoping to understand more for the sake of everyone. She says, "My Lord, please don't get tired of my questions. I'm not asking because I doubt, but because I want to be certain, just as you've taught us. My brothers and I want to share your teachings with the world so people can listen, turn away from their mistakes, and be saved from the control of the rulers of darkness. We're not seeking this knowledge just for ourselves, but for all people, so they can escape from those who rule with cruelty and find their way into the kingdom of Light."

Jesus, touched by her sincerity, responds kindly, "Mary, ask whatever you wish, and I will answer with complete clarity, holding nothing back."

Hearing this, Mary is overjoyed and asks, "My Lord, how much greater is the second Helper compared to the first? How do they differ in distance, light, and power?"

Jesus replies, "Mary, the second Helper is beyond the first in every possible way—height, depth, length, and width. The difference is so vast that even angels, archangels, and other divine beings cannot fully grasp it. In the same way, his greatness and brightness are beyond measure. His light shines far stronger than the first Helper's, and his glory is beyond comparison, just as I have told you before."

He continues, "This pattern continues with the third, fourth, and fifth Helpers. Each one is greater and shines even brighter than the one before. The distance and difference between them cannot be measured, not even by angels or higher beings. I will explain their unique qualities and roles as they unfold."

After Jesus finishes speaking, Mary Magdalene steps forward again and asks, "My Lord, what will happen to those who receive the mysteries of the Light within the realm of the last Helper?"

Jesus replies, "Those who receive the mysteries of the Light, once they are free from their physical bodies—which are ruled by earthly powers—will live in the level that matches the mystery they have received. Those who have received greater mysteries will be in higher places, while those with lesser mysteries will be in lower ones. Each person will be in the realm that fits the mystery they hold within the Inheritance of the Light. This is why I have told you before, 'Where your heart is, there your treasure will be also.' In other words, wherever your mysteries belong, that is where you will remain."

As Jesus finishes speaking, John steps forward with deep respect and says, "My Lord and Savior, may I ask something as well? You have promised to reveal everything to us, so I ask with your permission. Please do not hold back anything from what we seek to understand."

Jesus, full of kindness, responds, "Beloved John, you may ask freely. I will explain everything clearly, without parables, and I will answer your questions completely."

John then asks, "My Lord, will each soul be limited to the level that matches their received mysteries, or will they be able to rise to higher places or move to lower ones?"

Chapter 82

Jesus answered John with patience and kindness, saying, "Your questions are thoughtful and precise, which is good. Now, listen carefully so I can explain this fully. Everyone who receives the mysteries of the Light will stay in the place that matches the mysteries they have received. They do not have the power to move up to higher levels beyond their own.

"Those who receive the mysteries of the first Commandment can go down to the levels beneath them. This means they can move through all the spaces in the third realm, but they cannot go higher than their own level or beyond the mysteries they have received.

"For those who receive the mysteries of the First Mystery, which is the forty-eighth mystery from the farthest outer regions and the leader of the first realm beyond, they will be able to enter all the lower levels beneath them. However, they will not have the ability to go higher or move beyond the limits of their own mystery.

"The same is true for those who receive the mysteries within the twenty-four orders. Each person will stay in the place that matches their mystery. They can move freely through the lower levels but will not be able to rise higher. This is simply the way the mysteries work."

Jesus paused, allowing his words to sink in. He emphasized that every soul's position in the Light is connected to the mysteries they have accepted and understood.

Then, Jesus continued, explaining the deeper levels of the mysteries: "A person who has received the mysteries of the First Mystery within the third realm has the power to enter all lower orders beneath them and move freely through them. But they cannot rise to higher levels or go beyond the limits of their own order.

"Someone who has received the mysteries of the first Thrice spiritual—which rules over the twenty-four mysteries within the First Mystery—can go down into all the orders beneath them and move freely within those spaces. However, they do not have the power to go higher into the realm of the Ineffable.

"In the same way, a person who has received the mysteries of the second Thrice spiritual has control over all the levels ruled by the first Thrice spiritual. However, they cannot rise into the third Thrice spiritual, which exists above them.

"A person who has received the mysteries of the third Thrice spiritual—who rules over all three Thrice spirituals and their connected spaces—has power over all the orders beneath them. But even they cannot rise beyond their level or enter the higher spaces of the Ineffable.

"But the one who receives the ultimate mystery of the First Mystery of the Ineffable, which includes the twelve highest mysteries of the First Mystery, is different. This person has the ability to move through all the orders and spaces ruled by the three Thrice spirituals. They can travel freely from the farthest outer regions to the deepest inner realms, from the lowest spaces to the highest, and across all dimensions. In other words, this person can enter any place within the Inheritance of the Light and choose where they wish to dwell in the kingdom of Light.

"And I tell you the truth: At the end of time, this person will become a ruler over all the orders within the Inheritance of the Light. The one who receives the greatest mystery of the Ineffable—the same mystery that I hold—will have deep understanding and wisdom.

"This ultimate mystery holds the knowledge of where both light and darkness come from and why they exist.

"It understands how chaos began and why the treasury of the Light was created.

"It knows the purpose of judgment, the formation of the Light's kingdom, and the regions of its inheritance.

"It understands the reasons for punishment and the peace and rest found in the kingdom of Light.

"It knows why sinners came into existence and why the Light's inheritance was established.

"And this mystery holds the knowledge of why evil appears in the world and why the good have been brought forth.

"It also understands the purpose of punishment and judgment, knowing why they exist and how all beings of light came into existence.

"Finally, this mystery reveals the origin of sin and why the baptisms and mysteries of the Light were created to overcome it."

"This mystery understands where the fire of punishment comes from and why the seals of the Light were created to protect people, keeping them safe from harm.

"It knows the source of anger and why peace exists to balance it.

"It sees where lies and false accusations come from, but also how songs of Light rise to bring harmony.

"It understands why prayers of the Light were given, guiding people to connect with higher realms.

"It recognizes why curses exist and why blessings were created to cancel them out.

"It knows the roots of deception and dishonesty, as well as the power of truth and goodness to overcome them.

"It understands why violence and killing happen, but also why souls can be revived and life can be restored.

"It sees why acts of impurity exist and why purity was given to bring back holiness.

"It knows the reason for human desires and why self-control and discipline were introduced to keep them in check.

"It understands why arrogance and pride arise, but also why humility and gentleness were established to take their place.

"It knows the origins of sorrow and tears, but also why joy and laughter were given to balance them.

"It recognizes why people spread false stories, but also why truth and clarity emerge to bring understanding.

"It sees why some show gratitude while others hold resentment.

"It understands why people complain and feel unsatisfied, but also why innocence and humility exist as a response.

"It knows why sin exists and why purity was given to cleanse and restore divine order.

"It understands why strength and power appear, but also the reason for weakness and fragility.

"It knows the purpose of the human body and how it was designed to function.

"It sees the reason for both poverty and wealth, understanding their connection in the grand design.

"It understands why freedom exists in the world, but also why slavery and oppression arose alongside it.

"It recognizes why death came into being and why life was given as its counterpart, showing the eternal cycle of change."

When Jesus finished speaking, his disciples were overjoyed. They marveled at the wisdom and truth in his words.

Then Jesus continued, saying, "Listen carefully, my disciples, as I reveal the full knowledge of the mystery of the Ineffable.

"This great mystery understands why cruelty exists and why mercy was given as its healing force.

"It sees why destruction happens, but also why eternity was created as the ultimate reality.

"It knows why reptiles were made and why they will one day cease to exist.

"It understands the purpose of wild animals and why their time in the world is limited.

"It sees why cattle were created and why birds were placed in the sky.

"It recognizes why mountains rise above the earth and why precious stones are hidden within them, reflecting divine craftsmanship.

"It understands why gold exists and its role in the world's creation.

"It sees why silver was made and how it maintains balance with other materials.

"It knows why copper was formed and the purpose it serves.

"It understands the origins of iron and stone and how they shape the world around us.

"It sees why lead was created, its properties, and its role in the material world.

"It recognizes why glass and wax came into being, each serving a unique purpose in the grand design.

"It understands why plants and herbs grow, how they are connected, and how they sustain life on earth.

"It knows the origins of all materials, seeing their divine source and the roles they play in creation.

"It sees why the waters of the earth exist, their importance, and how they support life. It understands the creatures that live within them, from the smallest to the largest.

"It recognizes why the earth itself was formed, providing a foundation for life, and its significance in the universe.

"It understands the vast and mysterious nature of the seas, the role of water in creation, and the purpose of the creatures that live within the oceans.

"It sees why the material world exists, how everything is connected, and why one day, it will all come to an end as part of a greater plan."

Chapter 83

Jesus spoke again, his voice serious and full of meaning. He said, "My dear disciples, my friends and brothers, stay watchful and connected to the spirit within you. Listen carefully and stay focused on every word I am about to share. I will now reveal deep and complex knowledge about the Ineffable. It is important that you understand and absorb these truths because they contain the full wisdom that comes from the eternal source.

"This mystery understands how and why the west came into being, recognizing the forces that shaped it and the role it plays in the grand design.

"It also knows the reason the east was created, understanding its importance and how it balances with the other directions.

"This mystery reveals why the south exists, showing how different forces worked together to form it and how it connects with the rest of creation.

"And it understands the purpose of the north, seeing how it fits into the universe and maintains harmony in the world.

"Now, my disciples, continue listening with open hearts and clear minds as I reveal everything about the mystery of the Ineffable. Keep your spirits calm and ready to receive the great truths that I will share.

"This mystery knows why demons came into existence, understanding where they came from and the part they play in the larger plan of creation.

"It also reveals why humanity was created, explaining the divine purpose behind people's existence and the journey they must take.

"This mystery understands how heat was formed, recognizing its importance and its ability to change and shape the physical world.

"And it knows why the gentle, refreshing air exists, bringing comfort and balance to all living things.

"This mystery reveals how the stars were created, showing their role as guiding lights and their connection to the heavens.

"It also understands why clouds form, knowing how they sustain life and keep nature's cycles in motion.

"This mystery explains why the deep parts of the earth exist, revealing the purpose of its vast spaces and the waters that cover it, shaping and supporting life.

"And it knows why dry land rose from the earth, understanding the forces that lifted it and the balance it brings to all living things.

"This mystery also reveals why famine occurs, showing the lessons it teaches and the way it restores balance. At the same time, it understands why abundance exists, providing nourishment and ensuring that life continues to thrive."

Jesus continued to reveal deep truths, saying:

"This mystery understands why frost forms, recognizing how it affects the earth and its connection to the changing seasons.

"It also knows why morning dew appears, seeing its purpose in refreshing the land and providing nourishment to all living things.

"This mystery reveals why dust exists in the world and the role it plays, as well as why the cool, gentle breeze brings balance and peace to nature.

"It understands why hail forms, knowing its place in the natural cycle, and why soft, pure snow falls, covering the earth in beauty and stillness.

"This mystery perceives why the west wind blows, cooling the land, and why the east wind arises, carrying its own unique effects on both land and sea.

"It also knows why fire from above was created, understanding its power to transform, and why the waters of the earth appeared, essential for life and creation.

"This mystery understands why the warm south wind was formed and why the cold north wind arose, each playing an important role in maintaining balance in nature.

"It knows why the stars were placed in the sky, shining as lights in the vast universe, and why the great orbs of light—the sun and the moon—were created to bring cycles of day and night.

"This mystery perceives why the sky was formed, with all its layers and veils, surrounding and protecting the heavens.

"It also understands why the rulers of the celestial spheres were created, guiding the movement of the heavens, and why the spheres themselves, with all their regions, were formed to shape the cosmos.

"This mystery knows why the rulers of the ages came into being, organizing the divine order, and why the ages themselves, with all their hidden layers, were established.

"It sees why some rulers of the ages became tyrants, enforcing their own will, and why others turned to repentance, offering hope for change.

"This mystery understands why servants of the cosmos were created to help maintain order and why the celestial guardians, each with a unique role, were formed.

"It knows why angels were sent as messengers of the divine and why archangels, with even greater responsibilities, were brought forth.

"This mystery perceives why lords and divine beings exist, each representing different aspects of the higher order.

"It understands why jealousy first appeared in the heights, bringing conflict, and why peace was later restored to bring balance.

"This mystery knows why hatred emerged, creating division, and why love was given to heal and unite.

"It sees why chaos arose, leading to disorder, and why harmony followed to restore what was broken.

"This mystery perceives why greed came into existence, driving people to crave more, and why detachment arose, teaching the freedom of letting go.

"It understands why the desire for excess and indulgence appeared, and why satisfaction arose, bringing a sense of fulfillment.

"This mystery knows why some beings were created in pairs, symbolizing unity, while others exist alone, representing individuality.

"It perceives why some rejected the divine, and why reverence for God was given, leading people back to awe and respect.

"This mystery understands why great sources of light were created to illuminate the heavens, and why smaller sparks of light were formed, each playing a role in the vast design.

"It knows why the threefold powerful ones appeared, representing strength and authority, and why the unseen forces arose, working invisibly yet influencing all things.

"This mystery perceives why the first great beings, the forefathers, were created to form the foundation, and why purity emerged, symbolizing refinement and truth.

"It understands why a great self-willed being arose, seeking control, and why his followers were brought forth to carry out his desires.

"This mystery knows why an immensely powerful force came into existence, showing great strength, and why a hidden, ancient ruler emerged, remaining unseen yet influential.

"Finally, this mystery perceives why the thirteenth realm was created as a place of deep meaning and why the region of those in the Midst was formed, standing between worlds and holding secrets yet to be fully revealed."

Chapter 84

Jesus continued speaking to his disciples, saying:

"This mystery understands why the receivers of the Midst were created and why the virgins of the Light came into existence, each serving their divine purpose.

"It also knows why the ministers and angels of the Midst appeared, understanding their role in the divine order.

"This mystery reveals why the Lightland was formed—a place of endless brightness—and why the great receiver of the Light exists to gather and protect the forces of illumination.

"It understands why the guardians of the region of the Right were created and why their leaders were chosen to oversee and protect these sacred places.

"This mystery knows why the gate of life was established, marking the entrance to eternal truth, and why Sabaoth the Good was brought forth as a guardian of goodness and righteousness.

"It perceives why the region of the Right was formed as a place of divine justice and why the Lightland, known as the Treasury of the Light, exists as a storehouse of infinite radiance.

"This mystery understands the origin of the emanations of the Light and the purpose of the twelve Saviors, who guide and bring enlightenment to the universe.

"It also reveals why the three gates of the Treasury of the Light were established as pathways to divine mysteries, and why nine guardians were assigned to protect them.

"This mystery knows the origin of the Twin Saviors and the role of the three Amēns, whose combined presence sustains divine order.

"It perceives why the five Trees of divine wisdom came into being and why the seven Amēns were formed, each playing a part in maintaining the harmony of the Light.

"And it understands why the Mixture, which is not pure on its own, was created and why its purification is essential to restoring balance in the universe."

Jesus then turned to his disciples and said, "Now, my disciples, stay focused and aware. Each of you must find the strength to recognize the Light within and around you so that you may understand what I am about to reveal. From this moment on, I will explain to you the full reality of the region of the Ineffable and its true nature."

Hearing this, the disciples became overwhelmed and struggled to hold onto his words, their understanding slipping away. At that moment, Mary Magdalene stepped forward. She knelt before Jesus, kissed his feet, and wept, her voice filled with emotion.

"Have mercy on me, my Lord," she pleaded. "My brothers have heard your words, but they have struggled to grasp their meaning. They tried to hold onto what you said, but it has slipped from their minds. You spoke to us about the knowledge of all things being part of the mystery of the Ineffable. You also said, 'From now on, I will begin to reveal to you the complete knowledge of this mystery.' Yet, you have not fully explained its depth. Because of this, my brothers have lost their understanding and cannot fully grasp your teachings.

"Now, my Lord, regarding this knowledge of all things that you have spoken of—if it truly exists within the mystery of the Ineffable— who among mankind is capable of understanding it completely? Who among the living can comprehend the deep wisdom and truths of all that you have revealed?"

Chapter 85

When Jesus heard Mary's sincere words and saw that his disciples were struggling to understand his teachings, he spoke to reassure them, easing their worries. He said,

"Do not be troubled, my disciples, thinking that the mystery of the Ineffable is too difficult to understand. I tell you the truth: this mystery is meant for you, as well as for anyone who listens to your teachings— so long as they completely let go of this world, along with all its material things, negative thoughts, and concerns of this life.

"That is why I tell you with certainty: for those who choose to leave behind the world and everything in it, dedicating themselves fully to the divine, this mystery is easier to understand than any other mystery of the Light. It is the most accessible and the simplest to grasp. Those who reach this understanding do so by letting go of the distractions and worries of the material world.

"This is why I told you before, 'All of you who are burdened and tired, come to me, and I will give you rest. For my burden is light, and my path is easy.' Whoever chooses to receive this mystery must release all attachment to this world and its distractions. So, my disciples, do not fear or doubt your ability to understand. I promise you, this mystery is simpler than all others. It belongs to you and to anyone who is willing to leave behind the concerns of the world.

"Now, listen closely, my disciples, my companions, and my brothers, so I can guide you even further into the knowledge of the mystery of the Ineffable. This is the same mystery I have been revealing to you little by little, helping you understand how the universe itself has expanded. For the way the universe unfolds also reveals its divine knowledge.

"Now, pay attention as I continue teaching you, step by step, the deeper knowledge of this mystery. This mystery understands why the five Helpers separated and how they came forth from the Ones without a Source.

"It also reveals why the powers of the universe split apart and emerged from their origins.

"The great Light of lights understands why it divided itself and why it came forth from the One without a Source. This mystery holds the truth about why it broke apart and the divine purpose behind its emergence.

"This mystery also explains why the first Commandment divided into different parts, why it separated into seven mysteries, and why it is called the first Commandment. It knows why this division happened and what it means that it came forth from the One without a Source.

"The mystery understands why the Great Light of the Impressions of the Light divided, why it remained without sending forth emanations, and why it originally came from the One without a Source. It reveals the reason behind these actions and the divine order they follow.

"It also knows why the First Mystery, which is the twenty-fourth mystery from the outermost regions, divided itself and imitated the twelve mysteries, following the pattern of the Uncontainables and the Boundless. It understands why this separation took place and why it came forth from the One without a Source.

"This mystery reveals why the twelve Immoveables separated and how they formed their ranks in an orderly way. It knows the purpose of their coming forth and how they fit into the divine structure.

"The mystery holds the reason why the Unwaverables divided and why they created twelve distinct orders. It also explains why they emerged from the One without a Source and what role they play in the design of the Ineffable."

This mystery understands why the Incomprehensibles, who exist in the second space of the Ineffable, separated and why they came forth from the One without a Source.

It also explains why the twelve Undesignatables divided and arranged themselves according to the orders of the Unindicatables, even though they are limitless and beyond containment. This mystery reveals why they emerged from the One without a Source and their role in the grand design.

This mystery knows why the Unindicatables split apart, even though they remained hidden and did not reveal themselves, following the divine plan of the Ineffable. It understands their origin and how they fit into the universe.

It reveals why the Superdeeps separated and formed a single order when they emerged from the One without a Source, as well as their purpose and position in the divine hierarchy.

This mystery explains why the twelve orders of the Unspeakables divided into three sections and why they came forth from the One without a Source, revealing the reason for their existence.

It also understands why all the Imperishables, in their twelve orders, expanded into a single form before separating into different orders, despite being limitless. It explains why they emerged from the One without a Source and their purpose in creation.

This mystery holds the reason why the Impassables divided into twelve boundless spaces, organizing themselves into three groups according to the divine order of the Ineffable. It explains their origin and their place in the higher realms.

Finally, this mystery explains why the twelve Uncontainables, linked to the orders of the Ineffable, divided and came forth from the One without a Source. It understands how they moved through the cosmic structure until they reached the space of the First Mystery, which is considered the second space in the divine design.

This profound mystery also reveals why the twenty-four Praise

Singers separated and extended beyond the veil of the First Mystery. This First Mystery is a twin mystery, seeing both within and beyond, originating from the One and Only, the Ineffable. The mystery reveals why they emerged from the One without a Source and their purpose in the divine plan.

It also explains why all the Uncontainables I have mentioned divided in the second space of the Ineffable, which is linked to the domain of the First Mystery. It knows why these Uncontainables and Boundless beings came forth from the One without a Source and their role in the celestial structure.

Furthermore, this mystery reveals why the twenty-four mysteries of the first Thrice spiritual divided, explaining why they are known as the twenty-four spaces of the first Thrice spiritual. It understands why they came from the second Thrice spiritual and their place in the universe.

Similarly, it explains why the twenty-four mysteries of the second Thrice spiritual separated and appeared, revealing that they originated from the third Thrice spiritual and how they fit into the divine structure.

This mystery also reveals why the twenty-four mysteries of the third Thrice spiritual—the twenty-four spaces of the third Thrice spiritual—divided. It understands why this separation was necessary and how they emerged from the One without a Source, aligning with the greater cosmic order.

It also explains why the five Trees of the first Thrice spiritual separated and extended, standing in alignment with one another, each connected in an intricate way. It knows why they came forth from the One without a Source and their purpose in the divine plan.

This mystery reveals why the five Trees of the second Thrice spiritual divided, explaining their purpose and origin, as well as how they contribute to the cosmic order.

The mystery also understands why the five Trees of the third Thrice spiritual separated and why they emerged from the One without a Source, playing their part in the grand design of the universe.

It knows why the Foreuncontainables of the first Thrice spiritual divided and expanded into existence, understanding their divine origin and the role they serve in the higher realms.

This mystery also explains why the Foreuncontainables of the second Thrice spiritual separated and came into being, revealing their purpose and why they emerged from the One without a Source.

It further holds the reason why the Foreuncontainables of the third Thrice spiritual divided and expanded, knowing their origin and why their separation was necessary in the universe.

This mystery reveals why the first Thrice spiritual from below—those connected to the orders of the One and Only, the Ineffable—separated and came forth from the second Thrice spiritual, explaining their place in the divine structure.

It also understands why the third Thrice spiritual, known as the first Thrice spiritual from above, divided. It reveals why it came forth from the twelfth Prothricespiritual, located in the last region of the One without a Source, and its significance in the higher realms.

This mystery knows why all the regions within the space of the Ineffable, along with everything within them, expanded. It understands their origin from the last part of the Ineffable and their role in shaping the universe.

Finally, this mystery understands its own purpose and nature. It knows why it divided and emerged from the Ineffable, the Supreme Source that governs all things. It reveals how all these divine expansions are connected and how they align with the ultimate plan of creation.

Chapter 86

Jesus continued speaking to his disciples, offering them reassurance and a powerful promise:

"I will explain everything in detail about the mysteries of the Ineffable. I will reveal where they came from, how they expanded, and the way they are arranged. When the universe unfolds, I will uncover all of these truths for you—the ones who rise and the ones who descend, those who move outward and those who return inward, those who stand outside and lead, and those who are placed within. I will speak of those surrounding the First Mystery, as well as those who exist in the vast space of the Ineffable.

"I will not only share their mysteries but also explain how they are structured, including the Prothricespirituals and Superthricespirituals that oversee their order. Everything will be made clear according to its proper place and role. When the universe expands, I will reveal how all things are connected, where they came from, and what they were meant to be.

"The mystery of the Ineffable includes everything I have told you and everything I will tell you. It is the force that creates all things, the energy that moves them forward, and the power that lifts them up. This one mystery is the foundation, the source, and the final purpose of all existence.

"It is a single, indescribable truth of the Ineffable, containing the knowledge of everything that has existed and everything that will come to be—whether I have spoken of it yet or not. In time, I will reveal how all things are connected, showing how one great essence unites every mystery. This is the complete word of the Ineffable, holding every form, pattern, and process of fulfillment. Through it, all creation is maintained and understood.

"I will reveal to you the structure of every mystery—their shapes, their fulfillment, and the ultimate knowledge of the One and Only. This word of the Ineffable is the answer to all that I have explained and all that I will share. It is not only the source of creation but also the key to understanding how everything is connected.

"When you truly understand this one truth of the Ineffable, you will realize how simple and powerful it is. This knowledge, which I am now giving to you, will allow you to see the full design behind creation and the mystery of its beginning, flowing from the last extension of the Ineffable itself.

"For those who receive this one and only mystery and fully live by it, they will reach a higher state of being. When they leave behind the physical body that binds the soul under the rulers' control, they will shine like a brilliant stream of light. When the retributive receivers—who are responsible for releasing souls from the body—see this soul, they will be struck with fear. Its brightness will be so overwhelming that they will tremble and lose all power before the light they witness.

"This light is the direct expression of the one and only mystery, a true sign of the Ineffable's limitless power and wisdom.

"And the soul that carries the mystery of the Ineffable will become a pure stream of light, rising to the highest realms. The retributive receivers will be unable to stop it or even understand its path. This soul, now transformed, will ascend effortlessly beyond all powers, free from any force that could hold it back. It will move beyond reach, untouched and unstoppable.

"It will pass through every domain of the rulers and every region of the emanations of the Light. But unlike other souls, it will not be questioned, challenged, or required to give any sign or explanation. No ruler or power within the emanations of the Light will be able to approach it or delay its journey. Instead, as it moves through each

214

realm, every force—whether among the rulers or the emanations of the Light—will praise and honor it. They will be in awe, overwhelmed by the radiance of the light surrounding the soul. This soul will continue forward without interruption, passing through all regions until it reaches the inheritance of the mystery it has embraced—the ultimate mystery of the One and Only, the Ineffable. There, it will fully unite with the Light, becoming one with it.

"Truly, I tell you this: The speed at which this soul will pass through all these realms will be as swift as an arrow shot by a skilled archer, moving straight toward its goal without hesitation or resistance."

Jesus continued, giving his disciples a powerful promise:

"I tell you this: Anyone who receives the mystery of the Ineffable and follows it completely will rise above every level of existence. Even though he may live as an ordinary person in this world, his spirit will surpass all beings.

"He may walk among people, but his soul will rise far beyond all angels, continuing to ascend even higher.

"He may appear as an ordinary man, but his greatness will outshine all archangels, and his elevation will never stop.

"He may seem like any other person, yet he will stand above all rulers, surpassing even their strength and rising to heights they cannot imagine.

"Though he lives in the world, his majesty will be greater than all lords, shining beyond them in limitless glory.

"He may walk the earth, but his power will surpass all divine beings, reaching places they cannot enter.

"He may look like a man, but he will rise above all light-bringers, shining brighter than them and reaching realms beyond their reach.

"This is the high position of one who fully embraces the mystery of the Ineffable. He will continue to ascend, far above all creation, glowing with untouchable brilliance, until he is completely united with the Light of the One and Only."

"Though he appears as a man, his spirit is greater than all those considered pure, and he will rise even higher.

"He walks the earth, yet he will surpass all powerful beings, exceeding their combined strength and rule.

"He may seem ordinary, but his essence will lift him above all who came before him, rising far beyond their influence.

"Though he looks human, he will stand higher than all invisible forces, surpassing their ranks and reaching places they cannot go.

"He may live in this world, yet he will rise above even the great invisible forefather, standing beyond his presence.

"He will surpass all those in the Midst, moving beyond their realms.

"Though he exists in this world, he will rise above all emanations of the Treasury of the Light, surpassing even their combined radiance.

"He may seem bound to the world, but he will completely leave the Mixture behind.

"He will surpass the entire region of the Treasury, rising beyond all of its vast spaces.

"He may walk the earth, but he will rule with me in my kingdom, sharing in its glory.

"He may live among people, but he will be a king of the Light, with authority that comes from realms far beyond this world.

"He may exist in this world, but he is not of it—his soul is connected to something much greater.

"And truly, I tell you: That man is me, and I am that man.

"When this world comes to an end, when the universe rises and the perfect souls are counted—when I reign as king over the final Helper, ruling over all the Light's emanations, the seven Amēns, the five Trees, the three Amēns, and the nine guards—when I rule as king over the Child of the Child, who is the Twin Savior, and over the twelve Savior beings and all the perfect souls who have accepted the mysteries of the Light—then all those who have received the mysteries of the Ineffable will reign with me. They will sit at my right and my left in the kingdom, sharing in its power and majesty.

"And truly, I tell you: They are me, and I am them.

"That is why I told you before: 'You will sit on thrones at my right and left in my kingdom and rule with me.' This is why I have never hesitated or been ashamed to call you my brothers and companions, for you will share my reign as kings in the kingdom. I say this knowing that I will give you the mystery of the Ineffable—a mystery that is not separate from me, for I am that mystery, and that mystery is me.

"So not only will you rule with me, but all who receive the mystery of the Ineffable will also reign alongside me. We are one, though my throne will stand above all others. Because you will face the greatest suffering in this world, enduring more than anyone as you spread the words I give you, your thrones will be joined with mine in the kingdom.

"That is why I told you before: 'Where I am, there also will be my twelve ministers.' Among these, Mary Magdalene and John, the virgin, will rise above all other disciples and all who receive the mysteries of the Ineffable. They will sit at my right and left, for I am them, and they are me.

"They will be like you in all things, except that your thrones will be higher than theirs, and my throne will rise above yours.

"And every soul who discovers the word of the Ineffable—truly, I tell you—they will receive the highest understanding. Those who come to know that word will gain the perfect knowledge of the Ineffable itself."

Chapter 87

Jesus continued, explaining the difference between the knowledge of the universe and the mysteries of the Light:

"Anyone who understands everything I have told you—about the depth and the height, the length and the breadth—will fully grasp what I have revealed, including what I have not yet spoken. They will comprehend these truths one step at a time, as the universe expands and its mysteries are unveiled.

"I tell you truly, those who come to this understanding will see how the world itself was formed. They will know the nature of those in higher realms and discover the source from which the universe was created."

Hearing this, Mary Magdalene stepped forward and said, "My Lord, please forgive me for asking with such urgency and precision. I hope you are not displeased by my need to understand. Tell me, is the mystery of the Ineffable the same as the full knowledge of the universe, or are they different?"

Jesus answered, "They are different, Mary. The mystery of the Ineffable is one thing, and the knowledge of the universe is another."

Mary spoke again, "My Lord, I ask for your patience as I seek clarity. If someone lives but does not know the full knowledge of the Ineffable, does that mean they cannot enter the Kingdom of Light?"

Jesus replied with kindness, "No, Mary, that is not the case. Anyone who receives even one mystery of the Light will inherit a place in the

Light Kingdom that matches the mystery they received. However, they will not have full knowledge of the universe—understanding why all things exist—unless they first come to know the one and only word of the Ineffable. That word contains the knowledge of the entire universe.

"Listen carefully: I am the knowledge of the universe. But no one can fully understand this knowledge unless they first receive the mystery of the Ineffable. Still, even those who receive only part of the mysteries of the Light will have a place in the Light Kingdom that reflects the depth of the mystery they have accepted.

"That is why I told you before, 'Whoever believes in a prophet will receive a prophet's reward, and whoever believes in a righteous man will receive a righteous man's reward.' This means that each person will be placed in a region that corresponds to the mystery they received. Those who accept a lesser mystery will inherit a lesser region, while those who receive a greater mystery will inherit higher places. Everyone will have a place in my Kingdom, shining with an immeasurable light that even the gods and invisible beings cannot comprehend. They will be filled with immense joy and endless celebration.

"Now, listen closely, for I will tell you about the greatness of those who receive the mysteries of the First Mystery.

"Whoever receives the first mystery of the First Mystery, when the time comes for them to leave their physical body—the body ruled by the forces of this world—the divine receivers will come to guide their soul out of the body. That soul will transform into a brilliant stream of light in their hands. The receivers, overwhelmed by the brightness of the soul, will be struck with awe and fear. They will handle it with great reverence.

"The soul, now glowing like a radiant light, will ascend higher and higher, moving through every realm of the rulers and the Light. Unlike other souls, it will not be questioned, tested, or required to show proof to pass through these places. Instead, it will move freely and effortlessly, surpassing all barriers. It will rise above everything it encounters and reach its rightful place in the Kingdom, where it will be established in the glory of the First Savior, ruling above all the regions it has passed.

"In the same way, those who receive the second, third, fourth, or any of the twelve mysteries of the First Mystery—when their time comes to leave their physical body—the divine receivers will descend to guide their soul. These souls will also transform into magnificent streams of light. Their brightness will be so intense that the receivers will fall to their knees in fear and awe, unable to stand before such radiance.

"These souls will rise immediately, soaring through all the realms of the rulers and the Light. Nothing will be able to stop them. They will not have to answer to anyone or provide any sign, for their light will break through every barrier. They will pass through all realms with complete authority, ruling over every space they enter, including the realms of the twelve Saviors. Those who have received the second mystery of the First Mystery will rule over the entire domain of the second Savior in the Kingdom of Light."

In the same way, those who receive the third, fourth, fifth, and up to the twelfth mystery of the First Mystery will have authority over the regions connected to the Savior whose mystery they have accepted.

Now, anyone who fully receives the twelfth mystery of the First Mystery—the highest mystery I have spoken about—will have all twelve mysteries of the First Mystery. When this soul leaves the world, it will rise, passing through all the regions of the rulers and the Light, shining as a brilliant stream. It will rule over all twelve Saviors' regions. However, even this soul, as exalted as it is, will not compare to those who receive the one and only mystery of the Ineffable. That mystery is of a far greater order, beyond all comparison. Still, those who receive the twelve mysteries of the First Mystery will dwell in high places, among the domains of the twelve Saviors.

When Jesus finished speaking, Mary Magdalene stepped forward again. She knelt with deep respect, kissed his feet, and asked, "My Lord, forgive me for asking again. Please be patient with us and answer what we long to understand. How is it that the First Mystery contains twelve mysteries, while the Ineffable has only one?"

Jesus replied, "The Ineffable does indeed have one mystery, but this single mystery is made up of three distinct mysteries, even though they remain one. It also contains five mysteries, which all come from the same source. Each of these five mysteries has its own nature. These five are connected to the kingdom and the inheritances of the Light, but they are not the same. Their kingdom is far greater and more powerful than that of the twelve mysteries of the First Mystery, though they differ in nature from the highest mystery of the First Mystery in the Light Kingdom.

"Similarly, the three mysteries within the Light Kingdom are separate from one another, each unique in its essence. They are also different in structure and glory from the one supreme mystery of the First Mystery. Their nature, form, and purpose are distinct from each other in significant ways.

"The first mystery of the First Mystery—if followed completely and precisely, with every requirement fulfilled—will allow the soul to leave the physical body and transform into a magnificent stream of light. It will pass through all the realms of the rulers and all the regions of the Light. The brilliance of this soul will be so overwhelming that every being—both rulers and those in the Light—will stand in awe and fear as it ascends to its rightful kingdom.

"The second mystery of the First Mystery, if practiced carefully and in full detail, holds incredible power. If someone who has fully mastered this mystery speaks it over a person who is about to leave their body and whispers it into their ears, something extraordinary happens. If that person has already received mysteries and has followed the truth, then I tell you this: Their soul will immediately become a brilliant stream of light when they pass from their body. It will rise effortlessly through all realms and reach the kingdom connected to that mystery.

"But if the person leaving the body has never received any mysteries and is not aligned with the truth, yet someone who has mastered the second mystery speaks it over them as they die, something remarkable occurs. I tell you truly: That soul will not be judged in any of the rulers' realms, nor will it suffer punishment or harm from any fire. This will happen only because the great mystery of the Ineffable has been spoken over them.

"Those who govern the different regions will act quickly and with great respect, guiding the soul from one realm to the next, passing it along until it reaches the Virgin of Light. Along the way, every region will be filled with awe, recognizing the power of the mystery and the sign of the Ineffable's kingdom upon the soul.

"When the soul reaches the Virgin of Light, she will see the mark of the mystery of the Ineffable's kingdom upon it. She will marvel at its presence and examine the soul carefully. However, she will not allow it to fully enter the Light until it completes everything required to become a true citizen of the kingdom. This includes purification— letting go of all ties to the material world and freeing itself from everything that belongs to it."

The third mystery of the First Mystery is just as powerful and life-changing as the others. It acts as a bridge for the soul, ensuring a smooth transition without judgment, suffering, or obstacles. Each mystery is unique in its power and purpose, offering a way to freedom for those who follow it with sincerity and dedication. These mysteries guide the soul toward the ultimate Light, providing protection, safe passage, and eventually, unity with the divine.

The Virgin of Light places a special seal on the soul—one that is not described here—and within the same month of leaving its physical body, the soul is placed into a righteous new body. In this new form, the person will seek and find the true divine presence, gaining access to the higher mysteries and ultimately inheriting eternal Light. This Light is the reward given through the second mystery of the First Mystery of the Ineffable.

For the third mystery of the Ineffable, something even greater happens. If someone not only receives this mystery but fully understands and completes it with great care, they will gain more than just an inheritance in the kingdom connected to the mystery. If this person speaks the name of the mystery over another soul at the moment of death—even if that soul is suffering under the judgments and fires of the rulers—something incredible will occur. No matter how delayed or troubled the soul's journey may be, the power of this mystery will speed up its release.

I tell you truly: when the name of the mystery is spoken, the soul is quickly taken from one realm to the next until it reaches the Virgin of Light. There, the Virgin of Light places the same higher seal upon it. Within the same month, she ensures that the soul is placed into a righteous body that will come to know the true divine presence and receive the highest mysteries, allowing it to inherit the Light Kingdom. This is the great gift and purpose of the third mystery of the Ineffable.

Now, for all who receive one of the five mysteries of the Ineffable: when they leave their physical body, they will ascend and inherit the kingdom connected to their mystery. The kingdom of these five mysteries is greater than that of the twelve mysteries of the First

Mystery, surpassing all mysteries beneath it. Although each of the five mysteries is distinct, they share a single divine kingdom. However, they are different from the three mysteries of the Ineffable.

Those who receive one of the three mysteries of the Ineffable will inherit a kingdom even higher than that of the five mysteries. These three mysteries exist together in unity, but their greatness surpasses the five mysteries of the Ineffable. However, even these do not compare to the ultimate power of the one and only mystery of the Ineffable.

For those who receive the one and only mystery of the Ineffable, their inheritance has no limits. They will enter the kingdom in its entirety, experiencing it in its highest form, as I have already explained. Every soul that attains this mystery, or any of the mysteries within the space of the Ineffable, will move freely through the universe. They will not need to provide answers, prove themselves, or offer any signs. They are beyond all these things, without barriers or anything to hold them back. They will pass through all realms, ascending until they reach the kingdom tied to their mystery.

Similarly, those who receive mysteries from the second space of the Ineffable—connected to the first mystery of the First Mystery—will also move freely. They will not need tokens or face judgment in that divine space. Their journey will be uninterrupted as they move toward the final kingdom of the mystery they have embraced.

I tell you truly: every mystery of the Ineffable contains deep secrets that guide the soul's ascent and its place in the Light. When the universe expands, I will reveal every mystery, its meaning, its design, and how everything fits together. But for now, understand this: those who receive these mysteries will rise to the kingdom prepared for them, passing through all realms until they reach the divine Light that awaits them.

Those who belong to the third space, which is beyond the

outermost regions, will each have their own guides, explanations, and signs that help them on their journey. One day, I will explain everything about this space when the time comes to reveal its mysteries. However, this will happen after I have shown you how the universe expands and its true purpose unfolds.

But when the universe comes to an end—when the final number of perfected souls has been reached, and the mystery that created the universe has been completed—I will reign for a thousand years in the time of the Light. During this time, I will rule over all the emanations of the Light and over every perfected soul who has received and followed the mysteries given to them.

When Jesus finished speaking, Mary Magdalene stepped forward with great respect and asked, "My Lord, how many years in this world equal a single year in the Light?"

Jesus answered, "One day in the Light is equal to a thousand years on Earth. So, thirty-six myriads of years, plus half a myriad more in earthly time, equals a single year in the Light.

"Therefore, I will reign for a thousand years in the Light, within the presence of the last Helper, ruling over all the emanations of the Light and over all perfected souls who have received and lived by the mysteries of the Light.

"You, my beloved disciples, along with all who receive the mystery of the Ineffable, will stand with me in this kingdom. You will take your place at my right and left, reigning as kings alongside me.

"Those who receive the three mysteries of the Ineffable will also be kings in the Light Kingdom. However, they will not be equal to you or to those who have received the full mystery of the Ineffable. They will stand behind you, in their rightful place as kings.

"In the same way, those who receive the five mysteries of the

Ineffable will also reign, but their place will be behind those who have received the three mysteries.

"Likewise, those who receive the twelfth mystery of the First Mystery will stand in their position behind those of the five mysteries. Every soul will take its place according to the mysteries they have received and followed.

"Each one will be placed in their proper order, determined by the grace and the light they have embraced, within the kingdom of the Light."

All those who receive mysteries in any part of the space of the Ineffable will also be called kings and will stand ahead of those who have only received the mysteries of the First Mystery. Each soul will be placed according to the brilliance of its light, ensuring that those who receive greater mysteries will dwell in higher regions, while those who receive lesser mysteries will remain in the lower regions. In this way, everyone will reign as a king in the Light of my kingdom, shining according to the mystery they have embraced.

These are the roles assigned within the kingdom of the first space of the Ineffable. They are arranged according to the brightness of the Light and the rank given to each soul based on the mysteries they have received and followed.

Those who receive the mysteries of the second space, which is connected to the space of the First Mystery, will also dwell in the Light of my kingdom. They too will be placed according to their own brilliance, each one positioned in the region that matches the mysteries they have received. Just like in the first space, those who embrace higher mysteries will be in higher regions, while those with lower mysteries will remain in the lower regions of the kingdom's Light.

This structure forms the kingdom of the second space for those who receive the mysteries of the First Mystery.

Those who receive the mysteries of the third space—the outermost space—will be positioned behind the second king. They will be spread throughout the Light of my kingdom, each placed according to their own radiance, with every soul residing in the region that matches the mystery they have received. As before, those who attain the highest mysteries will be in the highest regions, while those who receive lesser mysteries will remain in the lower regions.

These three divisions form the structure of the Light Kingdom. Each division is designed to reflect the mysteries given to the souls who journey into the Light.

The mysteries within these divisions are vast and countless. They are recorded in the two great Books of Yew. However, I will share with you the most exalted mysteries of each division—those that surpass all others. These are the key mysteries that guide humanity toward the highest places in the Inheritance of the Light.

As for the lesser mysteries, they are not necessary for your mission. You will find them written in the two Books of Yew. These books were recorded by Enoch when I spoke to him from the tree of knowledge and the tree of life, which are in Adam's paradise.

When the time comes, after I have revealed to you how all things expand, I will also share the greatest mysteries of the three divisions of my kingdom. I will unveil the most important mysteries and provide you with their symbols, forms, codes, and seals from the last space, which is the first space from the outer regions. Additionally, I will teach you the responses, meanings, and signs connected to that space.

The second space, which lies within, is different. It does not have responses, explanations, signs, codes, or seals. Instead, it is made up only of its unique forms and figures, reflecting its special nature.

Chapter 88

When Jesus finished speaking, Andrew stepped forward humbly and said, "My Lord, please do not be upset with me. Have mercy on my confusion and help me understand something that I cannot fully grasp."

Jesus looked at Andrew with kindness and said, "Ask whatever is on your heart, and I will answer you clearly, without riddles or comparisons."

Encouraged, Andrew spoke, "My Lord, I am amazed and overwhelmed by what you have said. How is it possible for people, who are trapped in physical bodies in this world, to ascend after they die? How can they pass through the heavens, overcome the rulers, rise above the lords, gods, and even the great invisible beings? How can they journey beyond the Midst, travel through the entire region of the Right, and surpass all the powerful beings of the Light to finally enter the Kingdom of Light? This is difficult for me to understand."

Hearing Andrew's words, Jesus sighed deeply, filled with both compassion and frustration. He said, "How long must I wait for you to understand? How long will you continue to doubt? Have you not yet realized these truths? Are you still unaware?"

"Listen carefully: You, along with all angels, archangels, gods, lords, rulers, and even the greatest invisible beings—those in the Midst, the entire region of the Right, and all the powerful beings of the Light—you were all made from the same essence. Every one of you came from the same source, the same mixture of creation.

"At the command of the First Mystery, this mixture was gathered and held together so that all the great beings of the Light, along with their shining glory, could begin a process of purification. But they did not purify themselves by their own choice or power—it happened out

228

of necessity, according to the divine plan of the One and Only, the Ineffable.

"Unlike you, they have not suffered. They have not been changed or transformed as they moved through different realms. They have not been broken apart, placed into different kinds of bodies, or forced to experience pain and struggle.

"But you—you are the last remnants of creation. You are what was left over from the Treasury, from the region of the Right, and from the Midst. You are the leftovers of the invisible beings and the rulers. Because of this, you have suffered greatly. You have been placed in many different bodies, passing through many forms in this world.

"And yet, through all this pain and hardship, you have not given up. You have fought, rejected the distractions of this world, and freed yourselves from material desires. You never stopped searching until you discovered the mysteries of the Light. These mysteries have cleansed you, transforming you into pure, refined light."

"This is why I have told you before: 'Seek, and you will find.' What I meant was that you must seek out the mysteries of the Light, for they alone can purify the material body and transform it into pure light.

"I tell you truly: It is for the sake of humanity, who are bound to the material world, that I have come. I have given them the mysteries of the Light so that they may be purified. Without these mysteries, no human soul could be saved. They would never be able to enter the Kingdom of Light if I had not revealed these mysteries to cleanse them.

"The beings of the Light do not need these mysteries because they are already pure. But humanity does need them, for they are made from the lowest remains of creation. This is why I told you before, 'The healthy do not need a doctor, but the sick do.' In the same way, the beings of the Light do not need these mysteries because they are already cleansed, but humanity, being made of material things, must seek them out."

"That is why I command you to share this truth with all people: 'Do not stop searching, day and night, until you find the mysteries that purify you.' Tell them: 'Let go of this world and everything that ties you to it.' For anyone who buys and sells, who enjoys material pleasures—eating, drinking, or becoming caught up in the worries of this world—only adds more layers of materiality to themselves. But this entire world, along with everything in it, is nothing more than leftover matter. And in the end, everyone will be judged according to their purity."

This is why I told you before: "Let go of this world and everything that ties you to it, so that you do not add even more layers of material weight to yourself." Share this truth with all people: "Free yourself from the attachments of this world, so you do not burden yourself even further with the weight of material existence."

Tell them: "Do not stop searching, day and night. Do not rest until you have found the purifying mysteries that will cleanse you and transform you into pure light. Only then will you be able to ascend to the highest realms and inherit the Light of my kingdom."

Now, Andrew, along with your fellow disciples, think about this: Because of the sacrifices you have made, the suffering you have endured in every part of existence, and the many forms and bodies you have passed through, you have earned the purifying mysteries. These mysteries have refined you, making you into a light that is extraordinarily pure.

For this reason, you will rise above all realms, passing through every region of the great emanations of the Light. You will reign as kings in the Light Kingdom for all eternity.

When you leave this physical world and rise to the higher realms, reaching the regions of the rulers, they will feel ashamed before you.

The reason is this: You, who were once considered the lowest and made of the material world, will have become purer and more exalted than all of them.

And when you ascend beyond them, reaching the realm of the Great Invisible, the Midst, and the Right, all who exist there will see what you have become. They will stand in awe, realizing that the ones they once saw as the lowest and most unworthy have surpassed them. You will have reached a level of purity far beyond what they ever imagined.

Andrew, and all of you walking this path, hold onto this truth. Your suffering, your sacrifices, and your unshakable search for the Light have not been for nothing. Because of your dedication to purification and truth, you will rise above all rulers and powers, becoming leaders not only in the Light Kingdom but over all realms of existence.

Understand, my disciples, that your journey is proof of the power of letting go, the strength of the mysteries, and the promise of the Light. Through this path, the least will become the greatest, and those who were once cast aside will rise in glory and righteousness to reign forever.

Chapter 89

Jesus continued speaking and said, "When you rise to the higher realms of the great emanations of the Light, you will be honored and respected in all those places. This is because you, who were once considered the lowest, will have become purer than all who remain there. In every region you pass through, the beings will sing praises in your honor, celebrating your transformation and journey, until you reach the Kingdom of Light."

"This is the answer to the question you have asked. Now, Andrew, do you still have doubts?"

When Jesus spoke these words, Andrew suddenly understood, and so did all the disciples. They now fully realized that they were meant to inherit the Light Kingdom. Overcome with emotion, they fell at Jesus' feet, crying, weeping, and pleading, "Lord, forgive our brother for doubting."

Jesus, filled with kindness, said, "I forgive him, and I will always forgive. This is the reason the First Mystery sent me—to bring forgiveness for all sins and offer redemption to all who seek it."

Then, Jesus began to speak about the mysteries that remain in the Ineffable—the ones that have not been revealed but exist deep within that sacred realm. He explained that these mysteries are like the Limbs of the Ineffable. To help the disciples understand, he used an example.

"Think of these mysteries as the Limbs of the Ineffable, with each part representing a unique aspect of its greatness and glory. Just as the head has its own special purpose, and the eyes, ears, and all other parts serve their functions, each of these mysteries fulfills a specific role. Yet, together, they form a single, complete whole."

"This example is meant to help you understand, but it is not the full truth. It is only a glimpse of the mystery of the Ineffable— something too great to fully describe in human words."

"All the Limbs that exist within the Ineffable—just like in the example I have given you—are built upon the foundation of its mystery. These Limbs remain within the Ineffable itself, along with the three spaces that follow them, each connected to certain mysteries. And among all these, I am the true treasury, the one and only, with no equal in the world. But there are still more mysteries, regions, and truths waiting to be revealed."

"Blessed is the one who discovers the words of the mysteries of the first space, which exists on the outside. Such a person is like a god, for they have uncovered deep truths. Even greater is the one who finds the words of the mysteries of the second space, which is in the middle—they rise in power and become like a Savior, breaking free from the limits of the physical world. But the one who reaches the mysteries of the third space, which is the innermost, surpasses even the universe itself. They become like the uncontainables, those who dwell in that highest realm."

"Because they have found the mystery that allows these great beings to exist, they become like them. They reflect the divine nature of the realm they have understood.

"And anyone who discovers the words of the mysteries, as I have described them in the example of the Limbs of the Ineffable, reaches an even greater level. Truly, I tell you, the one who fully understands these mysteries becomes the highest among all and is like the First—the Ineffable.

"This is because these mysteries are the foundation of everything. Through them, the universe was created and continues to exist. It is by the power and wisdom of these mysteries that all things are held together. So the one who uncovers these truths becomes a reflection of the First. They embody the knowledge of the Ineffable—the ultimate truth I have shared with you today."

The Third Book of Pistis Sophia

Jesus continued teaching his disciples and said, "When I return to the Light, spread this message to the whole world: 'Never stop seeking, whether it is day or night. Do not allow yourselves to give up or grow tired until you have discovered the mysteries of the Light. These mysteries will cleanse you, transform you into pure light, and lead you into the eternal Kingdom of Light.'

"Tell them: 'Let go of the world completely. Turn away from material things, from all its worries, sins, and distractions. Only by doing this can you be worthy of the mysteries of the Light and be saved from the suffering that comes with judgment.'

"Say to them: 'Reject arguing and division, so you can be worthy of the mysteries of the Light and be spared from the fire of the dark one.'

"Tell them: 'Do not gossip or involve yourselves in matters that do not concern you, so you may reach the mysteries of the Light and avoid judgment.'

"Warn them: 'Avoid conflict and seeking legal battles, so that you may be worthy of the mysteries of the Light and escape the punishments of Ariēl.'

"Say to them: 'Reject lying, false accusations, and deception, so that you may discover the mysteries of the Light and be saved from the fiery rivers of the dark one.'"

Jesus instructed his disciples to share these teachings, emphasizing the importance of leaving behind worldly distractions and focusing on purification and enlightenment through the mysteries of the Light.

"Tell them: 'Do not bear false witness or give dishonest testimony, so you may be worthy of the mysteries of the Light. By doing so, you will escape the fiery rivers of the dark one, where suffering awaits those who refuse to turn away from their wrongdoings.

"Tell them: 'Let go of pride and arrogance, for these will keep you from the mysteries of the Light. Only through humility can you enter the mysteries and be saved from the consuming fire of Ariēl, which burns those who falsely lift themselves above others.

"Tell them: 'Do not give in to greed and the love of food, for being ruled by physical desires will tie you to the judgments of Amente. Instead, seek nourishment for your soul, which leads to salvation and the Light.

"Tell them: 'Stop wasting words on meaningless talk, so that you may become worthy of the mysteries of the Light. Those who control their speech will be freed from the fires of Amente, where careless words bring their own consequences.

"Tell them: 'Do not be deceitful or act with cunning intentions, for these things lead you away from the purity needed to inherit the Light. Those who let go of trickery will escape judgment and suffering in Amente.

"Tell them: 'Reject greed and selfishness, for these desires keep you trapped in darkness. Only by letting go of greed can you receive the mysteries of the Light and escape the fiery rivers of the dark one.

"Tell them: 'Do not cling to the world and its temporary pleasures, for they bind the soul to lower realms. By turning away from worldly attachments, you will escape the traps of fire and suffering that await those who love only the things of the world.

"Tell them: 'Do not steal or take what is not yours, for these actions will keep you from being worthy of the mysteries of the Light. Those who reject theft will be saved from the fiery rivers of Ariël, where such acts bring punishment.

"Tell them: 'Avoid corrupt and hateful speech, for a tongue that spreads lies and harm cannot approach the Light. Only by choosing words that bring peace can you avoid the suffering found in the fiery rivers of judgment.

"Tell them: 'Reject all forms of evil and malice, for only by freeing your soul from darkness can you be worthy of the Light. By doing this, you will escape the vast fires of Ariël, which consume those who refuse to turn away from wickedness.'"

Tell them: Let go of cruelty and lack of compassion, for those without kindness cannot receive the mysteries of the Light. Instead, choose love and mercy, and you will be saved from the harsh punishments of the dragon-faced ones.

Tell them: Abandon anger and uncontrolled rage, for these emotions lead to destruction and trap the soul in lower realms. If you overcome anger, you will be freed from the fiery rivers of the dragon-faced ones, where the flames never stop burning.

Tell them: Stop using hateful and hurtful words, for they not only harm others but also damage your own soul. If you let go of cursing and negativity, you will escape the fire-filled seas of the dragon-faced ones, where such actions lead to judgment.

Tell them: Reject stealing and dishonesty, for a soul that takes from others cannot enter the Light. Those who turn away from theft will be saved from the boiling seas of suffering ruled by the dragon-faced ones.

Tell them: Turn away from violence and robbery, for these actions pull the soul into darkness. Those who reject such ways will be freed from Yaldabaōth, the ruler of chaos and deception.

Tell them: Stop spreading lies and gossip, for words that destroy others prevent the soul from reaching the Light. Those who reject slander will escape the fiery rivers of the lion-faced one, whose judgment is severe.

Tell them: Let go of fighting and conflict, for division pulls the soul away from peace. Only by rejecting strife can you receive the mysteries of the Light and be saved from the raging rivers of Yaldabaōth.

Tell them: Do not remain in ignorance, for the Light cannot enter a soul that chooses darkness over understanding. Seek wisdom and truth, and you will be saved from Yaldabaōth's servants and the burning fire seas that await those who refuse to awaken.

Jesus taught his disciples to guide humanity toward a path of letting go, cleansing, and finding salvation in the Light.

Tell them: Turn away from all evil and harmful actions so that you may be worthy of the mysteries of the Light. By doing so, you will escape the grip of Yaldabaōth, his demons, and the harsh punishments they bring upon souls.

Tell them: Reject laziness and spiritual neglect, for these will keep you from seeking the Light with dedication. Only by striving for truth can you receive the mysteries of the Light and escape the burning seas of Yaldabaōth, where suffering awaits those who remain indifferent.

Tell them: Turn away from adultery and all forms of impurity, for such actions separate the soul from the divine path. Those who reject these acts will be worthy of the mysteries of the Light Kingdom and avoid the sulphur and fire-filled seas ruled by the lion-faced one.

Tell them: Reject violence and murder, for they cause deep harm and fill the soul with darkness. Those who choose a path of peace will find salvation through the mysteries of the Light and avoid the cold prisons of the crocodile-faced ruler, who reigns in the first chamber of outer darkness.

Tell them: Abandon cruelty, heartlessness, and a lack of reverence, for these close the soul to divine mercy. By embracing love and kindness, you will be worthy of the mysteries of the Light and escape the rulers who dwell in the outer darkness.

Tell them: Do not reject faith or deny the divine, for disbelief blocks the way to salvation. Only by embracing the truth of the Light can you avoid the deep despair and endless suffering that await those who turn away from it.

Tell them: Let go of sorcery, magic, and all forbidden practices, for these separate the soul from the truth. By rejecting them, you will avoid the freezing cold, hail, and emptiness of outer darkness.

Tell them: Do not speak against the divine or use disrespectful words, for such actions bring judgment from the great dragon in outer darkness. Only through reverence and humility can you escape this fate.

Tell them: Stay away from false teachings and misleading beliefs, for they lead souls away from the path of the Light. Those who spread or follow such lies without turning back will suffer the consequences of the great dragon and the darkness, where they will disappear at the end of time.

Warn those who have abandoned the truth of the First Mystery: You are in grave danger, for your punishment will be worse than all others. You will be trapped in the frozen wastelands of ice and hail, held by the dragon in outer darkness. You will neither return to this world nor find redemption, but when the universe fades away, you will vanish completely.

Tell the people: Remain calm in your hearts so that you may receive the mysteries of the Light and ascend to the Kingdom of Light.

Encourage them: Show love to one another, for love is the key to the Light. Through kindness, you may receive the mysteries and rise into the Light.

Tell them: Be gentle in your actions and in spirit, for this will bring you closer to the divine mysteries and lead you into the Light.

Tell them: Seek peace in all things, for those who choose peace will find their place in the Light. By living this way, you will receive the mysteries and enter the Kingdom of Light.

Tell them: Show mercy and kindness to everyone, for those who are compassionate will receive the mysteries of the Light and share in eternal joy.

Tell them: Give freely to those in need. Help others with an open heart, for generosity will open the path to the mysteries of the Light and lead you into the Kingdom of Light.

Encourage them: Care for the poor, the sick, and those who suffer. In serving others, you reflect the Light and become worthy to receive its mysteries and enter the Kingdom of Light.

Tell them: Love God and live according to His will, for by doing so, you will receive the mysteries of the Light and inherit the Kingdom of Light.

Tell them: Seek righteousness, for those who desire truth and justice will be found worthy of the mysteries of the Light and will share in eternal joy.

Finally, tell them: Be good in your thoughts, words, and actions. Let goodness guide you, and you will receive the mysteries of the Light and ascend to the eternal Kingdom of Light.

Speak to them and say: Let go of all attachments to the material world—its temporary pleasures, distractions, and false promises—so that you may be worthy to receive the mysteries of the Light. By doing this, you will rise above and inherit the endless joy and beauty of the

Kingdom of Light.

These are the steps for those who wish to follow the true path and receive the mysteries of the Light. Only by letting go of worldly distractions can one truly find the way to the Light.

Therefore, if someone fully commits to this path and turns away from the world's temptations, freely give them the mysteries of the Light. Do not judge them for their past. Even if they have lived in deep sin and have been weighed down by every kind of wrongdoing, do not hold back the mysteries from them. Instead, offer them the Light so they may find their way back, seek the truth, and be saved.

No matter how great their sins may have been, share with them the knowledge of the Kingdom of Light. Hide nothing from them, for the mysteries were not given for those who are already righteous, but for those who are lost. This is why I came—to reveal these mysteries so that even the worst sins may be erased.

This is why I told you before: 'I did not come to call the righteous.' I did not come for those who are already pure, but for those who are lost, so that they may return to the Light. I brought these mysteries into the world so that sin itself could be undone, and all who repent and seek the Light may be saved.

Remember this: The mysteries are a divine gift from the First Mystery, given through love and mercy. They exist to cleanse sins, remove burdens, and bring freedom to every soul who seeks redemption. Through these mysteries, even the greatest sinner can enter the Kingdom of Light and live forever in divine love and peace.

Chapter 90

When Jesus finished speaking, Mary stepped forward with deep respect and said, "My Lord, I have a question that troubles me. What happens to a righteous person who has lived a completely sinless life? If someone is pure in every way and has never done wrong, will they still have to go through suffering and judgment? Or will they be allowed to enter the Kingdom of Light because of their righteousness?"

Jesus looked at Mary and answered wisely, "A person who has lived a perfect life without sin, yet has never received the mysteries of the Light, will still follow a certain path when they leave this world. When their soul departs from their body, it will be met by the receivers of one of the great triplepowers. These are powerful beings whose job is to guide souls. Among them, there is a leader who commands them. They will take the soul and protect it from the retributive receivers, who seek to claim those who have not received the mysteries."

"For three days, they will carry the soul and travel through different parts of creation, observing its purity. Then, they will take it into the chaos, where it will briefly experience some of the troubles found in that realm. However, because the soul is righteous, the fires of chaos will not harm it deeply—only slightly and for a short time."

"Out of compassion, the receivers will quickly pull the soul out of chaos and lead it upward, past the rulers of the Midst. These rulers will not impose harsh punishments, but the fires in their regions will cause the soul some discomfort. When the soul reaches the domain of Yachthanabas, a pitiless ruler, he will not have full power over it. He may hold the soul for a short time, but his punishments will only cause minor disturbances before the soul is allowed to continue its journey."

"Once again, the receivers will have mercy and guide the soul past the realms of the æons. This is to keep the rulers of the æons from capturing the soul and pulling it into their domain. Instead, the receivers will lead it along the path of the sun and bring it before the Virgin of Light. She will carefully examine the soul and see that it is without sin. However, because the soul does not bear the mark of the mysteries, she will not allow it to enter the Light."

"Instead, she will place a special seal upon it and send it back into a new body within the realms of righteousness—a body that is prepared to seek out and receive the mysteries of the Light. In this new life, the soul will have the chance to discover the mysteries and, through them, inherit the Light forever."

"But if the righteous person has sinned once, twice, or even three times, they will return to a body that matches the nature of their sins. The kind of body they receive will depend on the specific mistakes they made. I will explain these details fully when I reveal the complete design of the universe."

"Listen carefully: Truly, I tell you, even if a person is completely righteous and has never sinned, they still cannot enter the Kingdom of Light unless they carry the mark of the mysteries. The mysteries of the Light are necessary. Without them, no soul can enter the Light. This is an unchanging truth: Only through the mysteries of the Light can a soul gain access to the eternal realms."

Chapter 91

When Jesus finished speaking, John stepped forward humbly and said, "My Lord, I have a question. Suppose there is a man who is a sinner, someone who has broken every law and done many wrong things. But then, he decides to change his ways for the sake of the Kingdom of Heaven. He turns away from his sins, gives up all worldly things, and we begin teaching him the mysteries of the Light, starting with the first ones. If he accepts these mysteries but later falls back into sin, returning to his old ways, what should we do?

"Now, imagine he repents again, completely turning away from sin and the world, coming to us with deep sincerity. If we are sure his desire for God is real, should we then give him the second mystery of the first space? But what if, after receiving it, he once again falls into sin and returns to the ways of the world? And later, if he repents again, sincerely turning back to the Light, should we start over and offer him the first mystery again?

"If this keeps happening—if he falls into sin many times but always comes back, seeking forgiveness and longing for the mysteries of the Light with all his heart—should we continue to forgive him and give him the mysteries up to seven times? Or should we stop at some point?"

Jesus looked at John with kindness and replied, "John, I tell you this: do not forgive him just seven times, but many times more. Every time he truly turns away from his sins, repents with sincerity, and seeks the mysteries of the Light, you must forgive him and offer him the mysteries again.

"Forgiving him is not just for his sake but for the salvation of his soul. Remember, when even one soul is saved, there is great joy in the Kingdom of Light. And those who work to save souls—guiding them to repentance and giving them the mysteries—will receive great rewards. They will have a special place among the saviors and will be honored in the Kingdom of Light forever.

"So never withhold forgiveness. Every time someone repents and returns to the mysteries, they move closer to the Light. It is not about how many times they fall, but how sincerely they get back up and seek the truth. Forgive them, guide them, and give them the mysteries as long as they truly repent. This is the will of the First Mystery and the purpose of the Light's mercy."

Chapter 92

John sincerely continued asking questions, eager to understand. He said, "Master, you have taught us that we must forgive not only seven times but many more times, and that we should continue offering the mysteries to save a brother's soul. But I ask you this: If we keep giving a person the mysteries of the first space, and he repeatedly fails to live in a way that is worthy of the Kingdom of Light, what should we do? Should we allow him to move forward to the mysteries of the second space, hoping that this might help him change and turn fully to the Light? Or should we stop him from progressing further?"

Jesus patiently answered John, saying, "If this person is not pretending and his heart truly longs for God, but he struggles because of the forces that shape his fate, then forgive him. Allow him to move forward and give him the first mystery of the second space. Maybe, through this, he will finally turn to the Light, truly repent, and inherit the Kingdom of Light.

"If, after receiving the first mystery of the second space, he stumbles again and falls back into sin but later repents with all his heart, turning away from the world and its distractions, and you are certain that his repentance is real, then forgive him again. Let him continue and give him the second mystery of the second space. Through your kindness, you may still guide him toward salvation.

"And if he once again fails to live by the mysteries, falling back into sin, but later returns with true repentance, rejecting the world completely and proving his longing for the Light, then forgive him once more. Accept his repentance, for the First Mystery is full of mercy and love. Let him advance further and give him the three mysteries together that belong to the second space of the First Mystery. Perhaps, by this grace, his soul will finally be saved.

"Never grow tired of forgiving, for saving souls is a sacred duty. The mercy of the First Mystery has no limits, and as long as someone returns with genuine repentance, they should be guided forward. Each mystery they receive brings them closer to their eternal inheritance in the Kingdom of Light, where they may live in the glory of the mysteries forever."

"However, if after receiving the three mysteries of the second space, he sins again and falls into all kinds of wrongdoing, at that point, do not forgive him anymore. Do not accept his repentance again. Let him remain among you as a warning, as someone who chose the path of sin even after being given many chances to return to the Light.

"Truly, I tell you, the three mysteries will stand as witnesses against him, marking the last opportunity he had to repent. After that, he will no longer have the chance to return to the higher realms. Instead, his soul will be sent to the domain of the dragon in outer darkness, separated from the Light."

"I have spoken of this before in a parable, saying: 'If your brother sins against you, speak to him in private. If he listens, you have won him back. But if he refuses, take another person as a witness. And if he still does not listen, bring him before the assembly. But if he does not listen even to the assembly, then let him be like a transgressor and a stumbling block.' This parable has a deeper meaning. It means this: If someone does not change after receiving the first mystery, give him the second. If he fails again, offer him the three mysteries together, which is like bringing him before the assembly. But if he still refuses to change, then let him be considered a transgressor, someone who has rejected all opportunities given to him."

"Also, I have told you before, 'By the testimony of two or three witnesses, every truth will be established.' This is fulfilled here because those three mysteries will serve as witnesses against him, proving that

245

he was given every chance to repent."

"And truly, I tell you this: If this person later seeks repentance after rejecting these mysteries, no ordinary mystery will be able to forgive him, and his repentance will not be accepted. He will not be able to find redemption through the common mysteries. Only the first mystery of the First Mystery or the mysteries of the Ineffable can offer him forgiveness. These are the highest and most merciful mysteries, filled with the endless love and forgiveness of the Ineffable. Only these mysteries have the power to extend mercy even after so many failures, because their compassion is infinite, their forgiveness immeasurable, and their mercy never-ending."

Chapter 93

When Jesus finished speaking, John continued asking questions in front of the other disciples. He said, "My Lord, what if there is someone who has lived in great sin but then completely turns away from the world? He gives up all worldly concerns, every sin, and everything tied to it. Suppose we test him carefully and find that he is not pretending, but is truly seeking God with honesty and sincerity. If we are certain of his commitment and see that he is worthy of receiving the mysteries of the second or even third space, should we give them to him before he has received any mysteries of the Inheritance of the Light? Or should we wait? What do you want us to do in this case?"

Jesus answered John in the presence of the disciples, saying, "If you are completely sure that this person has truly let go of the world—its distractions, attachments, and sins—and you believe without any doubt that he is not coming with deceit, curiosity, or false intentions but is honestly seeking God, then do not hold back the mysteries from him. Give him the mysteries of the second and third spaces and decide which one he is ready for. Whatever mystery he is worthy to receive, give it to him freely and do not hide it. If you refuse to give these mysteries to someone who deserves them, you will bring great judgment upon yourselves.

"If you give him the mysteries of the second or third space and later he falls back into sin, you must forgive him and offer them again, even a second and third time. However, if he continues to sin after receiving the mysteries three times, you must stop giving them to him. At that point, the three mysteries will stand as witnesses against him, marking the last chance he had to repent. And I tell you truly, if anyone gives him more mysteries after that, they will bring great judgment upon themselves. From then on, he should be considered a transgressor, someone who has chosen the wrong path despite many opportunities.

"I also tell you this: If a person rejects these chances and refuses to change even after receiving the mysteries three times, his soul can no longer return to the world for another opportunity. Instead, he will be sent to the place of the dragon in the outer darkness, where there is nothing but suffering, sorrow, and despair. When the world reaches its end, his soul will be trapped in unbearable cold and scorching fire until it completely ceases to exist.

"Even if he later changes his mind, leaves the world again, and repents with deep sincerity, no ordinary mystery can accept his repentance or forgive his sins. He will find no mercy or forgiveness in the lesser mysteries. Only the mystery of the First Mystery and the highest mystery of the Ineffable can grant him another chance. These are the only mysteries that hold infinite compassion and mercy, and they alone have the power to forgive and restore a soul at any time, no matter how serious the sin."

Chapter 94

When Jesus finished speaking, John stepped forward again and said, "My Lord, please be patient with me as I ask another question. I do not ask to challenge You but to understand clearly, so we may teach others with complete certainty."

Jesus, with kindness, replied, "Ask whatever is on your mind, and I will answer you plainly."

John then said, "Lord, suppose we enter a town or village, and the people there welcome us into their homes. If they seem kind and claim to seek God, but we do not yet know if they are sincere or deceiving us, what should we do? If we believe they are honest and give them the mysteries of the Lightkingdom, but later discover that they were lying, using the mysteries as a test or a spectacle, what will happen to them? What should we do in this situation?"

Jesus answered, "If you go to a town and are welcomed into someone's home, give them a mystery. If they are truly worthy, you will have saved their soul, and they will inherit the Lightkingdom. But if they were lying—if they mocked the mysteries, used them as a game, or tested you—then you must call upon the first mystery of the First Mystery, which is merciful to all, and say this prayer:

'O Mystery, which we have given to these unworthy and deceitful souls, who have misused it and mocked its truth, we ask that You take it back from them and make them forever unworthy of the mysteries of Your kingdom.'

"Then, shake the dust from your feet as a sign against them and say, 'May your souls be as the dust of your house.' I tell you truly, in that moment, the mysteries you gave them will be taken back. The wisdom, knowledge, and spiritual understanding they received will disappear from them, and they will be cut off from the mysteries forever.

"This is what I meant when I told you before: 'When you enter a house, say, "Peace be with you." If they are worthy, let your peace remain. If they are not, let your peace return to you.' This means that if someone sincerely seeks God, you may give them the mysteries of the Light. But if they deceive you, and you unknowingly share the mysteries with them, you can call upon the First Mystery to take them back. Those who mock or misuse the mysteries will be completely separated from them and will never enter the Lightkingdom.

"From that moment on, such people will not return to this world. Instead, they will be sent to the dragon in the outer darkness. However, if they later truly repent—if they renounce the world and all its sins, and fully submit to the Light—no ordinary mystery will forgive them. Only the highest mystery of the Ineffable, which is infinitely merciful, can accept their repentance and grant them forgiveness."

When Jesus finished, Mary stepped forward, knelt before Him, and kissed His feet. She said, "My Lord, please allow me to ask another question. Do not be angry with me, for I only seek to understand more deeply."

Jesus looked at her kindly and said, "Ask whatever you wish, and I will answer you."

Mary said, "Lord, suppose there is a righteous man who has already received all the mysteries of the Light. This man has a relative—perhaps a sibling, a cousin, or simply a friend—who has died. This relative may have been sinful or may not have been a sinner at all. But the righteous man is deeply saddened, grieving because he fears that the soul of his loved one is suffering in judgment and punishment. Is there anything we can do to help such a soul, Lord? Can we free them from their suffering?"

Jesus replied, "Mary, I have spoken of this before, but I will explain it again so you may understand fully and teach it to others.

"If you wish to not only free a soul from judgment but also ensure they are reborn into a righteous body—one that will find the mysteries of the Light and ascend to the Lightkingdom—you must perform the third mystery of the Ineffable. When doing so, say these words:

'O carriers of this mystery, take the soul of [name the person] out of judgment and punishment. Bring this soul quickly before the Virgin of Light. Let her seal it with the higher seal, and each month, let her send it into a righteous and pure body—one that will find the mysteries of the Light and ascend to the Lightkingdom.'

"If you do this, I tell you truly, those who oversee judgment and punishment will immediately release the soul. They will pass it from one to another until it reaches the Virgin of Light. She will then place the sign of the kingdom of the Ineffable upon the soul and give it to her messengers. They will guide the soul into a righteous body—one that is ready to seek the mysteries of the Light. From there, the soul will grow in goodness, ascend to the higher realms, and inherit the Lightkingdom.

"This is the answer to your question. Let this knowledge guide you."

Chapter 95

Mary, filled with concern, said, "My Lord, didn't you bring the mysteries into the world to save people from the deaths that Fate has decided for them? Some are sentenced to die by the sword, others by drowning, torture, or violent punishments ordered by law. There are many ways people suffer tragic deaths. Did you not give the mysteries so that someone might escape these fates and instead pass away peacefully and suddenly, without pain?

"We are facing great persecution because of you, Lord. Many seek to harm us because we follow your name. In such moments, can we use the mysteries to leave our bodies immediately and escape suffering entirely?"

Jesus looked at Mary and all His disciples with compassion and answered, "I have spoken about this before, but listen again so that you may fully understand.

"This is not only for you but for anyone who completes the first mystery of the First Mystery of the Ineffable. Whoever fulfills this mystery in every way—following all its steps and instructions—will have the power to rise above the fate assigned by the rulers. Through this mystery, a person can leave their body without facing the suffering that comes from a painful or violent death.

"Anyone who completes this mystery is no longer controlled by the suffering that Fate has planned for them. When the time comes for them to leave their body, they will be able to do so quickly and without pain. The power of this mystery allows them to escape the suffering that would normally come with death.

"This is why the mysteries were brought into the world: to free people from the control of the rulers, from the suffering caused by Fate, and from the hardships of the world. Those who receive and follow the mysteries gain the ability to overcome these struggles and enter the Lightkingdom, free from the pain of this world."

Jesus paused, letting His words sink in, making sure His disciples fully understood the power of the mysteries and the freedom they bring from the suffering of earthly life.

Chapter 96

Mary, deeply moved by Jesus' words, continued to ask, "My Lord, if someone completes this mystery in every way, will they be freed from what the rulers of Fate have decided for them? When the time comes, will their soul leave the body as a bright stream of light, rising high and passing through all the regions of the rulers and the Light? Will they reach their kingdom without needing to give explanations or show any signs?"

Jesus gently replied, "Yes, Mary, once this mystery is completed in all its steps, the moment its name is spoken, it will save the person from everything the rulers of Fate have planned. Their soul will leave the body as a shining light, rising beyond all the rulers and the Light without obstacles, until it reaches its rightful kingdom."

When Jesus finished speaking, Mary, overwhelmed with devotion, fell at His feet, kissed them, and said, "My Lord, I still have many questions. Please reveal everything to us and keep nothing hidden."

With patience and kindness, Jesus answered, "Ask whatever is in your heart, Mary, and I will explain it openly, without comparisons or riddles."

Mary then asked, "My Lord, didn't you bring the mysteries into the world for all people, no matter if they are rich or poor, weak or strong? If we go to a place where people do not believe in us or listen to our words, can we use these mysteries there so they will know that we are truly speaking the words of the God of the universe?"

Jesus turned to Mary and the disciples and said, "I have spoken about this mystery before, but I will explain it again so you understand fully. Mary, this is not only for you but for anyone who has mastered the mystery of raising the dead—the same mystery that can heal sickness, drive out demons, and cure all kinds of suffering, including blindness, paralysis, and deafness.

"Whoever receives and completes this mystery will have great power. Whenever they ask for something—whether to escape poverty, to become strong instead of weak, to heal the body, or even to bring the dead back to life—it will be granted. Whatever they request, as long as it aligns with the power of the mystery, will happen."

Hearing this, the disciples stepped forward together, their hearts overwhelmed. They cried out, "O Savior, your words fill us with amazement! The things you have told us are beyond anything we imagined. Our souls are longing more than ever to leave our bodies and come to you. You have lifted us up, and now we desire nothing more than to go to the kingdom of Light."

Jesus, seeing their passion and devotion, looked upon them with love, allowing His words to strengthen their faith and deepen their understanding of the mysteries and the promise of the Lightkingdom.

Chapter 97

When the disciples had finished speaking, Jesus continued, "When you go into cities, towns, or countries, tell the people this first: 'Never stop searching for the mysteries of the Light. Keep seeking until you find them, for they will guide you to the Lightkingdom.' Warn them to be careful of false teachers and misleading beliefs, for many will come in my name, claiming to be me, but they are not. They will lead many people astray."

He then explained further, "If people come to you with faith, listen to your teachings, and live in a way that makes them worthy of the mysteries of the Light, then share the mysteries with them freely. Give each person the mysteries they deserve—greater mysteries for those who are worthy of more, and lesser ones for those who need them. Do not hold back from those who sincerely seek the Light.

"However, the mystery of raising the dead and healing the sick must not be given to anyone, and you should not teach its instructions. This mystery is connected to the rulers and their domains. Because of this, do not share or teach it until faith has spread throughout the world. But you may use it wisely—if you come to a place where people reject you, refuse to listen, or do not believe in your words, then you may perform these miracles. When you raise the dead, heal the sick, the blind, or the lame, people in those places will see and believe. Through these acts, they will know that you speak the words of the God of the universe. This is why I have given you this mystery—to help bring faith to those who do not yet believe."

After saying this, Jesus turned to Mary and continued, "Now, Mary, listen carefully to the question you asked about what causes people to sin. Pay close attention to my words:

"When a child is born, its strength is weak, its soul is fragile, and even the false spirit within it is small. In the beginning, none of these parts—the power, the soul, or the false spirit—understands anything about good or evil. They are all weighed down by deep forgetfulness. The body itself is also weak and vulnerable.

"As the child grows and experiences the pleasures of the world— things created by the rulers—different parts of its being are affected. The inner power takes in the good portion from these experiences. The soul absorbs what is connected to righteousness and balance. But the false spirit, which is always drawn toward evil, takes in the part that leads to desire and wrongdoing. Meanwhile, the physical body simply absorbs the material essence of these things, without knowledge or understanding.

"However, the person's fate—their destined path—is separate from these things. It does not absorb anything from the world's pleasures and remains the same as when it first entered life."

With these words, Jesus explained the complex relationship between a person's inner power, soul, and false spirit, showing how they interact with the world and influence behavior.

As time goes on, these three parts—power, soul, and false spirit— continue to grow, each following its own nature. The power longs for the Light, reaching toward the divine realms. The soul, which is connected to both righteousness and the world, seeks a balance between good and earthly experiences. But the false spirit constantly pursues sin, temptation, and wrongdoing, as that is its true nature. The body itself remains inactive, needing physical energy to sense and act.

As each part develops, the spiritual watchers assigned by the rulers begin to observe. These watchers act as witnesses, recording everything the soul does—especially its sins—so that when the time comes, it can be judged and punished accordingly.

The false spirit plays a powerful and dangerous role. It does not simply influence the soul—it actively pushes it into sin, fulfilling the desires of the rulers who control fate. It forces the soul into wrong actions, leading it toward wickedness and disobedience.

The false spirit never stops working. It even influences the soul while it sleeps, creating dreams filled with temptation and earthly desires. It constantly tries to keep the soul focused on material things, dragging it away from the Light. It does not allow the soul to follow its true longing for the divine.

Jesus then said to Mary, "This false spirit is the real enemy of the soul. It constantly pressures the soul, forcing it to sin."

When a person reaches the end of their life, their destiny takes over, leading them toward death according to the path set by the rulers. After death, the watchers come to take the soul out of the body. For three days, the soul is taken through different regions of the world, while its destiny and false spirit travel with it. Meanwhile, the person's inner power returns to the Virgin of Light.

After three days, the watchers bring the soul down into the chaos of the underworld, where those responsible for punishment take control. At this point, the watchers return to their proper places, following the rulers' system for dealing with souls.

But the false spirit stays with the soul. It becomes both its accuser and its tormentor, ensuring the soul suffers for the sins it was pushed into committing. The struggle between the false spirit and the soul does not end with death—it continues in the afterlife.

Once the soul has suffered enough in the chaos, the false spirit leads it to new places where it must face more punishments for its past actions. It is taken to the region of the rulers in the middle realms, where they question it. If the soul does not know the mysteries that could free it, the rulers judge it further, adding more punishments based on its sins.

Jesus then said, "I will explain the details of these punishments when I reveal how the universe expands and functions."

He then began to explain how souls are brought back into new bodies, showing how destiny, the false spirit, and the soul continue their cycle through different lives.

Chapter 98

When the time comes for a good soul to leave the body, and it has received the mysteries of the Light, its journey upward begins, following the divine plan. The counterfeiting spirit, which had been attached to the soul during life, follows along as it ascends. This spirit, assigned by the rulers, stays with the soul to ensure it follows the proper path. The destiny also remains connected to the soul, keeping its hold until the moment of separation.

As the soul rises, it reaches the point where it must speak the sacred mystery that breaks the seals and bonds placed on it by the rulers of Fate and the counterfeiting spirit. If the soul successfully speaks this mystery, the chains binding it to the counterfeiting spirit are broken. At that moment, the counterfeiting spirit is released and returns to the realm of the rulers where it belongs. Likewise, the destiny lets go and returns to its own place.

At this turning point, the soul transforms into a brilliant stream of light. Its brightness is so overwhelming that the retributive receivers, who had been guiding it from the body, are struck with fear and awe. They fall to the ground, unable to bear the powerful radiance that now shines from the soul.

Now completely filled with light, the soul spreads its wings of light and soars upward. It passes through all the regions of the rulers, breaking through every barrier and rising beyond every limit. Nothing can hold it back as it travels to the kingdom that matches the mysteries it has received.

The Good Soul That Receives Higher Mysteries

If a soul has received the mysteries of the second or third space, it will ascend even higher after leaving the body. These mysteries act as both a key and a shield, allowing the soul to pass safely through the regions of the rulers without being stopped. The soul shines with an intense light, guiding its way, and no power can block its journey. It moves swiftly, overcoming all barriers, until it reaches its rightful place in the higher realms of the Lightkingdom.

The Soul That Sins After Receiving Mysteries

However, if a soul has received mysteries from the first space—the outermost regions of the Light—and later turns back to sin, its path becomes much more difficult. When its earthly life ends, the retributive receivers come to take the soul from its body. But because it had once known the sacred mysteries and then returned to wrongdoing, it does not go straight to the Lightkingdom.

Instead, the soul must face the judgments of the rulers. The counterfeiting spirit and destiny still hold power over it, keeping it tied to the consequences of its actions. The rulers carefully examine its deeds to determine the weight of its sins and what atonement is required.

The Savior warned of the seriousness of turning away from the mysteries after receiving them. While these sacred gifts provide a path to the Lightkingdom, the way a soul chooses to live after receiving them determines its fate. Those who abandon the path of righteousness must face the consequences before they can hope to ascend.

The Virgin of Light and the Soul's Redemption

When a soul comes before the Virgin of Light, she examines it based on its faithfulness to the mysteries and the purity of its actions. If the soul has failed to follow the mysteries or has not fully repented, she assigns it to a new body that reflects its past deeds. This allows the soul another chance to live righteously and redeem itself.

However, those who have remained faithful to the mysteries and resisted the temptation of sin will ascend immediately and receive their place in the Lightkingdom without delay.

The Savior assured His disciples that a detailed explanation of how souls are judged, redeemed, or sent back to be reborn would be given when He explained the full expansion of the universe. Until then, He urged them to stay focused on their mission—guiding souls toward the mysteries and teaching them how to live according to divine truth.

Breaking Free from the Counterfeiting Spirit and Destiny

After the soul leaves the body, destiny and the counterfeiting spirit follow closely behind. The counterfeiting spirit remains attached because it was bound to the soul by the rulers through seals and bonds.

However, if the soul possesses the knowledge of the mysteries of release, it can free itself. By reciting the sacred mystery, the soul breaks all the seals and bonds that tie the counterfeiting spirit to it. The seals dissolve, the bonds unlock, and the counterfeiting spirit immediately separates from the soul, returning to the rulers who first assigned it.

At this moment, the soul invokes another mystery, which removes both the counterfeiting spirit and destiny, completely freeing itself from their influence. However, even though the soul has the power to release itself, it is important to understand that the counterfeiting spirit and destiny once had authority over it because they were given power under the rulers' commands.

When the time comes for a soul that has received the mysteries of the Light to leave the body, the receivers of the Light arrive to take it. These sacred beings, carrying the power of the mysteries the soul has obtained, take the soul away from the retributive receivers, who have finished their task and return to their duties under the rulers, continuing their role in the cycle of guiding souls.

The Soul's Journey Through the Realms

The receivers of the Light wrap the soul in wings and robes of light, transforming it into a radiant being ready for its journey upward. Unlike souls that are unprepared and thrown into chaos, souls that hold the mysteries are protected. They are guided safely through the regions of the rulers of the midst.

As the soul reaches these rulers, they appear in terrifying forms, with faces of fire and auras of great power, trying to intimidate the soul. However, the soul is not afraid, for it carries the knowledge of the mysteries. It speaks the sacred words of apology assigned to these rulers, proving that it is no longer bound to them. The rulers, overwhelmed by the power of the mysteries, bow before the soul, unable to stop its progress.

The soul then declares its freedom, saying:

"Take back your destiny. I will not return to your regions. I no longer belong to you. I ascend to my true home."

Breaking Free from the Counterfeiting Spirit

As the soul continues upward, it reaches the regions ruled by Fate. Here, it addresses the rulers once more, using the mystery that breaks the bond between itself and the counterfeiting spirit—the deceptive force that influenced it during life. With this declaration, the soul releases the counterfeiting spirit, saying:

"Here is your counterfeiting spirit. I will not return to your region. I am free from you forever."

At that moment, the counterfeiting spirit is sent back to the rulers who created it, severing its connection to the soul once and for all.

Ascending Beyond the Lower Realms

Now free, the receivers of the Light lift the soul even higher, beyond the realm of Fate and into the higher aeons. In each region, the soul offers the proper apologies and presents its seals, proving its right to pass.

As it approaches the powerful rulers of the aeons, including Adamas, the soul again declares its knowledge of the mysteries, showing the seals and speaking the words of passage. The rulers, seeing that the soul holds the necessary mysteries, allow it to continue its ascent.

The soul moves even further, passing through the regions of the rulers of the Left. At every step, it speaks the sacred words and presents the seals it has earned, ensuring its safe journey. The mysteries it has received act as its credentials, allowing it to cross these cosmic barriers without opposition.

The Final Steps to the Lightkingdom

The Savior assured the disciples that a detailed explanation of these mysteries, apologies, and seals would be revealed when the full expansion of the universe was explained. Until then, He encouraged them to continue mastering the mysteries, for they would serve as the key to entering the Light and protect them from the forces of the material and spiritual rulers.

Entering the Presence of the Virgin of Light

At last, the receivers of the Light bring the soul to the Virgin of Light. Here, the soul offers its seals and sings praises before her. The seven Virgins of Light join her in examining the soul, searching for the seals, baptisms, and sacred anointings that prove its worth.

Once the soul has been confirmed to have these marks, the Virgin of Light seals it once more. The receivers of the Light then baptize the soul, anointing it with the spiritual oil. Each of the seven Virgins of Light places their seal upon it, ensuring it is fully prepared to continue.

Reaching the Gate of Life

The receivers then bring the soul to Sabaōth, the Good, who stands at the Gate of Life in the region of those who belong to the Right. Sabaōth, also called 'Father,' listens as the soul offers its praises, seals, and apologies. He then places his own seals upon the soul, acknowledging its passage.

The soul then presents its knowledge, praises, and seals to all who dwell in the region of the Right. In response, the beings of the Right seal the soul with their own divine marks.

Guided by Melchisedec Into the Treasury of the Light

After this, the soul is welcomed by Melchisedec, the great Receiver of the Light, who resides in the region of the Right. He places his seal upon the soul, followed by all the receivers of Melchisedec, who do the same. Together, they guide the soul into the Treasury of the Light—

the sacred realm where the souls of the righteous dwell.

Here, the soul presents its praises and all the seals it has gathered from the realms of Light. In return, all those in the Treasury of the Light seal the soul with their marks, welcoming it into the final stage of its journey.

Reaching the Eternal Inheritance

Now fully prepared, the soul continues forward, entering the region of its eternal inheritance—the place where it will dwell in Light forever.

Chapter 99

After Jesus finished speaking, he asked his disciples, "Do you understand what I am explaining to you?"

Mary stepped forward again and said, "Yes, my Lord, I understand your words, and I will remember everything you have said. As I listened, four ideas came to my mind, and my inner spirit has guided me. It has even filled me with joy and longing to be closer to you. Now, my Lord, let me share these four thoughts with you.

The first thought comes from what you said: 'Now the soul must answer to all the rulers in the kingdom of Adamas. It must also give honor, respect, and praise to the beings in the region of the Light.' This reminds me of when they brought you a coin. You saw it was made of silver and copper, and you asked, 'Whose image is on this coin?' They answered, 'The king's.' Then you said, 'Give to the king what belongs to the king, and to God what belongs to God.' In the same way, when a soul learns the sacred mysteries, it must acknowledge the rulers and also honor the beings of the Light. The silver in the coin represents the soul's connection to the Light, while the copper represents the material world and the false spirit that tries to deceive it. This, my Lord, is my first thought.

My second thought is about what you said regarding a soul that receives the mysteries. You told us that when the soul enters the realm of the rulers, they become fearful because the soul carries the mystery of fear. The soul gives each ruler what they are due and offers honor, glory, and praise to those in the region of the Light. You also spoke of this before through our brother Paul, who said, 'Give taxes to those who require taxes, fear to those who deserve fear, tribute to those who require tribute, and honor to those who deserve honor.' This means that when a soul gains knowledge of the mysteries, it must offer what is due to every realm. That is my second thought.

My third thought comes from what you have told us before: 'The false spirit fights against the soul. It pushes the soul to do wrong and later makes it suffer for those wrongs. It is always working against the soul.' You also once said, 'A man's enemies are those in his own household.' In this case, the 'house' of the soul is the false spirit and destiny, which constantly lead the soul astray. This, my Lord, is my third thought.

My fourth thought is about what happens when the soul leaves the body. If it has not learned the mystery to free itself from the false spirit, it remains trapped. If it does not know this secret, the false spirit takes the soul to the Virgin of Light, who is the judge. She examines the soul, and if she finds that it has sinned and lacks the mysteries of the Light, she hands it over to one of her servants. That servant then places the soul into a new body, and it must continue the cycle of rebirth until it completes its journey. You once told us, 'Make peace with your enemy while you are still on the way with him, or he may hand you over to the judge, who will send you to the servant, and you will be thrown into prison.'"

Mary continued asking Jesus, "If a soul is sent to prison, it will not be freed until it has paid its full debt. This connects to your teaching that every soul that leaves the body but has not learned the mystery to break its bond with the false spirit will remain trapped. Without this knowledge, the false spirit takes the soul to the Virgin of Light, who then passes it to her servant. That servant casts the soul into the cycle of rebirth, and it cannot escape until it has completed its final journey. This, my Lord, is my fourth thought."

When Jesus heard Mary's words, he said, "Well spoken, blessed Mary. You understand the meaning of what I have said."

Mary then said, "But my Lord, I still have more questions. I want to understand fully so that my brothers and I can share this knowledge clearly with everyone."

Jesus, filled with kindness, replied, "Truly, I tell you, I will not only answer what you ask, but I will also reveal even more—things you have not yet thought of, things no one has ever imagined, and things even unknown to the lower gods. So, Mary, ask whatever is in your heart, and I will explain it to you clearly, without hidden meanings or riddles."

Chapter 100

Mary asked, "My Lord, how do baptisms remove sins? I remember you once said, 'The enforcers of judgment follow a soul and record every wrong it does so they can use it as evidence against the soul.' So, do the mysteries of baptism erase those sins from their records? Do they make these enforcers forget the sins? Please, Lord, explain this to us clearly. We want to fully understand how baptisms forgive sins."

Jesus replied, "That is a good question. The enforcers of judgment do indeed record all sins. Their job is to accuse souls that have not received the mysteries and to keep them in a place of chaos where they are punished. However, these enforcers are limited to the lower regions of chaos—they cannot rise to the higher realms. They also have no power over souls that come from above their domain.

"These enforcers are not allowed to harm or take control of souls that have received the mysteries. They cannot drag them into chaos or hold them in judgment. Instead, they only have power over those who have not received the mysteries, keeping them trapped in chaos. But for those who have received the mysteries, these enforcers have no authority. Even if a soul passes through their territory, they cannot stop or capture it.

"Now, listen carefully, and I will explain how baptism truly removes sins. When a soul sins in the world, the enforcers of judgment witness and record everything, preparing to use it as evidence when the soul is judged. In addition, the false spirit attached to the soul also keeps track of these sins, marking them directly onto the soul. These marks allow the rulers of punishment to recognize the sins and decide the level of punishment for the soul. This happens to every soul that has sinned.

"But when someone receives the mystery of baptism, this mystery acts like a powerful and purifying fire. It burns away all sins, reaching deep into the soul and erasing every mark and seal placed on it by the false spirit. Once the soul is completely purified, the fiery mystery moves into the body, forcing out all negative forces that were attached to it. It separates them, breaking the connection between the soul and the false spirit.

"The baptism divides these forces into two separate groups—one for the false spirit, destiny, and the body, and another for the soul and its divine power. The mystery of baptism remains between them, making sure they stay apart. It continually purifies and protects the soul so that it is no longer influenced by the physical body.

"This, Mary, is how the mysteries of baptism remove sins and cleanse the soul completely."

Chapter 101

After Jesus finished speaking, he turned to his disciples and asked, "Do you understand what I am telling you?"

Mary stepped forward and said, "Yes, my Lord, I want to understand all your words. You once told us a parable about the forgiveness of sins, saying, 'I have come to bring fire to the earth, and I wish it were already burning!' You also explained this clearly, saying, 'I must go through a baptism, and I am anxious until it is finished! Do you think I came to bring peace to the world? No, I came to bring division. From now on, families will be divided—five people in one house will be split, three against two and two against three.' These, my Lord, are your exact words.

"The meaning of your words, 'I have come to bring fire to the earth, and I wish it were already burning,' is that you have introduced the mysteries of baptism, and your hope is that they will remove all sins from the soul, completely purifying it. Then you said, 'I must go through a baptism, and I am anxious until it is finished!' This means that you will remain in the world until baptisms have purified all the souls meant to reach perfection.

"Also, when you said, 'Do you think I came to bring peace? No, but division. Families will be split, three against two and two against three,' you were referring to how baptism creates a division within a person's physical body. It separates the false spirit, the body, and destiny into one group, while placing the soul and its inner power into another. That is why you described it as three being against two, and two against three."

When Mary finished, Jesus said, "Well spoken, Mary. You are pure in spirit and full of light. Your interpretation is correct."

Mary continued, "My Lord, I have more questions. Please be

patient with me as I seek more understanding. We now clearly understand how baptism forgives sins. But I want to ask about the mysteries of the three spaces, the First Mystery, and the Ineffable. Do these also forgive sins in the same way as baptisms, or is it different?"

Jesus answered, "No, they do not work the same way as baptisms. The mysteries of the three spaces forgive all the sins a soul has committed in the realms of the rulers from the very beginning. These mysteries not only erase past sins but also forgive any future sins a soul might commit, up until a specific point. I will explain the limits of each mystery when I reveal how the universe expands.

"The mysteries of the First Mystery and the Ineffable go even further. They not only erase all sins in the realms of the rulers, but they also ensure that no sin will ever be counted against that soul again, for all eternity. This is because of the great power and glory of these mysteries."

After Jesus said this, he turned again to his disciples and asked, "Do you understand what I am telling you?"

Mary spoke again, "Yes, my Lord, I understand. Regarding what you said—'The mysteries of the three spaces forgive sins and cover the wrongdoing of souls'—this was also foretold by David, the prophet. He spoke of this truth when he said, 'Blessed are those whose sins are forgiven and whose wrongdoing is covered.'

"And when you said, 'The mysteries of the First Mystery and the Ineffable forgive all people who receive them, not only for past sins but also for any sins they may commit in the future, forever, as those sins will no longer be counted against them'—David also spoke of this, saying, 'Blessed are those whose sins the Lord will never count against them.' This means that anyone who receives these mysteries will never have their sins counted from this moment forward."

Jesus responded, "Well said, Mary. You are pure and full of wisdom.

You have given the true meaning of my words."

Mary then asked, "My Lord, if someone receives the mysteries of the First Mystery but later sins or makes a mistake, then repents and prays using the mystery they received, will they be forgiven?"

Jesus answered, "Truly, I tell you: If someone receives the mysteries of the First Mystery and then sins, if they repent and pray using that mystery up to twelve times, they will be forgiven each time.

"But if they sin again after those twelve times and continue to do wrong, then from that point on, they will no longer be forgiven through that mystery. They will not be able to repent unless they receive the mysteries of the Ineffable. The mysteries of the Ineffable are filled with compassion and will always forgive sins."

Chapter 102

Mary asked again, "My Lord, what if someone receives the mysteries of the First Mystery but later turns away and does wrong? If they die before they have a chance to repent, will they still inherit the kingdom because they once received the First Mystery?"

Jesus answered, "Truly, I tell you, if someone who has received the mysteries of the First Mystery falls into sin once, twice, or even three times, and they die without repenting, their punishment will be more severe than anyone else's. They will be trapped in the jaws of the great dragon in the outer darkness, suffering for a long time. Eventually, they will be frozen in torment and completely destroyed. This is because they were given the great gift of the First Mystery but did not stay faithful to it."

Mary then asked, "My Lord, what about someone who receives the mysteries of the Ineffable but later loses faith and makes mistakes? If they realize their wrongs while still alive and sincerely repent, how many times will they be forgiven?"

Jesus replied, "I tell you the truth, anyone who has received the mysteries of the Ineffable will always be forgiven if they truly repent. It doesn't matter how many times they sin—if they turn back with a sincere heart, without lies or excuses, and pray using the mysteries they have received, they will be forgiven. This is because the mysteries of the Ineffable are filled with endless mercy and will always grant forgiveness."

Mary asked again, "My Lord, what happens to those who receive the mysteries of the Ineffable but later turn away, sin, and lose their faith—only to die before they have repented? What will happen to them?"

Jesus answered, "Truly, I tell you, how fortunate are the souls who receive the mysteries of the Ineffable! But if they turn away, commit sins, and die without repenting, their punishment will be more severe than any other. Even if their souls were new and this was their first time in the world, they will not return to the cycle of rebirth. They will have no second chance to act or change. Instead, they will be cast into the outer darkness, where they will completely disappear and cease to exist forever."

Chapter 103

After Jesus finished speaking, he turned to his disciples and asked, "Do you understand what I am telling you?"

Mary stepped forward and said, "I understand the meaning of your words. My Lord, when you said, 'Blessed are those who receive the mysteries of the Ineffable. But if they turn away, sin, and abandon their faith, and if they die without repenting, they will no longer return to the cycle of rebirth or accomplish anything further. Instead, they will be cast into the outer darkness, where they will disappear forever,' it reminded me of something else you taught us. You once said, 'Salt is good, but if it loses its flavor, how can it be made salty again? It becomes useless—not even fit for soil or a garbage pile—so it is thrown away.'"

She paused, then continued, "This is the same idea, Lord. Blessed are all the souls who receive the mysteries of the Ineffable. But if they turn away, fall into sin, and refuse to repent, they become like salt that has lost its flavor—no longer useful. These souls can no longer return to a body or fulfill any purpose. From that moment, they are cast into the outer darkness, where they will be completely erased."

When Mary finished, Jesus replied, "You have spoken well, Mary. You are pure in spirit and full of light. Your understanding is correct."

Mary then asked, "My Lord, what about those who receive the mysteries of the First Mystery and the Ineffable, and who remain faithful—never abandoning their belief or acting with deception—but still make mistakes because of fate? If they realize their wrongdoing, repent, and pray using one of their mysteries, how many times will they be forgiven?"

Jesus answered Mary in front of his disciples, saying, "I tell you the truth, anyone who has received the mysteries of the Ineffable or the First Mystery, and who sins because of fate, will always be forgiven if they repent while still alive and continue practicing their mysteries. These mysteries are full of mercy and will always accept sincere repentance. That is why I have told you before that these mysteries not only erase all past sins but also do not hold future sins against those who receive them. From the moment they are forgiven, their sins are completely removed. This is why these mysteries accept repentance at any time and continue to forgive new sins.

"But if someone receives the mysteries of the Ineffable or the First

Mystery, then sins and dies without repenting, they will face the same fate as those who never repented at all. Their souls will be trapped in the jaws of the dragon in the outer darkness, where they will be completely erased and cease to exist forever. That is why I have told you that if those who receive the mysteries knew when they were going to die, they would stay watchful and avoid sin, ensuring that they could inherit the Light Kingdom forever."

Chapter 104

After Jesus finished speaking to his disciples, he asked, "Do you understand what I am telling you?"

Mary replied, "Yes, my Lord. I have listened carefully to everything you said. Earlier, you taught us, 'If a homeowner knew when a thief was coming in the night, he would stay awake and not let his house be broken into.'"

After she spoke, Jesus said, "Well said, Mary. You have understood the meaning of this teaching correctly."

Then Jesus turned back to his disciples and said, "Go and share this message with everyone who receives the mysteries of the Light. Tell them, 'Be mindful of your actions and do not fall into sin. Do not stack one wrongdoing upon another and leave this world without repenting, because such souls will lose their place in the Light Kingdom forever.'"

Hearing this, Mary said, "My Lord, the kindness of these mysteries, which offer forgiveness at all times, is truly incredible."

Jesus responded to Mary in front of his disciples, saying, "Think about this: Even a king in this world gives gifts to his people and sometimes shows mercy, even to those guilty of terrible crimes like murder or other serious offenses. If a human ruler can show compassion, then how much greater is the mercy of the mysteries of the higher realms? These mysteries belong to the Light Kingdom, which is far beyond anything in this world. If earthly kings can forgive, then imagine the boundless compassion of the Light, which lasts forever and has no limits."

Chapter 105

Jesus Tests Peter

Jesus continued speaking and said, "Imagine a king of this world giving a soldier a royal uniform and sending him to faraway lands. Even if that soldier commits terrible crimes, including murder, he won't be punished because he wears the king's robe. If this is true for an earthly king, how much more true is it for those who are clothed in the mysteries of the Ineffable and the First Mystery? These mysteries come from the highest authority, beyond all understanding, and they grant forgiveness and protection to all who receive them."

At that moment, Jesus saw a woman approaching with a repentant heart. He had baptized her three times, but she had not yet lived in a way that was worthy of the mysteries. Wanting to test Peter's kindness and willingness to forgive—just as he had taught his disciples—Jesus said to him, "Look at this soul. I have baptized her three times, yet she has not lived according to the Light's mysteries. Why then does she continue wasting this opportunity? Peter, now perform the mystery that removes souls from the inheritance of the Light. Cut her off from the Light's promise."

Jesus said this to see if Peter would show mercy despite her failures. After hearing these words, Peter answered, "My Lord, let her have one more chance. Let us offer her the higher mysteries, and if she proves herself worthy, then she may receive her place in the Light Kingdom. But if she still does not live up to it, only then should she be removed

272

from the Light's inheritance."

When Peter said this, Jesus saw that he truly had compassion and forgiveness, just as he had been taught. Then Jesus turned to the rest of his disciples and asked, "Do you understand the meaning behind this lesson and the story of this woman?"

Mary stepped forward and said, "My Lord, I understand the mysteries and the lesson shown through this woman's story. You once told us a parable about this: 'A man had a fig tree planted in his vineyard. Every year, he came looking for fruit but found none. So he said to the gardener, "For three years, I've been checking this tree, and it hasn't produced any fruit. Cut it down! Why let it take up space?" But the gardener replied, "Master, give it one more year. Let me dig around it and add fertilizer. If it produces fruit next year, then let it stay. But if it still does not, then you may cut it down."' My Lord, this parable has the same meaning as this woman's story."

Pleased with her understanding, Jesus said to Mary, "Well said. You have correctly understood the meaning of the parable and how it connects to this lesson."

Chapter 106

Mary continued asking Jesus, "My Lord, if someone has received mysteries but then failed to live according to them, later turned away, and sinned—then deeply and sincerely repents—what should we do? Should my brothers and sisters give them the same mystery again, or should they offer a lower one? Is either option allowed?"

Jesus answered, "I tell you the truth, neither the same mystery nor a lower one will respond to them or forgive their sins. Only a mystery that is greater than the one they previously received will hear their repentance and cleanse them. So, Mary, tell your brothers and sisters that they must offer this person a mystery that is higher than what they had before. They should accept their repentance and forgive them. The higher mystery will remove their sins because it is more powerful than the ones they had before. The previous mysteries cannot forgive them anymore because they have already moved beyond them. But the greater mysteries, being stronger, will accept their repentance and cleanse them completely.

"However, if someone has already received three mysteries from either the two outer spaces or the third, innermost space, and then turns away and sins, no mystery—whether higher or lower—will hear them or help them repent. In this case, only the mystery of the First Mystery and the mysteries of the Ineffable have the power to hear their repentance, accept it, and forgive their sins. Only these highest mysteries have the mercy and compassion to cleanse them."

Mary then asked, "My Lord, what about someone who has received two or three mysteries from either the second or third space but has never turned away or sinned? If they have remained faithful, honest, and true, without any deception—what will happen to them?"

Jesus replied, "Anyone who has received mysteries from the second or third space and has remained faithful, never turning away or sinning, can receive mysteries from any space they desire—whether from the first, the last, or anywhere in between. Because they have remained steadfast and true, there is no limit to what mysteries they may receive. Their faithfulness gives them full access to all mysteries without restriction."

Chapter 107

Mary continued and asked, "My Lord, if someone has come to know God and received the mysteries of the Light but later turns away, sins, and lives without repentance, and another person has never known God or received these mysteries and also lives in sin, what will happen to them when they die? Which one will face a harsher judgment?"

Jesus answered, "I tell you the truth, the person who knew God and received the mysteries of the Light but still chose to sin without repenting will face much greater suffering in judgment. Their punishment will be far more severe than that of the person who never knew God or received the mysteries. Those who have been given knowledge and understanding carry a greater responsibility, and their judgment will reflect that. Let those who are willing to listen take this lesson to heart."

When Jesus finished speaking, Mary stepped forward again and said, "My Lord, I understand your words clearly. I see how this connects to what you have taught us before. You have shown us that receiving the Light brings great responsibility, and turning away from that knowledge leads to a far greater judgment than ignorance ever could."

Chapter 108

Mary continued speaking to Jesus and said, "My Lord, you have explained everything clearly. You have taught us about those who delay, thinking they have many lifetimes to receive the mysteries. Your words leave no doubt. When you said, 'If a servant knows what his master wants but does not prepare or follow his instructions, he will be punished severely. But if another servant does wrong without knowing better, his punishment will be lighter. To whom much is given, much will be required, and to whom more is entrusted, even more will be expected,' you made it clear, my Lord, that greater knowledge comes with greater responsibility. If someone knows the truth and receives the mysteries of the Light but still chooses to turn away and sin, their judgment will be much harsher than that of someone who was never given the same knowledge. That is the meaning of your words."

Mary then continued asking, "My Lord, if faith and the mysteries are already revealed, and if souls continue to be reborn into the world, what happens to those who keep delaying? If they keep putting off receiving the mysteries, believing they have more lifetimes to do so, won't they risk losing their chance forever? Isn't that a dangerous mistake?"

Jesus answered, speaking to his disciples, "Spread this message to everyone: Do not wait. Seek now to receive the mysteries of the Light in this time of difficulty so that you may enter the Light Kingdom. Do not think you have time to delay, or that you can wait for another life to receive them.

"Those who put it off do not understand how urgent this is. They do not know when the number of perfect souls will be complete. When that moment comes, I will close the gates of the Light. After that, no one else will be able to enter, and no one inside will be able to leave. This will mark the completion of the First Mystery—the very reason the universe was created. And I am that First Mystery.

"When that time comes, no soul will have another chance to enter the Light. No one will be able to receive the mysteries anymore. When the number of perfect souls is reached, I will purify the world with fire. This fire will cleanse everything—the realms, the skies, the veils, the earth, and everything that exists in the material world. But even while this purification is happening, people will still be living on the earth, unaware of how close the end truly is."

"In those days, faith will be even more obvious, and the mysteries will become even clearer to those still on earth. Many souls will continue to be reborn, moving through different lives and bodies. Some of them will have heard my teachings and my call in this present time. They will return in another life, thinking they still have time to receive the mysteries of the Light. But when they finally come forward, the number of the perfect souls will already be complete. They will reach the gates of the Light, hoping to enter, only to realize that it is too late. The First Mystery will have been fulfilled, and the final purpose of the universe will be revealed. By then, I will have already shut the gates, and no one else will be allowed to enter or leave."

"These souls will cry out at the gates, saying, 'Lord, let us in!' But I will answer them, 'I do not know you or where you came from.' They will plead, 'But we received your mysteries and followed your teachings! We did everything you commanded. You taught us as we walked the roads, and we listened!' But I will say, 'I do not know who you are. You continued to do wrong, even until now. Leave me and go into the outer darkness.'

"At that moment, those souls will be sent into the outer darkness, where they will suffer, crying out in anguish.

"That is why you must proclaim this message to the whole world: 'Give everything you have to seeking the Light. Let go of your attachment to material things so that you may receive the mysteries before the number of perfect souls is reached. Do this so that you will not find yourselves locked out of the Light Kingdom and cast into the outer darkness.'

"Let those who are willing to listen hear and understand these words."

When Jesus finished speaking, Mary stepped forward again and said, "My Lord, not only has my heart understood, but my soul has fully absorbed your words. When you said, 'Proclaim this to the people of the world—tell them to seek the mysteries of the Light now so that they may inherit the Light Kingdom,' I have grasped its meaning completely. I am ready to share this wisdom with others."

The Fourth Book of Pistis Sophia

Chapter 109

Mary asked Jesus, "My Lord, what is the outer darkness like? How many places of punishment exist within it?"

Jesus answered, "The outer darkness is a massive and terrifying dragon. Its tail is curled around and held inside its mouth, surrounding the entire world and stretching beyond its borders. Inside this great dragon, there are twelve enormous dungeons, each ruled by a different being. These rulers all have different appearances from one another.

"The first dungeon is ruled by a being with the face of a crocodile, whose tail is also in its mouth. From this dragon's jaws come ice, dust, freezing cold, and many diseases. In its region, this ruler is called 'Enchthonin.'

"The second dungeon is ruled by a being with the face of a cat, and its true name in that region is 'Charachar.'

"The third dungeon is overseen by a ruler with the face of a dog, and it is called 'Archaroch.'

"The fourth dungeon is controlled by a being with the face of a serpent, known in its region as 'Achrōchar.'

"The fifth dungeon is ruled by a being with the face of a black bull, and its name in its region is 'Marchūr.'

"The sixth dungeon has a ruler with the face of a wild boar, called 'Lamchamōr.'

"The seventh dungeon is ruled by a being with the face of a bear, whose true name in its region is 'Luchar.'

"The eighth dungeon is controlled by a ruler with the face of a vulture, known as 'Laraoch.'

"The ninth dungeon has a ruler with the face of a basilisk, and its name in its region is 'Archeoch.'

"The tenth dungeon is home to many rulers, each with seven dragon heads. The leader of them all is called 'Xarmarōch.'

"The eleventh dungeon is also filled with many rulers, but each of them has seven heads with cat-like faces. The highest ruler in this region is called 'Rōchar.'

"The twelfth and final dungeon contains an enormous number of rulers, each with seven dog-faced heads. The most powerful ruler of this dungeon is known as 'Chrēmaōr.'"

Jesus then explained the terrifying nature of the outer darkness, revealing the structure of its dungeons and their dreadful rulers.

"All of these rulers live within the dragon of the outer darkness. Their names are not fixed—they change every hour, just as their faces do. Their constantly shifting forms reflect the chaos and horror of the outer darkness.

"Each of the twelve dungeons has a doorway that opens upward to the regions above. The dragon of the outer darkness contains these twelve dungeons, and each one has its own entrance leading upwards. At every doorway, there is an angel stationed as a guardian, placed there to maintain order and prevent any disturbances.

"These angels were not randomly assigned. They were put there by Yew, the First Man, who oversees the Light. Yew is also the messenger of the First Commandment, and with great wisdom, he established these angelic guardians to watch over the dragon and its dungeons. Their purpose is to ensure that the dragon and the rulers within do not rise up in rebellion or disrupt their designated places."

Chapter 110

After Jesus finished speaking, Mary Magdalene asked, "My Lord, will the souls who are sent to that terrible place enter through the twelve doors of the dungeons, each according to their punishment?"

Jesus replied, "No, souls do not enter the dragon through those doors. The ones who will be sent into the dungeons of the outer darkness are those who have committed the worst sins and never repented. These include those who blaspheme, spread false teachings, or commit unnatural acts. It also includes atheists, murderers, adulterers, sorcerers, and anyone who lives in wickedness without seeking forgiveness. Additionally, souls that have completed all their lifetimes but never repented will also be sent there.

"When their final lifetime is over, these unrepentant souls—along with all the others I have described—will be pulled into the dragon's grasp. They will enter through his tail, and then he will close his mouth around it, trapping them inside. From that moment on, they will be imprisoned in the dungeons of the outer darkness.

"The dragon of the outer darkness has twelve true names, each written on one of the doors of his dungeons. These names are different from each other, yet so closely connected that saying one is like speaking them all. I will reveal these names to you when I explain the deeper mysteries of the universe. This is the nature of the outer darkness—a great dragon that captures the souls of the wicked."

Hearing this, Mary asked, "My Lord, are the punishments in the dragon's dungeons worse than all other judgments?"

Jesus answered, "Yes, they are the most terrible of all. The souls sent there will suffer endlessly. They will be frozen by unbearable cold, pounded by violent hail, and burned by a fire that is far beyond anything in this world. But their suffering won't last forever. At the end of time, when the universe is transformed, these souls will be completely destroyed. The extreme cold and raging fire will consume them entirely, and they will disappear forever."

Mary was filled with sorrow and said, "What a terrible fate for those who sin! My Lord, tell me, is the fire in the human world more intense, or is the fire in Amente stronger?"

Jesus answered, "I tell you the truth: The fire in Amente is nine times hotter than the fire in the human world.

"The fire in the punishments of the great chaos is nine times stronger than the fire in Amente.

"The fire in the judgments of the rulers in the middle regions is nine times more powerful than the fire in the great chaos.

"But the fire in the dragon of the outer darkness, along with the flames in all its punishments, is seventy times stronger than the fire in all the other judgments combined."

Chapter 111

When Jesus finished speaking, Mary Magdalene and the disciples were deeply troubled. Mary clutched her chest, wept, and cried out along with the others, saying, "How terrible it is for sinners! Their punishments are many and severe!"

She then moved closer to Jesus, fell at his feet, kissed them, and said, "My Lord, please be patient with me as I ask more questions. Do not be upset that I keep asking, but I want to understand everything fully."

Jesus, with kindness, replied, "Ask whatever you wish to know, and I will explain it to you clearly, without hidden meanings or parables."

Encouraged, Mary asked, "My Lord, suppose a righteous person has followed all the mysteries and lived a good life, but he has a close relative—someone he loves—who is sinful. This person has done all kinds of wrongs, never repented, and wasted his time in the world. If he dies without asking for forgiveness and is sent to the outer darkness to face severe punishment, is there any way to save him? Can we help his soul escape such suffering and be reborn into a righteous life, where he may find the Light and have the chance to reach the kingdom?"

Jesus answered, "If someone has truly lived in sin, refused to repent, and reached the end of their lifetimes without turning to righteousness, then when they die, they will be taken to the outer darkness. However, if you wish to help such a soul and give them a chance to find the Light, you must perform the sacred mystery of the Ineffable, which can forgive sins at any time. After performing the ritual, you must say this prayer:

'The soul of [name of the person], whom I carry in my heart, whether suffering in the dungeons of the outer darkness, trapped in the dragon's punishment, or enduring torment elsewhere, let it be set free. If this soul has completed its cycle of rebirth, let it be taken before the Virgin of Light. May she seal it with the mark of the Ineffable and place it in a righteous body for its next life. Let this body find the mysteries of the Light, so the soul may grow in goodness, rise higher, and reach the Light kingdom. And if this soul has already finished its journey through reincarnation, let it be brought before the seven virgins of the Light, who oversee baptisms. May they prepare it, seal it with the sign of the Ineffable kingdom, and allow it to enter the orders of the Light.'

This is the prayer you must say when performing the mystery.

I tell you the truth: If the soul for which you pray is trapped in the dragon's grasp in the outer darkness, he will release it, letting it go free. If it is caught in the judgments of the rulers, the receivers of

Melchisedec will come quickly to rescue it. No matter where the soul is suffering—whether in the dragon's punishment or under the rulers' judgment—the receivers of Melchisedec will take it and bring it to the region of the Midst, where it will stand before the Virgin of Light.

If the soul has not yet completed its cycle of rebirth, the Virgin of Light will mark it with a sacred seal and send it into a righteous body for its next life. In this new body, it will have the chance to find the mysteries of the Light, live righteously, and one day inherit the Light kingdom."

Chapter 112

The Pathways of Light and the Journey of the Soul

"When a soul has completed all its lifetimes, the Virgin of Light carefully examines it. Since the soul has finished its journey, she does not send it to punishment. Instead, she entrusts it to the seven virgins of the Light. These seven virgins evaluate the soul, baptize it with their sacred blessings, anoint it with spiritual oil, and lead it into the Treasury of the Light. There, the soul is placed in the last order of the Light, where it will stay until all perfected souls ascend together. When the time comes to open the veils of the higher realms, the soul is purified once more, cleansed of all remaining impurities, and lifted into the first Savior's order within the Treasury of the Light."

When Jesus finished speaking, Mary said, "My Lord, I have heard you say that those who receive the mysteries of the Ineffable or the First Mystery become beams of pure light. They move freely through all regions until they reach their eternal home."

Jesus replied, "Yes, Mary. If someone receives the mystery while they are still alive and then leaves their body, they truly become radiant streams of light. These beams of light move through all realms without obstacles until they reach their destined place.

"But if a sinner dies without repenting, and then someone performs the mystery of the Ineffable on their behalf to free them from punishment—either so they may be reborn in a righteous body or be placed in the last order of the Light—their journey is different. These souls cannot move as beams of light because they did not receive the mystery themselves. Instead, the receivers of Melchisedec take charge of them, guiding and escorting them to the Virgin of Light.

"In these cases, the messengers of judgment, assigned by the rulers, move quickly. They carry the souls from one guardian to the next, ensuring that they reach the Virgin of Light without delay."

Chapter 113

Mary continued speaking to Jesus, saying, "My Lord, suppose someone receives the mysteries of the Light but later becomes careless. He forgets to say the prayer that removes impurity from his food and drink, and because of this, he becomes tied to the forces of fate. If he sins again after the mysteries have stopped protecting him—due to his own neglect—and he dies without repenting or receiving the higher mysteries that could forgive him, what will happen to him?

"What if we later learn that this person has been taken into the dragon of the outer darkness because of his sins? If he has no one on earth to help him—no one to perform the mystery of the Ineffable to save him from suffering and bring him to the Light—what will become of him? How long will he remain in the dragon's punishment before he is freed? My Lord, I ask this because such a soul may have suffered greatly in life, faced hardships, and tried to follow the truth, even if imperfectly.

"So, Lord, I beg for your mercy. Do not let any soul, whether they are our loved ones or strangers, be left in such a terrible fate. Have compassion on those who may find themselves in this condition, for you hold the power over the doors of the universe. Your mysteries extend over all things. Show kindness to these souls, Lord, because even if they called upon your name for only a single day with true faith, without deceit, they deserve your mercy. Grant them your grace and give them rest."

Jesus looked at Mary with deep compassion and blessed her for her words. Then he said to her with great kindness, "Mary, if someone finds themselves in the situation you described, while they are still alive, give them the mystery of one of the twelve sacred names connected to the dungeons of the dragon of the outer darkness. I will reveal these names to you once I have finished explaining the universe from both the inside and the outside.

"Anyone who learns one of these twelve names—whether they are among the worst sinners, whether they once received the mysteries of the Light but turned away, or even if they never followed the mysteries at all—if they die without repenting, they may be sent into the depths of the dragon's punishment. There, they will suffer through cycles of torment.

"But if, while trapped in the dragon's grasp, they remember and speak one of these sacred names, something extraordinary will happen. The entire dragon will tremble violently, its body shaking in turmoil. The door of the dungeon where the soul is held will suddenly open, releasing them. The ruler of that dungeon will be overwhelmed by the power of the name and will have no choice but to cast the soul out, setting them free.

"When this happens, the angels of Yew, the First Man—who oversee the dungeons—will quickly take action. They will seize the freed soul and bring it to the presence of Yew, who serves as the messenger of the First Commandment. There, the soul will be examined. Yew will determine whether the soul has completed its lifetimes and whether it is lawful for it to return to the world. However, for souls sent to the outer darkness, returning to life in the world is usually not permitted.

"If Yew finds that the soul has not yet completed its cycles, his receivers will take it into their care. They will then perform the mystery of the Ineffable on its behalf, transferring it into a righteous body where it will have the chance to seek the mysteries of the Light and inherit the Light Kingdom.

"But if Yew confirms that the soul has already completed its journey and finds that it does not carry the sacred sign of the Ineffable, he will still show mercy. He will bring the soul before the seven virgins of the Light, who will baptize and purify it. However, because it lacks the sign of the Ineffable, the virgins will not anoint it with spiritual oil or grant it the seals of inheritance. The soul will be allowed to enter the Treasury of the Light but will be placed separately from those who received the full inheritance.

"Even though these souls do not receive the same rewards as those who carried the sign and seal, they are still saved from all punishments. They will remain in a quiet part of the Treasury of the Light, apart from the main orders, until the time of the universe's final ascension. When the veils of the Treasury are lifted, these souls will be purified again with great care. They will then be given mysteries and placed in the last order of the Treasury of the Light, ensuring that they are fully freed from judgment and suffering."

When Jesus finished speaking, he turned to his disciples and asked, "Do you understand what I am telling you?"

Mary stepped forward and answered, "My Lord, I understand your words. This is what you told us before in a parable when you said,

'Make for yourselves a friend out of the Mammon of unrighteousness, so that if you are left behind, he may receive you into the everlasting tents.' My Lord, isn't the Mammon of unrighteousness the dragon of the outer darkness?

"The meaning of this teaching is now clear: If someone learns the mystery of one of the names of the dragon of the outer darkness, even if they are trapped there or have completed their lifetimes, when they speak the name, they will be set free. They will rise from the darkness and be received into the Treasury of the Light. This, my Lord, is the true meaning of your words."

Jesus looked at Mary with great love and said, "You have spoken well, Mary. You are pure in spirit and full of wisdom. What you have said is the true understanding of my teaching."

Chapter 114

Mary continued asking, "My Lord, does the dragon of the outer darkness ever come into this world, or does he stay apart from it?"

Jesus answered, "When the light of the sun shines outside the world, it hides and blocks the dragon's darkness. But when the sun sets and disappears below the world, the dragon's darkness remains, filling the space where the sun's light has withdrawn. At night, this darkness spreads like a mist or smoke. If the sun did not return to shine its light, the world would not be able to withstand the full force of the dragon's darkness. Without the sun, the world would collapse into ruin."

Mary then asked again, "My Lord, I still have more questions. Please help me understand everything. What causes a person to sin?"

Jesus replied, "It is the rulers of Fate who influence a person and lead them toward sin."

Mary asked, "My Lord, do these rulers of Fate physically come down into the world to make people sin?"

Jesus explained, "No, they do not come into the world in a physical way. Instead, when an old soul is preparing to return to the world through the paths controlled by the rulers of Fate, these rulers play a role in shaping its journey.

"These rulers exist in a region called the head of the æons, also known as the kingdom of Adamas, which is near the Virgin of Light. When a soul is about to be born into the world, they give it a cup of forgetfulness. This cup contains a mixture that makes the soul forget everything it has learned in past lives, including the lessons and punishments it once experienced. Along with this forgetfulness, the cup also carries seeds of wickedness—desires and influences that pull the soul toward wrongdoing.

"The moment the soul drinks from this cup, something strange happens. A shadowy copy of the soul is created, known as the counterfeiting spirit. This spirit mirrors the soul in every way and attaches itself to it, becoming its unseen companion throughout life."

Jesus continued, "If the soul is a new one—created from the sweat, tears, or breath of the rulers—then the process is different. The five great rulers of Fate take sweat from all the rulers of the æons and mix it together, dividing it into portions to form new souls.

"If the soul is formed from the leftovers of the purification of the Light, then Melchisedec, the great Receiver of the Light, gathers these remnants from the rulers. The five great rulers of Fate then knead this material together and shape it into different souls. Each ruler contributes something to the soul's creation, which is why all of them share a connection to it.

"When the five rulers portion and form souls, they usually use the sweat of the rulers. But if the soul comes from the purification of the Light, Melchisedec retrieves it. If it is made from the tears or breath of the rulers, the five rulers shape it into separate souls.

"For older souls returning to the world, the ruler at the head of the æons personally prepares the cup of forgetfulness. This cup is mixed with the seed of wickedness and given to every soul passing through. The cup of forgetfulness becomes the counterfeiting spirit attached to that soul. This spirit stays outside the soul, acting like a covering or shadow, copying the soul's every detail and surrounding it as it moves through life."

The five great rulers of Fate, along with the rulers of the sun and the moon, breathe life into the soul. When this happens, a small part of my own divine power, which the last Helper placed in the Mixture, enters the soul through their breath. This divine power exists separately within the soul, untouched by any outside force, and serves a specific purpose in the divine plan. It allows the soul to think, understand, and seek the Light from above.

This divine power is just like the soul in every way—it shares its form and nature. But unlike the counterfeiting spirit, which stays outside the soul, this divine power remains inside it. From the beginning, I commanded that it would always be part of the soul to fulfill the purpose of the First Mystery's divine plan.

When the time comes for the universe to expand, I will reveal all of this to you in greater detail. I will explain the true nature of the soul—how it is created, which rulers take part in its formation, and the different types of souls that exist. I will also tell you how many beings shape the soul and reveal their names. I will explain how the counterfeiting spirit and destiny are prepared, as well as the soul's original name before it is purified and the name it receives once it has been cleansed.

I will also reveal the name of the counterfeiting spirit and the name of destiny. I will tell you about all the bonds and chains that the rulers use to keep the counterfeiting spirit attached to the soul. Additionally, I will reveal the names of the rulers who shape souls inside bodies and explain how each soul is formed. I will describe the different types of souls, including those of humans, birds, wild animals, and reptiles. I will even explain the souls of the rulers who are sent into the world, so you can have complete knowledge.

After I have told you all this, I will explain why it all came to be.

Listen carefully, and I will describe the light and the soul as clearly as I can. The five great rulers of Fate, the deceptive spirit, time, and the rulers of the sun and moon breathe life into the soul. During this process, a portion of my own power enters the soul, as I have just explained. This power stays inside the soul, giving it strength and independence. Meanwhile, the deceptive spirit is placed outside the soul, keeping watch over it and taking control.

The rulers bind this deceptive spirit to the soul with seals and chains, making sure it stays firmly attached. Because of this, the soul is forced into wrongdoing, following its selfish desires and serving the rulers who control it. It remains under their influence as the body changes and moves through life, always being pulled toward sin and worldly desires.

That is why I have brought the mysteries into this world. These mysteries exist to break the chains of the deceptive spirit and remove the seals that trap the soul. They are here to set the soul free, releasing it from the grip of the deceptive spirit and its control.

Chapter 115

Salome felt unsure about what she had heard and struggled to understand it. Seeing her confusion, Mary tried to help her see the truth more clearly.

Jesus spoke and said, "Let go of your earthly parents, the rulers of this world, so that I can transform them into pure light and lead them to the eternal kingdom of their true Father—the First Source, the First Mystery, forever. This is why I have told you before: 'Whoever does not leave behind father and mother to follow me is not worthy of me.' What I meant is that you must release yourself from the rulers who act as your parents so that I can make you children of the First Mystery for all eternity."

After Jesus finished speaking, Salome stepped forward and asked, "My Lord, if our parents are the rulers of this world, then how can the Law of Moses say, 'Whoever abandons their father and mother must be put to death'? Doesn't this contradict what you just told us?"

As Salome spoke, Mary Magdalene felt a deep understanding awaken within her. She turned to Jesus and said, "My Lord, may I explain this to my sister Salome and help her understand?"

Jesus, recognizing Mary's wisdom, smiled and said, "Yes, Mary. Speak and reveal the answer to her question."

Encouraged by his words, Mary stepped forward, gently placed her hands on Salome's shoulders, and said, "My dear sister, the words you quoted from the Law of Moses—'Whoever abandons their father and mother must be put to death'—are not about our physical parents, our souls, or even the deceptive spirit that exists within us. These things were created by the rulers of this world and belong to them.

"But the Law is actually speaking about something much greater—the divine power that comes from the Savior, the light within us that gives us true life."

Mary continued, her voice steady and full of understanding, "The meaning of this commandment is this: Anyone who turns away from the Savior and rejects his mysteries will not only die physically but will also face spiritual destruction. Their soul will be lost. This is the real meaning behind the words of the Law."

Hearing this, Salome's heart softened, and she stepped forward to embrace Mary. With gratitude shining in her eyes, she said, "Truly, the Savior has given you great wisdom. I pray that he grants me the same understanding."

When Jesus heard Mary's explanation, he looked at her with great love and called her blessed in front of all his disciples. Then he turned to her and said, "Listen carefully, Mary, as I reveal who is responsible for leading people into sin and deception.

"The rulers of the æons attach the counterfeiting spirit to every soul. They do not do this just to let it exist but to make sure that it constantly pushes the soul toward sin and wrongdoing. The counterfeiting spirit follows the orders of these rulers, acting as their servant.

"They command it, saying, 'When the soul leaves the body, do not leave it in peace. Take hold of it and drag it through every place of judgment, one after another, as punishment for the sins you led it to commit. Make sure it suffers in each place of judgment so that it cannot rise to the Light or escape the cycle of rebirth.'

"The rulers continue their instructions, telling the counterfeiting spirit, 'Do not stop unless the soul speaks the mysteries of the Light and breaks all the seals and chains we have placed upon it. If the soul speaks the mysteries, undoes the seals, and declares its freedom, then let it go, because it belongs to the Light and no longer has anything to do with us. From that moment on, you will have no power over it.

"'But if the soul does not speak the mysteries, does not break the seals, and does not declare its freedom, then you must seize it and make sure it does not escape. Drag it through the punishments and all the places of judgment as payment for the sins you caused it to commit. In the end, bring the soul before the Virgin of Light, who will decide its fate and send it back into another body to begin the cycle again.'

"The great rulers of Fate are the ones who control this process. They keep souls trapped under their power, making sure they move through endless cycles of judgment and suffering. These rulers hand the souls over to the counterfeiting spirit, which keeps them lost in the illusions and hardships of the material world. This prevents them from rising to the Light of the Heights or finding true freedom."

The rulers call upon their servants—365 in total—and give them the soul and the counterfeiting spirit, which are bound together. The counterfeiting spirit forms an outer layer around the soul, while the soul's core power sits deep inside, giving it life and stability. This inner power helps both the soul and the counterfeiting spirit function properly. The rulers then instruct their servants, saying, "This is the form and pattern you must place into the body that will be created from the material world."

They continue, explaining, "First, place the soul's core power inside, as this power keeps it upright and stable. Next, place the soul itself, and finally, add the counterfeiting spirit, which will remain as the outermost layer, bound to the soul."

Following these orders, the rulers' servants prepare the different components—the core power, the soul, and the counterfeiting spirit. They bring them down to the world and place them in the region controlled by the rulers of the midst. These rulers oversee the counterfeiting spirit, while destiny—represented by Moira—is set into motion to guide the person through life until their appointed death. The rulers of Fate determine this destiny and attach it to the soul as part of its earthly existence.

The servants of the sphere then bind the soul, its power, the counterfeiting spirit, and destiny together. They divide these parts into two portions and look for a man and a woman in the world—people they have already marked as destined to receive these portions. When they find the right individuals, they transfer one portion to the man and the other to the woman. This transfer happens in different ways, such as through food, air, water, or other substances entering the body.

Jesus continued, "I will explain all of this to you—how every soul is formed, what type it is, and how it enters bodies. Whether a soul is placed in a human, a bird, an animal, a reptile, or any other creature, I will reveal the process by which it is assigned to a body. I will explain how all of this happens according to the unfolding of the universe."

"When the servants of the rulers divide the portions, they secretly place one into the woman and the other into the man. This process ensures that the destined individuals will come together according to the signs given to them. Through this union, the soul, its power, and the counterfeiting spirit become further entangled in the physical world, continuing the cycle of birth and life in the material realm."

The Soul's Incarnation

Even if the soul and counterfeiting spirit are placed far apart, they are pulled toward each other by a force that aligns them in the material world. The counterfeiting spirit, which is in the man, moves toward the portion that was placed within his body. It then lifts this portion and directs it into the womb of the woman, guiding it toward the part that carries the seed of wickedness.

At that moment, the 365 servants of the rulers descend into the woman's womb and begin their work. They join the two portions— the soul and the counterfeiting spirit—inside the womb, starting the process of forming a new life. They also manage the blood from the food and drink the woman consumes, gathering it for forty days to prepare for the body's formation. After these forty days, they mix the blood thoroughly, using it as the foundation for the developing body inside the womb.

After this initial period, they spend another thirty days shaping the physical body. They carefully form its structure to resemble the shape of a human. During this time, different celestial beings, known as decans, each take responsibility for forming different parts of the body. Jesus said, "I will tell you the names of these decans and their roles when I explain the mysteries of the universe."

Once the seventy days are complete and the body is fully formed, the next phase begins. First, they summon the counterfeiting spirit and place it inside the body. Then, they call the soul and position it alongside the counterfeiting spirit. After that, they place the core power deep within the soul, making it an essential part of the being. Lastly, they assign destiny to follow the body throughout life, influencing it from the outside but not mixing directly with the other elements.

After completing these steps, the servants seal all these parts together using special seals given to them by the rulers. These seals are placed on the body at key moments in its creation and throughout its existence.

- The day the elements entered the womb is sealed on the left hand.
- The day the body's formation was completed is sealed on the right hand.
- The moment the rulers gave the soul and spirit to the servants is marked at the center of the skull.
- The day the soul was released from the rulers is marked on the left side of the skull.
- The moment the body was fully formed and received a soul is sealed on the right side of the skull.
- The attachment of the counterfeiting spirit to the soul is marked on the back of the skull.

- The infusion of power into the body by the rulers is sealed in the brain at the center of the head and deep within the body, including the heart.
- The number of years the soul is meant to live in the body is sealed on the forehead.

Through these steps, the rulers ensure that the soul, its power, and the counterfeiting spirit are tightly bound together in the physical world, continuing the cycle of life and destiny.

Every important event and moment in a person's life is marked by these seals, preserving the details of how their body was formed and their fate. I will reveal the names of these seals to you when the universe expands and explain why these processes take place. Once you understand these mysteries, you will see that I am the very essence of this divine plan.

This is how the servitors complete the creation of a person. After placing all the seals on the body, they finish their work, following the instructions given to them by the rulers as part of the grand design of the universe.

Here's how the process works: The servitors take the unique signature of the seals, which holds the person's identity, and bring it to the rulers of judgment. These rulers oversee punishments and determine each soul's fate. They then pass this information to their assigned receivers, who are responsible for taking the soul from the body at the right time. The signature of the seals acts as a record, allowing the receivers to know exactly when the soul must leave the body and when the physical body is ready to be born.

The receivers also pass this knowledge to their servitors, who closely observe the soul throughout its life. These servitors remain near the soul, keeping track of all its actions, sins, and mistakes. They work alongside the counterfeiting spirit, documenting every wrongdoing. This detailed record is later used to determine the punishments the soul will face in judgment. The severity of its punishment is based on the choices and actions it made while alive.

After delivering the unique signature of the seals to the rulers of judgment, the servitors return to their other tasks, carrying out the duties assigned to them by the rulers of Fate. The cycle continues, and when the time for birth arrives—after the months of pregnancy are complete—the child is born into the world.

At birth, the different components within the newborn are still small. The soul is faint, the counterfeiting spirit is weak, and the core power within the soul is minimal. However, destiny, which exists outside the body, is fully formed and strong. Unlike the other components, destiny does not mix with the soul, body, or counterfeiting spirit. Instead, it follows the person throughout their life, staying close until the moment the soul must leave the body. Destiny determines the kind of death the individual will face, as planned by the rulers of Fate.

If a person is meant to die from an animal attack, destiny ensures they cross paths with a wild beast. If their fate is to be bitten by a snake, destiny leads the snake to them. If they are meant to fall into a pit, drown in water, or suffer another type of accident, destiny arranges the circumstances to make sure it happens as planned. Whether the death is quick or slow, peaceful or painful, destiny is responsible for making sure it happens as it was decided.

This is the sole purpose of destiny—to bring about the appointed death of every person. It has no other task or function. From birth, destiny follows each person closely, watching and guiding them until the moment they leave the world. It remains unseen but is always there, waiting until the time comes for the person to meet their end.

Chapter 116

Mary asked Jesus, "Is everything that happens to a person—whether good or bad, whether sin, death, or even life—already decided by the rulers of Fate? Is there no way to escape what has been set for them?"

Jesus answered, "I tell you the truth, everything that Fate has planned for each person—whether blessings, mistakes, or even the way they die—will happen as it has been decided. The rulers of Fate control the world, and whatever they have set in motion unfolds as planned."

"That is why," he continued, "I have brought the keys to the mysteries of the kingdom of heaven into the world. Without these mysteries, no person could ever be saved. Without their power, not even the righteous could enter the kingdom of the Light. Sinners would remain trapped by their wrongdoings, and even those who live righteously would have no way to rise beyond this world."

"This is why I have brought these mysteries—to free those who believe in me and follow my teachings. These mysteries give me the power to break the bonds and seals that the rulers of Fate have placed on them. Through these mysteries, I bind them instead to the Light—to its seals, garments, and divine order. So, whoever I free from the chains of the world will also be free in the heavenly realms. Likewise, whoever I connect to the Light's mysteries in this world will be connected to the eternal inheritance of the Light above."

"I have come at this time to bring these mysteries, not just for sinners but also for the righteous. Sinners need them to break free from the power of the rulers, and the righteous need them to ascend into the Light. Without these mysteries, no one—whether good or bad—can enter the kingdom of the Light."

"This is why I have not kept these truths hidden but have spoken them openly for all to hear. I have not separated sinners from the righteous in my message. Instead, I have shared it with everyone, saying: 'Seek, and you will find. Knock, and the door will be opened for you. For everyone who truly seeks will find, and to everyone who knocks, the door will be opened.' I have called all people to search for the mysteries of the kingdom of the Light because these mysteries will cleanse them, make them worthy, and lead them into the Light."

Jesus then reminded them of John the Baptizer's prophecy, saying: "John spoke about me when he said, 'I have baptized you with water for repentance, to cleanse you of your sins. But the one who comes after me is greater than I am. He carries a winnowing fan in his hand, and he will purify his threshing floor. He will burn the chaff with fire that never goes out, but he will gather the wheat into his barn.'"

"The Spirit within John gave him these words, predicting my coming. He knew that I would bring these mysteries into the world, mysteries that would cleanse the sins of those who believe in me and follow my teachings. Through these mysteries, I will transform them into pure and radiant light, and I will lead them into the eternal Light of the kingdom."

Chapter 117

After Jesus finished speaking, Mary asked him, "My Lord, if people go out searching for the truth but come across false teachings, how can they tell whether those teachings come from you or not? How will they know what is truly yours?"

Jesus replied, "I have told you before: 'Be as skillful as moneychangers. Accept what is real and reject what is fake.' Now, share this with everyone who seeks the truth: 'Just as you recognize signs in nature—when the north wind blows, you expect cold; when the south wind stirs, you prepare for heat—so too must you learn to recognize the signs of true divine teachings.'

"Tell them: 'If you can understand the natural world by observing the weather and the seasons, you must also learn to recognize spiritual truth. When someone comes to you claiming to speak about God, listen carefully. Check if their words match the teachings I have given you. See if their message aligns with the patterns of the sky, the stars, the sun and moon, the earth and all its creatures, the waters and everything within them. Test their words against these things.'

"Say to them: 'If their teachings fit perfectly with the knowledge I have shared, then they are speaking the truth, and you can trust them. But if their words do not match, then they do not belong to us.' This is what you must tell people when you spread my message, so they can guard themselves against false teachings."

Jesus continued, "This is why I have come into the world and sacrificed myself for the sake of sinners, so I can save them. Even the righteous—those who have never done great wrong—still need to seek out the mysteries in the Books of Yew. These mysteries are necessary for salvation.

"I first revealed these mysteries to Enoch in Paradise. I spoke to him from the Tree of Knowledge and the Tree of Life, telling him to write them down. He hid these sacred writings in the rock of Ararad. To protect them, I placed the ruler Kalapatauroth as their guardian. He rules over Skemmut and carries the authority of Yew, surrounding all the aeons and Fates. I assigned him to watch over the Books of Yew so that the rulers of this world, driven by envy, would not destroy them—especially during the great flood. When the right time comes, I will give you these mysteries, but only after I have revealed the full expansion of the universe."

Hearing this, Mary asked, "My Lord, who in this world could claim to be completely free from sin? Who is pure enough to receive the mysteries in the Books of Yew? Even if someone avoids one type of sin, they will still be guilty of another. I believe no one is without fault. If a person is cleansed of one wrongdoing, they will still have another to account for. How, then, can anyone hope to receive the mysteries?"

Jesus answered, "I tell you the truth: out of a thousand, only one will be found worthy, and out of ten thousand, only two will succeed in completing the mystery of the First Mystery. I will explain this in greater detail when I reveal the expansion of the universe.

"This is why I have come into the world and given myself up—to bring the mysteries to everyone. All people are affected by sin, and all need the gift of these mysteries. Without them, no one can rise into the Light, for the burden of sin weighs down every soul. Only the mysteries can release them and guide them into the kingdom of the Light."

Chapter 118

Mary asked Jesus, "My Lord, before you came down to the world of the rulers and entered this world, had any soul ever reached the Light? Did anyone find their way to the Light before your arrival?"

Jesus answered, "I tell you the truth: Before I came, no soul had ever entered the Light. The gates to the Light were closed, and the path leading there was not open. It is only now, with my coming, that I have unlocked the gates and revealed the way. Now, those who live in a way that is worthy of the mysteries can receive them, follow the path, and enter the Light."

Mary, wanting to understand more, asked, "But my Lord, I have heard that the prophets entered the Light. Is that not true?"

Jesus replied, "I tell you the truth: No prophet has ever entered the Light. Instead, the rulers of the lower realms spoke to the prophets from their own domains. They gave them the mysteries of the lower realms, but those mysteries could not lead them into the Light. When I entered these realms, I transformed Elias and sent him into the body of John the Baptizer so that he could prepare the way for my work. The others, I also placed in righteous bodies—bodies that could receive the mysteries of the Light, ascend, and inherit the kingdom of the Light."

Jesus continued, "As for Abraham, Isaac, and Jacob, I forgave their sins and purified them. I gave them the mysteries of the Light within the lower realms and placed them in the region of Yabraoth, where the rulers who repented now reside. When I return to the highest realms and enter the Light completely, I will take their souls with me. But Mary, I tell you truly, they will not enter the Light before I have brought your soul and the souls of all your brothers and sisters with me."

"The other patriarchs and all the righteous people from the time of Adam until now—those still under the rule of the lower realms—when I entered these realms, I changed them through the Virgin of Light. I placed them into righteous bodies, ones that could receive the mysteries of the Light. These are the ones who will find the mysteries, enter the Light, and inherit the kingdom of the Light."

Hearing these words, Mary said, "We are truly blessed above all people because of the great things you have shown us. My Lord, we are honored to receive these mysteries."

Jesus responded to Mary and the other disciples, saying, "I will continue to reveal to you the wonders of the higher realms, from the deepest inner places to the farthest outer reaches. I will explain everything so that you may reach complete knowledge, understand all things fully, and grasp both the highest heights and the deepest depths."

Mary spoke again, saying, "My Lord, now we know with certainty that you have brought the keys to the mysteries of the kingdom of the Light. These mysteries forgive sins, cleanse souls, transform them into pure light, and lead them into the eternal Light."

The Fifth Book of Pistis Sophia

Chapter 119

After Jesus had been crucified and risen from the dead on the third day, his disciples gathered around him. Filled with awe and respect, they fell to their knees and worshiped him, saying, "Lord, have mercy on us. We have left our families and everything we knew behind to follow you. We have given up everything and placed our trust in you completely. Please show us compassion and continue to guide us."

At that moment, Jesus stood with his disciples on the shore of a great ocean. The waters stretched endlessly before them, reflecting the vast sky above. As his disciples stood close, Jesus lifted his eyes to the heavens and began to pray. He spoke a sacred prayer, calling upon the eternal Light, saying, "Hear me, O my Father, the father of all creation, limitless and eternal Light. Grant us your grace and presence: aeēiouō iaō aōi ōia psinōther thernōps nōpsither zagourē pagourē nethmomaōth nepsiomaōth marachachtha thōbarrabau tharnachachan zorokothora ieou sabaōth."

As Jesus spoke these sacred words, his disciples formed a circle around him in deep reverence. Thomas, Andrew, James, and Simon the Cananite stood in the west, facing the east as they listened. Philip and Bartholomew stood in the south, looking north, while the rest of the disciples and the women who followed Jesus stood behind him in quiet devotion. Jesus stood at the center, in front of an altar, symbolizing his connection to the divine.

Jesus continued his prayer, turning in all four directions as he spoke. His disciples, dressed in simple white linen robes to show their spiritual readiness, followed his movements with great seriousness. With deep solemnity, Jesus called out, "iaō iaō iaō." He then turned to his disciples and explained, "This name holds deep meaning. The letter iōta represents the universe and everything that has come from the Light. Alpha stands for the return of all things to their original source, the eternal Light. And ōmega signifies the final completion when everything reaches its ultimate fulfillment."

Then, Jesus lifted his hands again and called upon the divine with more sacred words, saying, "iaphtha iaphtha mounaēr mounaēr ermanouēr ermanouēr." He turned to his disciples and said, "This prayer means: O Father of all creation, who exists beyond all time and space, hear me on behalf of my disciples. These are the ones I have led to you so they may believe in the truth of everything you have revealed. Grant them the blessings I now ask for, because I know the sacred name of the Father of the Treasury of the Light."

As he spoke, the air around them seemed to carry the power of his words, and the sky above reflected the great mystery he was revealing. The disciples stood in complete silence, their hearts filled with awe, knowing they were witnessing something beyond human understanding.

Then, Jesus—also known as Aberamenthō—lifted his voice once more, calling upon the sacred name of the Father of the Treasury of the Light. He summoned the power of the divine, saying, "Let all the mysteries of the rulers, the authorities, the angels, the archangels, and all the powers—everything that belongs to the unseen god Agrammachamarei and Barbēlō—draw near to the Leech on one side and move toward the right."

At that moment, a powerful shift took place in the heavens. Everything in the sky moved toward the west—the aeons, the great sphere, their rulers, and all the forces connected to them. These mighty powers gathered to the left of the sun and the moon.

The sun took the form of a huge dragon, its long tail curled into its mouth, forming an endless loop. This dragon stretched across the seven ruling powers of the Left and was carried through the sky by four glowing white horses. The moon, however, appeared as a large vessel, shaped like a ship. Two dragons, one male and one female, steered it from below, while two majestic white bulls pulled it forward. At the back of this ship sat the figure of a child, guiding the dragons as they stole light from the rulers. At the front of the vessel was the face of a cat, watching everything closely.

As this great event unfolded, it seemed as if the entire world moved along with it. The mountains and seas shifted westward, pulled by an invisible force. Amidst this cosmic movement, Jesus and his disciples remained standing in a space between earth and heaven, floating beneath the great sphere. They had arrived at the first level of the Way of the Midst.

Jesus stood firmly in this region, with his disciples gathered around him. Filled with awe at their surroundings, they turned to Jesus and asked, "Master, where are we? What is this place?"

Jesus answered, "This is the Way of the Midst. A long time ago, the rulers of Adamas rebelled against the divine order. They continued creating more rulers, archangels, angels, and servitors, going against what was meant to be. Because of this, Yew, the father of my father, came from the Right and put a stop to their rebellion. He bound these rulers and their creations to a fate inside the great sphere."

He continued, "Inside this sphere, there are twelve aeons. Six of them are ruled by Sabaōth, the Adamas, and the other six by his brother Yabraōth. But at one point, Yabraōth and his rulers chose to believe in the mysteries of the Light. They turned away from the rebellion and stopped creating more rulers. However, Sabaōth and his rulers refused to change. They continued their defiance, creating even more beings in disobedience to the divine order."

"When Yew, the father of my father, saw that Yabraōth and his followers had placed their faith in the Light, he acted quickly. He rescued Yabraōth and all those who had remained faithful, taking them away from the sphere of corruption. He placed them in a purified region, a bright and radiant space in front of the sun. This place is between the Way of the Midst and the hidden realms of the invisible god. There, Yew gave Yabraōth and his rulers a home in the Light as a reward for their faithfulness."

"As for Sabaōth, the Adamas, and his rulers, Yew left them to their fate. They remained trapped within the sphere, their defiance shaping the future of their existence."

Chapter 120

The rulers who refused to follow the mysteries of the Light and instead continued their ways of corruption were bound within the great sphere by Yew. He limited their power and influence, placing 1,800 rulers in each aeon and assigning 360 rulers to oversee them. Over these, he appointed five great rulers to take charge. These five rulers are known in the world as Kronos, Arēs, Hermēs, Aphroditē, and Zeus.

Jesus continued, "Listen carefully, and I will explain their mystery to you. When Yew bound these rulers, he saw that they still needed power to keep balance and prevent chaos. So, he took a power from the Great Invisible and gave it to Kronos. He then took a power from Ipsantachounchaïnchoucheōch, one of the triple-powered gods, and gave it to Arēs. Another power was taken from Chainchōōōch, another of the triple-powered gods, and given to Hermēs. He also took a power from Pistis Sophia, the daughter of Barbēlō, and bound it to Aphroditē.

Yew understood that if these rulers were left without control, they could bring great destruction to the world and the aeons. So, he needed someone to guide and control them. He went into the Midst and took a power from little Sabaōth, the Good, who lives in the Midst, and gave it to Zeus. Because Zeus had qualities of goodness, Yew made him the leader, ensuring that the rulers and the sphere did not bring complete ruin through their wickedness.

Yew also set the cycles of Zeus's rule. He decided that Zeus would spend thirteen months—some say three months—in each aeon. During this time, Zeus would restore order and free the rulers in that aeon from their own evil ways. Yew gave Zeus two aeons to live in, positioned opposite those of Hermēs.

Jesus then said, "I have now told you the names by which these five rulers are known in the world. But now, listen closely, for I will reveal their true, incorruptible names. These names do not decay or change like their earthly ones. Kronos's true name is Ōrimouth. Arēs's name is Mounichounaphōr. Hermēs is truly called Tarpetanouph. Aphroditē's real name is Chōsi. And Zeus's true name is Chōnbal. These are their original names, untouched by corruption."

When the disciples heard these revelations, they were filled with awe. They fell to the ground in gratitude, worshiping Jesus, and said, "We are blessed beyond all people because you have revealed these great mysteries to us."

Eager to learn more, they begged him, "Lord, please tell us even more. What are these ways of the Midst that you have spoken of? What is their purpose, and why do they bring such great punishments?"

Mary, filled with devotion, stepped forward. She knelt at Jesus's feet, kissed his hands, and said, "Yes, my Lord, please explain to us the purpose and workings of the ways of the Midst. We have heard you mention their connection to severe punishments. How can we escape their influence? How do these ways trap souls, and for how long do they keep them in suffering? Please have mercy on us, Lord, so that the enforcers of these punishments do not capture our souls or drag us into their cruel judgments. Give us your wisdom and grace so that we may avoid their traps and inherit the Light."

Chapter 121

Mary, overwhelmed with sorrow and longing, spoke through her tears, saying, "Lord, please don't leave us lost and without your Light, the Light of your Father. We cannot bear to be separated from you or the radiance of the divine."

Seeing Mary's sadness, Jesus, full of compassion, answered her and the disciples, saying, "My beloved brothers and sisters, you who have given up your families and all worldly attachments for my sake, I will not abandon you. I will give you all the mysteries and knowledge you need so that you may be completely filled with the Light and never be without it.

"I will reveal to you the mystery of the twelve aeons of the rulers. You will learn their seals, their sacred codes, and the prayers needed to access and understand their realms. I will show you the hidden knowledge of their power and the way to rise above their control.

"Beyond that, I will give you the mystery of the thirteenth aeon. I will teach you how to call upon its sacred power, show you its codes, and reveal its seals so that you may reach its realm and understand its deeper mysteries.

"I will also give you the mystery of the baptism of those of the Midst. You will learn how to call upon this baptism, its codes, and its seals, as well as the prayers that allow you to ascend to these regions.

"Moreover, I will give you the baptism of those of the Right, which is our true home—the region of the Light. I will teach you its sacred codes, seals, and prayers so that you may reach this holy place and remain there.

"Finally, I will give you the great mystery of the Treasury of the Light itself. You will learn the sacred invocation needed to enter it, and I will show you the full path to this most sacred and glorious place.

"I will share all these mysteries and all this knowledge with you so that you may be called 'children of the fullness'—perfected in wisdom and truth. You are more blessed than anyone else in the world, for the children of the Light have come in your time to guide you and reveal these sacred truths."

Jesus continued, "After this, the father of my Father, Yew, took action again against the rulers who refused to believe in the mystery of the Light. From the rulers of Adamas who remained in disbelief, Yew took 360 of them and bound them in the skies where we now stand, just below the great sphere. Over these rulers, he placed five great rulers to take charge of them. These are the rulers of the Way of the Midst, and they oversee the workings of this realm."

Jesus then explained further, "The first ruler of the Way of the Midst is called Paraplēx. She takes the form of a woman, and her long hair flows down to her feet like a rushing river. Under her command are twenty-five arch-demons, each leading a large number of lesser demons. These demons, controlled by Paraplēx, enter into people, tempting them to acts of anger, slander, and cursing. They are the ones who seize souls, pulling them away and subjecting them to their dark mist and harsh punishments."

Hearing this, Mary, still eager to understand, spoke again. "I hope I am not asking too many questions or seeming foolish," she said. "My Lord, please do not be upset with me for asking so much."

Jesus, patient and kind, replied, "Do not be afraid to ask, Mary. Speak freely, and I will answer everything you wish to know."

Mary, filled with a deep desire to understand, said to Jesus, "My Lord, please explain to us how these rulers capture souls and carry them away. Tell us this mystery clearly so that my brothers and sisters may understand and be prepared."

Jesus, also called Aberamenthō, answered Mary, saying, "Listen carefully, and I will explain this to you. The father of my Father, Yew, is the great overseer of all rulers, gods, and powers that came from the Light of the Treasury. He is joined by Zorokothora Melchisedec, who is responsible for gathering and guiding the purified lights that escape from the rulers. These two are the highest of all Lights, and their purpose is to bring back the trapped light into the Treasury of the Light, where all purified beings belong.

"When the time and conditions are right, Yew and Melchisedec descend to the regions of the rulers. They act with power, forcing the rulers to release the purified light, which they then lead into the Treasury of the Light. After this, Yew returns to the regions of the Right, while Melchisedec continues his work.

"But when Yew and Melchisedec are not present, the rulers grow angry and rebellious. They seek revenge for what has been taken from them. In their rage, they capture and drag away the souls they can find, destroying them with dark smoke and wicked fire. In their fury, they torment and corrupt these souls, seeking to undo the Light's work."

Jesus continued, "One of the most powerful of these rulers is Paraplēx, who takes the form of a woman. Her long hair flows down to her feet, symbolizing her power. She commands twenty-five arch-demons, each leading groups of lesser demons. These demons enter into people, causing them to give in to anger, violence, cursing, and lies. They are the ones who capture souls and drag them into darkness. Once there, Paraplēx and her demons punish them with relentless torment, surrounding them with dark smoke and burning them with an evil fire. Under her control, these souls begin to break apart and weaken.

"The souls that fall into her grasp suffer in agony for 133 years and 9 months. During this time, they endure constant torment in the fires of her wickedness, their very essence being destroyed by her power.

"But at the appointed time, a shift occurs in the universe. The great sphere turns, and little Sabaōth, also known as Zeus, reaches the first aeon of the sphere. This aeon is called the Ram of Boubastis and is linked to Aphroditē. When Boubastis moves into the seventh house of the sphere, called the Balance, something incredible happens. The barriers between the regions of the Right and the Left are lifted, revealing hidden realms. At that moment, the great Sabaōth, the Good, looks down from the heights of the Right and casts his gaze upon Paraplēx's domain.

"When Sabaōth looks upon her region, his powerful gaze causes it to collapse and disappear. Her strongholds fall apart, and she loses her power. The souls that were trapped in her torments are freed and thrown back into the cycle of the sphere. However, they are deeply damaged by the suffering they endured in Paraplēx's grasp and must begin their journey again, bound to the cycles of fate."

Jesus then spoke with great seriousness, "This is what happens to souls that fall under the control of these wicked rulers. This is why the mysteries of the Light are so important. Without them, no soul can escape from these rulers or find the way to the Treasury of the Light."

Chapter 122

Jesus continued teaching, saying, "The second ruler is called Ariouth the Ethiopian. She is a dark and powerful being, her form completely black, representing the darkness of her domain. She commands fourteen arch-demons, each of whom controls a large number of lesser demons. These demons enter the hearts of those who seek conflict, stirring up anger and arguments. They harden people's hearts, filling them with rage until they are driven to violence. Through their influence, wars begin, and murders are committed, leaving destruction wherever they go.

"The souls that Ariouth and her demons capture are taken into her domain, where they suffer terribly. For 113 years, these souls are trapped in her regions, experiencing endless torment. They are surrounded by thick smoke and burned by wicked fire, suffering without relief.

"But a time comes when the balance of the universe shifts. The great sphere turns, and little Sabaōth, the Good—who is known as Zeus in the world—enters the fourth aeon of the sphere, called the Crab. At the same time, Boubastis, known as Aphroditē, moves into the tenth aeon, called the Goat. In that moment, the barriers between the Left and the Right are removed, and Yew, the father of my Father, looks down from the heights of the Right. The entire world is shaken, the aeons tremble, and fear spreads through all their inhabitants. When Yew casts his gaze upon Ariouth's domain, her regions collapse and are destroyed. The souls who had been trapped in her punishments are released and sent back into the cycle of the sphere, though they are broken and weakened by the suffering they endured."

Jesus continued, "The third ruler is called Triple-faced Hekatē. She is a strong and dangerous authority who commands twenty-seven arch-demons, each controlling many more demons beneath them. These demons spread lies and deception among people, leading them to swear false oaths, steal, and desire things that do not belong to them. They tempt people to chase after greed and dishonesty, pulling them deeper into corruption.

"The souls that Hekatē captures are handed over to her demons, who torment them without mercy. These souls are burned in dark smoke and wicked fire, suffering for 105 years and 6 months. As they are punished, their very essence starts to fade, breaking apart under the weight of the fire and torment.

"But even her domain is not beyond change. When the great sphere turns, little Sabaōth, the Good—known as Zeus—enters the eighth aeon of the sphere, called the Scorpion. At the same time, Boubastis, or Aphroditē, moves into the second aeon, called the Bull. In that moment, the veil separating the Right from the Left is pulled away, and Zorokothora Melchisedec looks down from the heights. His powerful gaze shakes the earth, causing mountains to tremble and the aeons to be filled with fear. When he looks upon Hekatē's domain, her strongholds collapse and are destroyed. The souls that were suffering in her punishments are set free and cast back into the cycle of the sphere. However, the pain they endured has left them damaged, their essence weakened by the fires of her judgment."

Jesus continued his teaching, saying, "The fourth ruler is called Parhedrōn Typhōn. He is a mighty and powerful being who commands thirty-two demons. These demons enter the hearts and lives of people, pulling them away from the Light. They tempt people into lust and uncontrolled desires, leading them toward adultery, fornication, and an endless pursuit of physical pleasure. They trap people in a cycle of indulgence, keeping them blind to higher truths and preventing them from seeking the Light."

"When Parhedrōn Typhōn and his demons capture the souls of those who have given in to temptation, they suffer great torment. For 128 years, they are trapped in his regions, punished by thick smoke and fierce fire. These punishments wear them down, breaking them apart as they are burned by the flames of his cruelty.

"But even Parhedrōn Typhōn's power does not last forever. When the great sphere turns, and little Sabaōth, the Good—known in the world as Zeus—reaches the ninth aeon of the sphere, called the Archer, a great shift takes place. At the same time, Boubastis, known as Aphroditē, moves into the third aeon, called the Twins. At that moment, the barriers separating the Left and the Right are removed. From the heights, Zarazaz, a mighty ruler known among the rulers as 'Maskelli,' looks upon Parhedrōn Typhōn's domain. The power of Zarazaz's gaze destroys Typhōn's regions completely, causing them to collapse. The souls that were trapped in his torment are freed and sent back into the sphere. However, these souls are left weak and broken, scarred by the suffering they endured in Typhōn's fire and smoke."

Jesus paused before continuing, "Now, I will tell you about the fifth ruler. His name is Yachthanabas, and he is a powerful authority who commands many demons. These demons corrupt people's sense of justice, leading them to make unfair decisions. Under their influence, people take bribes, favor the guilty over the innocent, and ignore the needs of the poor. They fill people's minds with worries about things that do not matter, distracting them from what is truly important—the mysteries of the Light. When these people die, their souls are easily taken by Yachthanabas and his demons."

"The souls that fall into Yachthanabas's grasp are tormented for 150 years and 8 months. They are burned by his fierce fire and choked by his dark smoke. The pain they experience is unbearable, and their very essence is slowly broken apart by the suffering they endure."

"But, just like the other rulers, Yachthanabas's power is not forever. When the sphere turns again, and little Sabaōth, the Good—called Zeus in the world—enters the eleventh aeon of the sphere, known as the Waterman, and Boubastis moves into the fifth aeon, called the Lion, the barriers between the Left and the Right are removed. In that moment, the great Iaō, the Good, who watches over the Midst, looks

315

down upon Yachthanabas's domain. The power of Iaō's gaze destroys Yachthanabas's regions completely. The souls that were suffering in his punishments are freed and sent back into the sphere. However, they are deeply wounded by the pain they endured, weakened and broken by the fire and smoke of his torments."

Jesus finished by saying, "These are the workings of the Midst, the places you have asked me about. Now you understand their purpose and their effects."

Chapter 123

When the disciples heard these words, they were filled with fear and amazement. They fell to the ground before Jesus and cried out, "Lord, help us and have mercy on us. Protect us from these terrible punishments that are waiting for sinners. How terrible it is for them! How lost are the people of this world! They stumble like the blind, unable to see or find their way. They are confused and do not understand where they are going.

"Have mercy on us, Lord, and rescue us from this deep ignorance we are trapped in. Have mercy on all people, because their souls are being hunted like prey. The rulers of darkness take advantage of their forgetfulness and lack of knowledge, leading them into suffering.

"Save us, Lord, our Savior! We feel lost, frozen in fear, and unable to escape. Free us from these dangers and the traps set by the wicked rulers."

Jesus saw how troubled his disciples were, and he spoke to them with kindness and reassurance. He said, "Do not be afraid. Take comfort in knowing that you are truly blessed. I will give you power over all these things. You will have authority over the rulers and their worlds, and they will be placed under your command.

"Remember what I promised you before my crucifixion when I said, 'I will give you the keys to the kingdom of heaven.' Now I tell you again—I will keep my promise and give you the power to overcome all obstacles."

Jesus then prepared to reveal even greater mysteries to them. Together, they rose to a higher place, where the air was filled with a brilliant, pure light. The very forces of the Midst seemed to fade away in the presence of this great brightness. As Jesus and his disciples stood within this dazzling light, he turned to them and said, "Come closer to me."

The disciples stepped forward with reverence, eager to learn what he would reveal. Then, Jesus turned to face the four corners of the world. He spoke a sacred name over their heads, blessing them with its power. Then, he breathed onto their eyes, giving them the ability to see beyond the physical world.

Jesus said, "Lift your eyes and tell me what you see."

The disciples looked up, and before them appeared something beyond words. They saw an incredible light, greater than anything they had ever imagined—so bright and magnificent that human words could not describe its beauty.

Then Jesus told them, "Now look away from the light and tell me what you see."

The disciples answered, "We see fire, water, wine, and blood."

Jesus—also called Aberamenthō—said to them, "Truly, I tell you, when I came into this world, I brought only these four things—this fire, this water, this wine, and this blood. These are the gifts I have given to humanity. The fire and water came from the highest regions of Light, from the Treasury of the Light. The wine and the blood came from Barbēlō, the divine mother of all.

"And later, my Father in the highest sent the Holy Spirit in the form of a dove to complete my mission."

Jesus continued, "The fire, the water, and the wine are given to cleanse the world of its sins. They are gifts of the Light, meant to purify and renew. The blood, however, is a special sign. It was given to me because of the human body I took on when I came into the world. I passed through the region of Barbēlō, the great power of the invisible God. The blood represents the covenant and the sacrifice that was necessary to save humanity."

"The breath of life reaches all souls. It lifts them up and guides them toward the Light. This breath is a divine spark that awakens the soul and leads it back to its true home.

"This is why I said, 'I have come to cast fire upon the earth.' The fire I bring is meant to purify the world, burning away sin and cleansing souls so they can enter the Light.

"This is also why I told the Samaritan woman at the well, 'If you knew the gift of God and who is speaking to you, saying, "Give me a drink," you would ask him, and he would give you living water. This water would become a spring inside you, bringing eternal life.' The living water I spoke of is the divine power that cleanses and nourishes the soul, making it ready for everlasting life.

"For the same reason, I took a cup of wine, blessed it, and gave it to you, saying, 'This is my blood of the covenant, poured out for you for the forgiveness of sins.' The wine represents my sacred blood, which seals the promise between the Light and humanity—a promise of forgiveness and salvation.

"And this is why, when I was on the cross, they pierced my side with a spear. When they did, water and blood flowed out together. This was not an accident—it was a sign of the mysteries of the Light. The water and blood that flowed from me are symbols of purification and the eternal covenant. These mysteries are what cleanse sins. They are the sacred truths and divine names of the Light that I have brought into the world."

When Jesus finished speaking, he gave a command: "Let all the powers of the Left return to their own places." By his authority, he sent them away to their proper regions. Then, Jesus remained with his disciples on the Mount of Galilee.

Still searching for reassurance, the disciples came to him and asked, "Lord, have you not yet forgiven our sins? Have you not yet freed us from our faults? Will you now make us worthy to enter the kingdom of your Father?"

Jesus, full of kindness, looked at them and said, "Truly, I tell you, your sins will be forgiven. I have brought the mysteries of forgiveness into the world so that everyone who believes in me and follows the path of the Light may be saved. The kingdom of my Father is open to those who purify themselves through these mysteries and live in faith."

Jesus then spoke to his disciples with great love, saying, "Not only will I cleanse you of your sins, but I will also make you worthy of my Father's kingdom. I will give you the mystery of forgiveness so that you may have the power to forgive and to bind. Whoever you forgive on earth will also be forgiven in heaven, and whoever you bind on earth will also be bound in heaven.

"Moreover, I will give you the mysteries of the kingdom of heaven so that you may share them with others, helping them to enter the divine Light."

Then Jesus told his disciples, "Bring me fire and vine branches." The disciples quickly gathered these items and brought them to him. Jesus carefully arranged the offering with great respect. He placed two vessels of wine—one on the right side and one on the left. In front of the vessel on the right, he set a cup of water, and in front of the vessel on the left, he placed a cup of wine. In the center, between these cups, he laid loaves of bread, one for each of his disciples. Behind the loaves, he placed another cup of water.

When everything was set, Jesus stood before the offering and told his disciples to stand behind him. He instructed them to wear pure linen garments as a sign of spiritual cleanliness and readiness. In their hands, they held the sacred sign of the name of the Father of the Treasury of the Light. With deep reverence, Jesus raised his voice in prayer and called upon the divine:

"Hear me, O Father, the source of all fatherhood, endless Light:

iaō iouō iaō aōi ōia psinōther therōpsin ōpsither nephthomaōth nephiomaōth marachachtha marmarachtha iēana menaman amanēi israi amēn amēn soubaibai appaap amēn amēn deraarai amēn amēn sasarsartou amēn amēn koukiamin miai amēn amēn iai iai touap amēn amēn amēn main mari mariē marei amēn amēn amēn.

"Hear me, O Father, the father of all fatherhood. I call upon you, the one who forgives sins and purifies the soul. Forgive the sins of these disciples who have followed me faithfully. Cleanse them of all wrongdoing and make them worthy to be called children of the kingdom of my Father, the Father of the Treasury of the Light. They have remained loyal to me and followed my teachings.

"So now, O Father, I call upon the forgivers of sins, whose sacred names are these:

siphirepsnichieu zenei berimou sochabrichēr euthari na nai dieisbalmērich meunipos chirie entair mouthiour smour peuchēr oouschous minionor isochobortha.

"Hear my prayer and cleanse these souls. Remove their sins and purify them from all wrongdoing. Let them be counted among the children of my Father's kingdom, the Father of the Treasury of the

Light.

"I know your great and mighty power, and I call upon you:

auēr bebrō athroni ē oureph ē ōne souphen knitou sochreōph mauōnbi mneuōr souoni chōcheteōph chōche eteōph memōch anēmph.

"Forgive these souls and wipe away their sins, whether they acted knowingly or unknowingly. Purify them from all wrongdoing, whether it be impurity, unfaithfulness, or any other transgression they have committed. Father, forgive them and make them worthy to be counted among the heirs of your kingdom. Let them take part in this sacred offering with clean hearts and purified spirits.

"Holy Father, if you have heard my prayer and have forgiven their sins, if you have cleansed them and made them worthy, then let them receive this offering in purity and peace."

When Jesus finished praying, the disciples stood in amazement, feeling the presence of the divine surrounding them. The offering glowed with a holy light, and a deep sense of transformation filled the air.

Then Jesus turned to his disciples and gave them instructions for the future. "This sacred practice is a gift. Through it, sins are forgiven, and souls are purified. Protect it well, for it is a mystery of the Light, a path to the kingdom of my Father."

Chapter 124

Jesus stood before the offering and said, "Father, if these souls have truly been forgiven and are now counted among your kingdom, show me a sign in this offering as proof."

At that moment, the sign Jesus had asked for appeared, confirming that the offering had been accepted and that the disciples' sins had been cleansed. Jesus turned to them and said, "Rejoice and be glad, for your sins have been forgiven, your mistakes erased, and you are now part of my Father's kingdom."

Hearing this, the disciples were filled with joy. They praised Jesus, their hearts full of gratitude, knowing they had been redeemed. The air was filled with their voices of celebration, a moment of pure happiness.

Then Jesus spoke again, saying, "This is the sacred practice and mystery you must perform for those who believe in you—those who are sincere, who have no deceit in their hearts, and who listen to your words with faith. For those who meet these conditions, when you perform this mystery, their sins will be forgiven up until the moment you do this for them. But be careful to protect this mystery. Do not reveal it to just anyone, but only to those who follow my commandments and show through their actions that they are worthy.

"This mystery is the true baptism that cleanses sins and removes wrongdoing. It is the baptism of the first offering, the gateway to the regions of Truth and Light."

After Jesus had finished speaking, the disciples came to him and said, "Teacher, we ask you to reveal to us the mysteries of the Light of your Father. We have heard you speak about different baptisms—the baptism of fire, the baptism of the Holy Spirit of the Light, and a sacred anointing. Please tell us about these mysteries, so that we may also inherit the kingdom of your Father."

Jesus, full of patience and wisdom, answered, "There are no greater mysteries than the ones you ask about. These are the highest and most important mysteries because they lead the soul into the Light of lights, into the realm of ultimate Truth and Goodness. They guide the soul into the most sacred place, where there are no physical forms, no male or female—only an endless, indescribable Light.

"Nothing is greater than these mysteries, except for the mystery of the seven Voices and their forty-nine powers, along with their sacred symbols. And there is no name more powerful than the great name in which all names, all lights, and all powers exist. Whoever knows this name, when their soul leaves the body, will not be stopped by darkness, fire, rulers, or any powers of Fate. No angel or archangel will be able to hold them back. That soul will be free.

"If this name is spoken to fire, the fire will be put out. If it is spoken in darkness, the darkness will disappear. If it is spoken to demons, or to the beings that control outer darkness, or to their rulers and powers, they will all collapse. Their own flames will destroy them, and they will cry out in fear, 'Holy, holy, you are the most holy of all!'

"If this name is spoken to those who carry out punishments, to their rulers, or to all their powers—even to Barbēlō, the invisible god, and the three triple-powered gods—they too will fall apart. They will be undone and destroyed, and they will cry out, 'O Light of all lights, which lives in the endless Light, remember us and purify us.' Such is the power of this name."

When Jesus finished speaking, the disciples were deeply moved. They fell to their knees, tears streaming down their faces, their cries echoing around them. Overwhelmed by the mysteries he had revealed and the greatness of the Light he described, they called out to Jesus in awe and devotion.

The Sixth Book of Pistis Sophia

Jesus answered, "When a person who has spoken curses or blasphemed dies, their soul is taken to a place of punishment. There, it is thrown into rivers and seas of fire, where it suffers for six months and eight days. These burning waters strike the soul like whips, scorching it with unbearable heat. Though the fire cleanses the soul of its wrongdoings, the suffering is intense and painful.

"After this time, the soul is brought to the path called the way of the midst. Here, each ruler of this path takes turns punishing it in different ways. This continues for another six months and eight days. The purpose of these punishments is to strip away the soul's sins, but they leave it exhausted and tormented.

"When this is complete, the soul is brought before the Virgin of Light, who judges all souls—both good and bad. She weighs its actions and determines what will happen next. If the soul is still unworthy, she gives it to her servants when the sphere turns. They then cast the soul into the aeons of the sphere, where more purification is required.

"The servants of the sphere take the soul to a boiling fire below. This fire is like a burning liquid that eats away at the last traces of wrongdoing. The suffering is severe, but it fully cleanses the soul of its sins.

"After this purification, Yaluham, the receiver of Sabaōth, the Adamas, comes forward. He carries the cup of forgetfulness, filled with the water of oblivion. The soul is made to drink from this cup, and the moment it does, it forgets everything—its past journeys, its suffering, and all knowledge of the higher realms. Completely stripped of memory, the soul is sent back into the world, placed in a new body where it will live a life full of hardship and struggle. This is the punishment of the one who curses."

Mary, troubled by this, asked, "My Lord, what happens to someone who constantly spreads lies and slander? If such a person dies, where does their soul go? What is their punishment?"

Jesus replied, "A person who is guilty of slander and does not repent will face judgment when their time on earth is over. When they die, the receivers of Ariēl, named Abiout and Charmōn, come to take their soul. For three days, they lead it around the world, showing it the things of the earth and the creations of man.

"After these three days, they take the soul down into Amente, where it is brought before Ariēl. There, the soul is punished for eleven months and twenty-one days. It is burned, whipped, and tormented in endless suffering, as its wrongdoing is stripped away.

"Once its time in Amente is finished, the soul is taken into the chaos and brought before Yaldabaōth and his forty-nine demons. Each of these demons takes turns punishing it for another eleven months and twenty-one days. The soul is beaten with fiery whips and burned in their unholy flames.

"When its time in chaos is over, the soul is thrown into boiling rivers and seas of fire. There, it suffers another eleven months and twenty-one days, its pain beyond measure. Though these torments purify the soul, they also break it down, leaving it in a ruined state.

"After this, the soul is taken back to the way of the midst. Just like before, each ruler on this path punishes it again. This continues for another eleven months and twenty-one days.

"Finally, the soul is brought before the Virgin of Light again. She examines it once more and decides its fate. If the soul is still unworthy, she hands it over to her receivers when the sphere turns. They throw it into the aeons of the sphere, where it is led to the boiling fire beneath. This fire completely consumes all remaining traces of wrongdoing.

"When this final purification is complete, Yaluham, the receiver of Sabaōth, the Adamas, comes forward again. He brings the cup of forgetfulness, filled with the water of oblivion, and gives it to the soul. The moment the soul drinks, all its memories are erased. It forgets the punishments it endured, the higher realms it once knew, and everything about its past existence. Empty of knowledge, it is sent into a new body, where it will live a life filled with difficulty and pain.

"This is the punishment of the slanderer."

Hearing this, Mary cried out in sorrow, "How terrible it is for those who sin! Their punishments are great, and their ignorance leads them to such suffering!"

Salome then asked, "My Lord, what about a person who has killed another? If a murderer dies, what happens to their soul?"

Chapter 125

Jesus answered, "If a person has committed murder but no other sin, and their time in this world has come to an end, their soul will face a harsh judgment. When they die, the servants of Yaldabaōth come down to take their soul. These beings tie the soul by its feet to a powerful and terrifying demon with the face of a horse. This demon has burning eyes filled with anger and is a force of great destruction.

"For three days, this demon drags the soul around the world, forcing it to witness the pain and suffering it has caused. The soul sees the consequences of its actions, reliving the harm it has done. It is tormented with guilt, but its punishment has only just begun.

"After these three days, the soul is taken to a place of endless cold and snow, a dark and empty land filled with suffering. Here, it faces unbearable pain, with icy winds cutting through it and the freezing air burning deep into its very being. For three years and six months, the soul remains in this frozen wasteland, isolated and in agony. This cold is not just physical—it represents the soul's separation from the warmth and grace of the Light.

"Once this punishment is over, the soul is taken even deeper into chaos, where it is brought before Yaldabaōth and his forty-nine demons. These terrifying beings, full of hatred and destruction, take turns whipping the soul with fiery lashes. Each strike burns and scars the soul, stripping it of its sins. This torture continues for another three years and six months, with the soul trapped in a place of endless screaming and suffering, surrounded by the cries of others who share its fate.

"After this torment, the soul is taken even lower into the depths of chaos, where it is brought before Persephonē, the queen of the underworld. Here, the soul faces a new level of suffering, as Persephonē herself delivers her own punishments. Her judgment is severe, bringing both physical and spiritual pain. For another three years and six months, the soul endures her wrath, unable to escape the torment she inflicts.

"This is the fate of a murderer. Taking a life is a grave act, and the punishment that follows is severe. Yet, these trials are not just for suffering—they are meant to cleanse the soul, to burn away its sins, and to prepare it for the chance of redemption."

Chapter 126

Jesus continued, "After these punishments, the murderer's soul is taken to the path known as the way of the midst. Here, each ruler in this realm takes turns punishing the soul, making it suffer according to their own laws. For another three years and six months, the soul endures these torments, each ruler adding to its suffering until it is nearly broken.

"When this time is finished, the soul is brought before the Virgin of Light, the ultimate judge of both good and evil souls. She carefully examines its actions and sins, weighing its worth. If the soul is found unworthy, she orders it to be cast into the outer darkness, where it will remain until the darkness itself is removed. There, the soul is completely destroyed, fading into nothingness.

"This is the punishment of a murderer."

As Jesus finished, Peter, clearly frustrated, spoke up and said, "Lord, let the women stop asking questions so that we, too, may speak and learn from you."

Jesus, always patient, turned to Mary and the other women, saying, "Let your brothers speak now, so they may also ask what is in their hearts."

Peter then asked, "Lord, what happens to a thief, someone who steals without regret? When such a person dies, what punishment awaits their soul?"

Jesus answered, "When the thief's time in this world is complete and they die, the receivers of Adōnis come to claim their soul. These beings pull the soul from its body and take it around the world for three days. During this time, they show the soul the harm it caused through its greed and selfishness, making it witness the effects of its actions.

"After these three days, the soul is taken to Amente, where it is judged by Ariēl. There, it is punished for three months, eight days, and two hours. The suffering is relentless, forcing the soul to face the misery it caused through its theft.

"When this punishment is complete, the soul is taken into chaos and brought before Yaldabaōth and his forty-nine demons. One by one, these demons take their turn torturing the soul. For another three months, eight days, and two hours, the soul is whipped with fiery lashes and tormented without mercy, breaking down its arrogance and defiance.

"Next, the soul is led to the way of the midst, where it faces yet another series of punishments. Each ruler in this realm punishes it according to their own laws. The soul suffers here for another three months, eight days, and two hours, surrounded by thick smoke and burning fire. Every new punishment weakens it further, leaving it in agony.

"When this period of suffering is over, the soul is once again brought before the Virgin of Light. She examines its past, judging whether it has changed. If it is still unworthy, she hands it over to her receivers as the sphere turns. These beings throw the soul into the aeons of the sphere, leading it to a strange water below. But this is no ordinary water—it burns like fire. The flames consume the soul, cleansing it of its remaining sins through intense suffering.

"When this purification is complete, Yaluham, the receiver of Sabaōth, the Adamas, approaches the soul. He carries the cup of forgetfulness, filled with water that erases all memory. The soul drinks deeply from the cup, and at that moment, it forgets everything—the places it traveled, the punishments it endured, and even the higher truths it once knew.

"With its memory wiped clean, the soul is placed into a new body. However, this new life is filled with hardship. The person may be born blind, crippled, or sick, carrying the burden of their past actions into this life.

"This is the punishment of the thief."

Jesus continued, "When a man filled with pride and arrogance dies, his soul does not escape judgment. If his time in this world has ended, the receivers of Ariēl come to take his soul. These beings remove the soul from its body and, for three days, carry it around the world. During this time, they show the soul the realities of creation, revealing the true consequences of its pride and self-importance. The soul is forced to see what it ignored in life.

"After these three days, the soul is taken down into Amente, where it stands before Ariēl. There, it is punished for twenty months, enduring relentless suffering meant to strip away the arrogance and selfishness it carried in life. These torments are not just painful but serve to break down the pride that once controlled the soul.

"Once this punishment is complete, the soul is taken even deeper into chaos, where it is brought before Yaldabaōth and his forty-nine demons. Here, the torment becomes even more severe. Each demon takes its turn punishing the soul for another twenty months. Their punishments burn away what remains of the soul's arrogance, leaving it shattered and humbled.

"Next, the soul is led to the way of the midst. Along this path, every ruler takes turns punishing the soul in their own way. For another twenty months, the soul suffers in fire, smoke, and spiritual affliction. These punishments force it to face the full weight of its past actions, breaking it down even further.

"When this suffering is finished, the soul is taken before the Virgin of Light, who judges all souls, both good and bad. She carefully examines the soul's deeds and determines if it is worthy. If the soul is still unworthy, she orders it to be cast into the aeons of the sphere when the sphere turns. The servitors of the sphere then lead the soul to a body of water beneath the sphere, but this is no ordinary water—it burns like fire. The soul is thrown into these flames, which purify it by consuming the last of its impurities, leaving it weak and empty.

"After this purification, Yaluham, the receiver of Sabaōth, the Adamas, comes forward. He carries the cup of forgetfulness, filled with water that erases all memory. The soul drinks from this cup and instantly forgets everything—its past, its punishments, and any knowledge of the higher realms. With no recollection of what it once was, the soul is sent into a new body, one that is crippled, deformed, and rejected by others. This life of struggle and humiliation serves as a reminder of the arrogance it once held.

"This is the punishment of the arrogant man."

Hearing this, Thomas asked, "Lord, what happens to someone who constantly speaks against the Light? What is the punishment for a person who insults the divine and rejects the truth?"

Jesus answered, "If a blasphemer has completed their time on earth, the receivers of Yaldabaōth come to claim their soul. Because their sin was with their tongue, these beings bind their tongue to a massive demon with the face of a horse. This terrifying creature drags the soul through the world for three days, showing it the damage caused by its words and actions. During this time, the soul suffers greatly as the demon and the receivers take their revenge.

"After these three days, the soul is cast into a realm of never-ending cold and ice. There, it suffers for eleven years, completely frozen in a wasteland of misery. The soul is tormented by the same coldness it had in life, a reflection of its rejection of warmth, love, and truth.

"When this time is over, the soul is taken even deeper into chaos and placed before Yaldabaōth and his forty-nine demons. One by one, these demons punish the soul for another eleven years, burning it with fire and tearing away what remains of its defiance.

"From there, the soul is cast into the outer darkness—a place of complete emptiness and despair. It remains there, frozen and unmoving, trapped in its own rejection of the Light. The soul stays in this darkness until the time comes for the great ruler with the face of a dragon, who encircles this realm, to be judged. When that moment arrives, the darkness itself will be lifted, and the soul will be completely destroyed, erased from existence as a result of its own rejection of the Light.

"This is the judgment of the blasphemer."

Chapter 127

Bartholomew asked, "What happens to a man who engages in relations with another man? What is his punishment?"

Jesus answered, "The judgment for a man who lies with another man is the same as that of someone who continuously speaks against the divine. In the eyes of justice, their sins are equal.

"When such a man's time on earth is over, the servants of Yaldabaōth come to take his soul. They bring it before Yaldabaōth and his forty-nine demons, where his punishment begins. Each demon takes turns punishing the soul, tormenting it for eleven years. The soul is whipped, burned, and broken under their wrath.

"After this, the soul is thrown into fiery rivers and boiling pits of tar. These places are filled with demons that have the faces of pigs, and they attack the soul, tearing away its essence for another eleven years. The burning rivers and molten tar continue to torture the soul, consuming it in unbearable suffering.

"When this punishment ends, the soul is taken into the outer darkness, a place of complete emptiness. There, it will remain until the final judgment, when the darkness itself will be destroyed. When that day comes, the soul will be erased completely, disappearing into the void."

Thomas then asked, "We have heard of people who mix male seed with the monthly blood of women, cook it into porridge, and eat it, saying, 'We believe in Esau and Jacob.' My Lord, is this right or is it a sin?"

Jesus became deeply upset and spoke with great anger, saying, "I tell you the truth: this is the worst of all sins, greater than any other wrongdoing. Those who do such things will not be given another chance. They will not return to the world, nor will they be sent into another body. Instead, they will be thrown straight into the outer darkness, a place without mercy or light, filled only with the cries of suffering souls. There, they will be completely destroyed, wiped from existence forever."

John then asked, "My Lord, what happens to a man who has lived a good life, has never done evil, but has not received the sacred knowledge needed to pass through the rulers? When he dies, where does his soul go?"

Jesus answered, "When the time comes for such a man to leave his body, the servants of Bainchōōōch—one of the triple-powered gods— come to collect his soul. Unlike the others, they come with joy, greeting the soul with happiness and celebration.

"For three days, they guide the soul around the world, teaching it about the creation of the earth and the works of the Light. They rejoice with the soul, showing it the beauty and purpose of the world.

"After these three days, they take the soul to Amente, the place of judgment. However, this soul is not punished. Instead, it is shown the tools of punishment used for sinners, but it does not experience any pain. Still, the heat and smoke from the fires of judgment lightly touch the soul, reminding it of the weight of justice.

"Next, the soul is taken to the way of the midst, where it is taught about the punishments of the rulers in that region. Again, the soul is not harmed, though the heat and smoke brush against it as a warning.

"Finally, the soul is brought before the Virgin of Light, who judges all souls fairly. Seeing its goodness, she sends the soul to be with the little Sabaōth, the Good, in the Midst. The soul waits there until the sphere turns and the cosmic alignment occurs—when Zeus and Aphroditē stand before the Virgin of Light, and Kronos and Arēs take their positions behind her.

"At that moment, the Virgin of Light hands the righteous soul to her servants. They cast it into the aeons of the sphere, where it is taken to a body of water below the sphere. This water, like a burning fire, purifies the soul completely, washing away any remaining impurities.

"Once the soul is cleansed, Yaluham, the receiver of Sabaōth, the Adamas, approaches. He carries the cup of forgetfulness, filled with water that erases all memory. The soul drinks from the cup and forgets everything—its journey, its lessons, and all the places it has been. Stripped of all past knowledge, the soul is prepared for its next life."

Then, a servant of little Sabaōth, the Good, steps forward. He carries another cup, one filled with wisdom, understanding, and clarity. This is the cup of wisdom. He offers it to the soul, and as the soul drinks, its heart is awakened. Because of this cup, the soul cannot rest or forget—it begins to seek truth, constantly questioning and searching for the mysteries of the Light.

The soul is then placed into a new body, one that is driven by a deep desire to uncover the secrets of the Light. This longing, given by the Virgin of Light through the cup of wisdom, pushes the soul to seek the divine until it finally discovers the mysteries and enters into the Light forever.

Mary asked, "What about someone who has committed every possible sin and has never found the mysteries of the Light? Will he suffer for all his sins at once?"

Jesus answered, "Yes, such a person will receive punishment for every wrongdoing. If he has committed three sins, he will be punished for each of those three sins. His chastisements will match the exact nature of his transgressions. But even the worst sinner can still be saved if he truly repents and seeks the Light with all his heart."

John then asked, "Lord, if someone has committed all sins and done much evil, yet later finds the mysteries of the Light, can he still be saved?"

Jesus replied, "Yes. If such a person finds the mysteries of the Light, faithfully follows them, and completely turns away from sin, then he will inherit the Treasury of the Light. The mysteries have the power to transform even the most sinful soul and bring it into the fullness of the Light."

Jesus continued to teach his disciples about the times when souls are more likely to find the mysteries of the Light. He said, "When the sphere turns and Kronos and Arēs align behind the Virgin of Light, while Zeus and Aphroditē stand before her in their proper places, the veils of the Virgin are drawn aside. At that moment, the Virgin of Light is filled with joy as she sees the two bright stars shining before her. During this time, all the souls she sends into the world will be righteous and good. These souls will find the mysteries of the Light and have the chance to be saved.

"But if the alignment changes, and Arēs and Kronos appear before the Virgin while Zeus and Aphroditē stand behind her, hidden from view, then the souls she sends into the world at that time will be wicked and full of anger. These souls will not find the mysteries of the Light. Their lives will be marked by forgetfulness and distraction, leading them away from the path of salvation."

When Jesus spoke these words, his disciples were deeply moved. They cried out and wept, saying, "How terrible it is for sinners! How awful for those who live in ignorance, trapped by forgetfulness, until they leave their bodies and suffer such painful punishments. Lord, have mercy on us! Son of the Holy One, be compassionate toward us, so that we may escape these terrible judgments. For we too have sinned, O Lord, our Light and Savior."

Seeing their distress, Jesus was filled with compassion. He comforted them, reminding them that through the mysteries of the Light, they could find redemption and salvation.

After their time with Jesus, the faithful disciples went out to share his teachings. They traveled in groups of three, spreading the message of the kingdom of the Light to all corners of the world. They proclaimed the goodness of God's kingdom, bringing the promise of salvation to everyone who would listen.

Through their words, Christ himself worked within them, confirming their message with miracles and wonders. Signs followed their teachings, proving the truth of what they spoke.

In this way, the kingdom of God was made known across the entire earth, reaching every part of Israel and serving as a testimony to all nations, from the rising of the sun to its setting. Through their efforts, the mysteries of the Light were revealed to humanity, offering a path of redemption and salvation to all who were willing to seek it.

Thank You for Reading

Dear Reader,

We hope this timeless classic has sparked your imagination and enriched your literary journey. Now that you've turned the final page, we want to share a vision for the future of reading—one where every classic you've ever wanted to explore is at your fingertips, in a format that best suits your life.

We'd like to invite you to gain immediate, unlimited digital & audiobook access to hundreds of the most treasured literary classics ever written—along with the option to secure deluxe paperback, hardcover & box set editions at printing cost. Together, we can spark a new global literary renaissance alongside our small, independent publishing house called "The Library of Alexandria."

Thousands of years ago, the Library of Alexandria stood as a beacon of knowledge—until it was lost to history. We aim to reignite that spirit of preservation and discovery right now, in the modern age—only this time, it's accessible to all, in every language and every format.

Picture a world where every timeless classic, novel, poem, or philosophical treatise is not only available to read but also updated for today's readers—modernized, translated into any language or dialect, and ready to enjoy in any format you choose, whether that is in an eBook, audiobook, paperback, or deluxe hardcover & box set version a printing cost.

By joining our movement to rebuild the modern Library of Alexandria, you become part of an unprecedented mission to offer:

- **Unlimited Audiobook & eBook Access to the Greatest Classics of All Time**

  Instantly explore thousands of legendary works, from Plato and Shakespeare to Jane Austen and Leo Tolstoy. All are instantly ready to read or listen to, giving you a complete literary universe at your fingertips.

- **Paperback & Deluxe Editions at Printing Costs:**

  Purchase any title in a paperback, deluxe hardbound, or deluxe boxset edition at printing costs, shipped right to your doorstep. Curate your personal library of Alexandria with editions worthy of display—crafted to last, designed to captivate, and delivered straight to your door.

- **Modern translations for Contemporary Readers in all languages and dialects**

  Discover a vast selection of classics reimagined in clear, current language—no more struggling with outdated phrases or obscure references. Next to the original versions, we aim to offer translations in as many languages and dialects as possible.

  As we continue our translation efforts and add new languages, readers everywhere can connect with these works as if they were written today. By bridging linguistic divides, you're contributing to ensuring that these timeless stories become more meaningful, accessible, and inspiring for people across the globe.

- **Your Personal Library of Alexandria:**

  Over the months and years, you'll curate a unique physical archive of classics—each volume a testament to your taste, curiosity, and love of knowledge. It's not just about owning books—it's about curating a cultural legacy you'll cherish and pass down for generations to come.

- **Join a Global Literary Renaissance:**

  Your support fuels an ongoing mission: allowing us to reinvest in offering deluxe print editions (including special boxsets) at their true cost, broaden the range of available formats and translations, and extend the reach of these works to new audiences worldwide. By joining today, you're not just preserving a legacy of masterpieces; you set in motion a powerful wave of literary accessibility.

  We are more than a publisher—we're a movement, and we can't do it alone. Your support lets us scale our mission, preserving and reimagining history's greatest works for tomorrow's readers.

Become a Torchbearer of knowledge.

Thank you for picking up this book and allowing us into your literary journey. As you turn the pages, know that you're part of something larger: a global effort to keep these stories alive, share their wisdom across borders and generations, and spark a true cultural revival for the modern era.

If this resonates with you—please consider taking the next step by visiting:

www.libraryofalexandria.com

With gratitude and a shared love of knowledge,

The Modern Library of Alexandria Team

Visit:

www.libraryofalexandria.com

Or scan the code below: